INFORMATION TOMORROW

Reflections on Technology and the Future of Public and Academic Libraries

Edited by
Rachel Singer Gordon

Information Today, Inc.
Medford, New Jersey

First printing, 2007

Information Tomorrow: Reflections on Technology and the Future of Public and Academic Libraries

Copyright © 2007 by Rachel Singer Gordon

Publisher's Note: The editor and publisher have taken care in preparation of this book but make no expressed or implied warranty of any kind and assume no responsibility for errors or omissions. No liability is assumed for incidental or consequential damages in connection with or arising out of the use of the information or programs contained herein.

Many of the designations used by manufacturers and sellers to distinguish their products are claimed as trademarks. Where those designations appear in this book and Information Today, Inc. was aware of a trademark claim, the designations have been printed with initial capital letters.

Library of Congress Cataloging-in-Publication Data

Information tomorrow : reflections on technology and the future of public and academic libraries / edited by Rachel Singer Gordon.
     p. cm.
  Includes bibliographical references and index.
  ISBN 978-1-57387-303-1
   1. Public libraries--Information technology. 2. Academic libraries--Information technology. 3. Libraries and the Internet. 4. Libraries and electronic publishing. 5. Library users--Effect of technological innovations on. 6. Public libraries--Forecasting. 7. Academic libraries--Forecasting. I. Gordon, Rachel Singer.
  Z678.9I534 2007
   020.285'4678--dc22

                                      2007028391

President and CEO: Thomas H. Hogan, Sr.
Editor-in-Chief and Publisher: John B. Bryans
Managing Editor: Amy M. Holmes
VP Graphics and Production: M. Heide Dengler
Book Designer: Kara Mia Jalkowski
Cover Designer: Shelley Szajner
Copyeditor: Dorothy Pike
Proofreader: Pat Hadley-Miller
Indexer: Beth Palmer

Contents

PART 1: FORMATS AND FUNCTIONS

CHAPTER 1

CHAPTER 2

CHAPTER 3
Mouse Bites Cat: Taking Back the 21st-Century ILS **31**
John Blyberg

CHAPTER 4
Six Years Too Late: Chasing Our Destiny in the Electronic Publishing Age **43**
Jill Emery

CHAPTER 9

CHAPTER 10

PART 3: 2.0—AND BEYOND

CHAPTER 11

Jenny Levine

CHAPTER 12

Rhonda B. Trueman, Tom Peters, and Lori Bell

CHAPTER 16

Foreword

Don't worry about what anybody else is going to do. ... The best way to predict the future is to invent it. Really smart people with reasonable funding can do just about anything that doesn't violate too many of Newton's Laws!

—Alan Kay in 1971

I've had the opportunity to read and re-read the book you're holding, and you are in for a treat. It is rare for one book to cover so much of the horizon for an entire sector, but *Information Tomorrow* outlines so many of the major building blocks for our future. And it is written by some of the freshest and best library thinkers of our times. This is a fabulous team of authors—the newest thinkers, the new breed of librarian—dare I say, Librarian 2.0?! Each chapter offers new approaches and new thinking for the exciting library world of the new Millennium.

Once again, Information Today, Inc. has incubated a book that meets a need. Reading it is almost like attending one of its conferences—all the best speakers in one place. Creating a collection based on the theme of innovation risks two things: being too shallow or being too visionary. Either results in a nice read, but does little to point readers in the right direction with explicit advice and views you can use. You, however, are holding a book that is the culmination of a timely, brilliant concept and the hard-earned insights of its stable of contributors. Some advice: Read these chapters in any order. This book is the perfect airplane or commuter standby. After you're finished with it, recommend it to others; pass this book around.

Books like this are meant to be more than read. They need to be experienced. Plan now to make the ideas in this book take flight. Pass chapters around and use them as launching pads for lunchtime brown bag discussions. There are no right answers. We do know, though, that the wrong answer is ignoring the potential changes in our world and not delving into the strengths, weaknesses, opportunities, and threats. Using the ideas and insights of these authors to have informed discussions at your shop is like creating your own 16-week mini-conference.

For these past few years I have been traveling to many countries, continents, libraries, and conferences. If there is any one theme, one thread that I keep hearing, it's about the struggle to discover the magic sauce that will launch the new generation of library success. Worldwide, all types of libraries and all sectors of librarianship are asking themselves the key questions: How do we best serve our users and learners? How do we stay relevant? How do we harness technology while remaining true to our traditions and values? We're all in this boat together, and all libraries will float higher as we learn from the successes in other libraries, in other sectors, by other professionals.

For the last two decades or more we've focused as a profession on building the technological framework and foundation for a new hybrid library—digital and print, human and objects, communities and learning, and more. We've explored new concepts and engaged in a discussion that sometimes seemed to extend to rethinking and reassessing the foundations and principles of librarianship as a field. It has been an exciting Renaissance. Now the library world finds itself at another tipping point; we're moving forward beyond the technocratic focus of the past few decades to one that is primarily focused on people, our beloved end-users. And lord knows those users have changed!

Sometimes it seems that all of society is not at the top of the parabola on Moore's adoption curve. Libraries find themselves in a new normal, where significant portions of our user populations are moving beyond experimenting with new technologies as innovators and early adopters to seamlessly integrate these into their daily lives of work, study, and play. That has required many adjustments—not just to our sector, but to society in general, especially in our host communities, enterprises, and institutions. The selection of chapters in this book speaks not just to the technology but also to policy and legislative shifts, as well as to the evolution that must happen in traditional institutional settings. Joel Barker's famous dictum that our past success guarantees nothing is never more true than today. Revolution requires evolution.

So, in this text you'll find a guided tour through the top 16 issues facing libraries today. There are no right answers, and no one answer will work in all situations. It is an exciting time to be in libraries—as long as we keep the conversation going and try to invent the future, we are guaranteed a future. Here are the gems you'll find in this book:

- Megan K. Fox's informed view on the potential of mobile devices to transform information work

- Daniel Chudnov's take on the emerging role of open source, open access, and open content in our world

- John Blyberg's views on the future of the ILS and OPAC

- Discussions on changing publishing models by Jill Emery

- The challenges facing scholarly publishers and academic libraries by Dorothea Salo

- Beth Gallaway on the new and positive role gaming is playing in education and libraries

- Joseph Janes on competing with the Googles of the world

- Michael Stephens on the Read/Write Web

- Robert Bocher on the emerging critical issue of libraries and privacy

- David Lee King on positive user experiences on library Web sites

- Jenny Levine, the Shifted Librarian, on Library 2.0

- Rhonda B. Trueman, Tom Peters, and Lori Bell on Second Life Library 2.0 and libraries' roles in virtual worlds

- John D. Shank and Steven J. Bell on the blended librarian's role in academic learning

- Meredith G. Farkas on the future of library and information science education

- Jessamyn West on the negative side of technology—technophobia, technostress, and technorealism

- And lastly, Alane Wilson, who reads the tea leaves and points to the opportunities

I can't agree with every position in this work, and that is just wonderful! It's a two-way street, and informed conversations create change. To be intellectually challenged is a great gift. I get discouraged if I am not pushed out of my box often enough. I need to have my buttons pushed regularly. I believe there's enough in this book to push a few buttons for you and your organization. And that, to me, is what a collection should do—educate, inform, irritate, and inspire.

So, do yourself a favor, and get your juices flowing—read on.

Enjoy. Learn. Grow. Share.

—Stephen Abram, MLS
Vice President, Innovation, SirsiDynix
Chief Strategist, SirsiDynix Institute
Stephen's Lighthouse Blog
President-elect, SLA
Past President, Canadian Library Association
Past President, Ontario Library Association
stephen.abram@sirsidynix.com

Preface

I never think of the future—it comes soon enough.
—Albert Einstein

Our technological future begins now, and we need to pay attention to trends, technologies, and possibilities in order to remain relevant in the lives of our users. While prediction in this field can prove less than fruitful, if not embarrassing (remember when CD-ROMs were the wave of the future?), the essays in this book speak to trends that affect libraries' directions and decisions more than to any specific technology. The threads of interactivity, openness, and collaboration—combined with changing user expectations and technological possibilities—intertwine throughout these chapters, as each addresses one piece of the emerging technological puzzle.

Recurring themes throughout hark to the call of Library 2.0 and its focus on user-centered change. The contributors to this volume ask us to:

- Meet our users where they are.

- Base technological decisions on user needs and library missions, rather than on the new and the cool.

- Keep the principles and foundations of librarianship in mind when making technology decisions—as when making all our decisions.

- Re-envision our roles in an environment where we all can be content creators, as well as content consumers.

- Remember the importance of collaboration and community, and extend our partnerships beyond the traditional.

- Remain open to new technologies and new possibilities, maintaining our sense of wonder and thirst for lifelong learning.

Although each tackles one piece of our technological future, when taken as a whole, these essays bring to light the ways in which technological and societal change interact to demand changes in the way we operate our institutions.

Part I, "Formats and Functions," begins with Megan K. Fox's discussion of our role in an increasingly mobile, always-on age. How do we shift our services and mindsets to meet expectations of always available information, wherever and whenever users need us? Daniel Chudnov and John Blyberg extend the conversation with a respective look at open-source software and 21st-century OPACs. As each makes clear, not only do we face changing user expectations, but our approach to technology needs to draw on the foundations and principles of librarianship. When we treat technology as a creature separate and apart, we find ourselves taken advantage of by outside forces and unable to best serve either our institutions or our users.

Open source can also apply to our approach to electronic publishing. As Jill Emery so simply points out in her investigation into the issue: "We must accept that our future is driven by our users, not by our collections." Dorothea Salo next takes up the call, asking how and why libraries should shape the future of academic publishing within the larger context of the open-access movement.

Part II, "Change and Challenges," revisits the themes of changing user expectations and meeting our users where they are. Beth Gallaway kicks off this section by outlining why and how to use technology to reach out to our patrons, especially teens, by implementing gaming programs and friendliness to gaming within our institutions; she also shows what librarians can learn from gamer culture. Joseph Janes tackles the Google elephant in the room, taking a reasoned approach to what Google can do, what it can't do, and where that leaves libraries—again, in part, in the position of needing to meet our users where they are.

Michael Stephens also calls for a user-centric focus, writing about the Read/Write Web (or Web 2.0) and the ways it has changed both our online environment and our expectations. When traditional barriers to content creation crumble, how do we need to re-envision our role? Robert Bocher continues the discussion with a look at privacy issues from both a legal and a professional perspective; talking about ways to protect patrons' electronic information and to consider privacy issues when implementing new technologies in our institutions.

Beyond looking at patrons' online activities and ways to reach them via newer tools and technologies, David Lee King steps back to look at the bigger picture: doing (and redoing) our Web sites with an eye to experience design and planning. The most important step? Focus on your users when creating anything!

Part III, "2.0—and Beyond," extends the concepts in the earlier chapters, showing how we're beginning to blend new technological tools and a new mindset to envision the library of the future. No discussion of the future of libraries would be complete without a look at Library 2.0, and Jenny Levine outlines its main themes and the necessity of putting the user at the heart of all of our services, whether physical or virtual. Rhonda B. Trueman, Tom Peters, and Lori Bell take this call to heart with their activities in Second Life Library 2.0, and discuss libraries' presence and activities in the virtual world Second Life—a proactive approach to meeting users wherever they are.

From the academic library perspective, John D. Shank and Steven J. Bell address "blended librarianship," or the intersections between academic librarianship, technology, and instructional design. Beyond a new approach to academic librarianship, blended librarianship also emphasizes collaboration and community through "The Blended Librarian Online"; Shank and Bell discuss their project and its future direction.

Education also comes into play in our decisions on how best to educate current and future librarians, and library schools would do well to pay attention to Meredith G. Farkas's plea for the integration of technology throughout LIS education. As we weave technology through every aspect of our institutions, we need librarians who both understand and are comfortable with technology as implemented in a library setting; we need to rethink our LIS programs with an eye to educating 21st-century professionals.

The last couple of chapters step back and take a broader view, recognizing that any discussion of technology and libraries really boils down to a discussion of people and the way they learn, adapt, implement, and react to it. Jessamyn West explores technostress, technophobia, and technorealism, talking about the social and emotional component of implementing technology within our institutions. Alane Wilson shares ways to develop foresight in our technology planning, taking the people factor—and the ways they are using and will use technology—into account.

These glimpses into technology and the future of libraries begin to paint a picture of directions and possibilities. What this volume's contributors stress throughout, however, is the need to plan for that future in terms of themes and trends, balancing our professional foundations and principles against new possibilities and user demands. When we look at technology as woven into our institutions and professional practices rather than as an entity apart, we begin to be able to approach it more realistically. When we look at technology as a means to an end rather than an end in and of itself, we begin to give ourselves permission to envision new ends and new roles for both ourselves and our institutions. When we look at technology as enabling us to carry out our missions in new ways, we give ourselves the luxury to experiment and explore.

I look forward to seeing all of us experiment, explore, and envision, extending these ideas as appropriate for our own institutions and communities.

—Rachel Singer Gordon
rachel@lisjobs.com

Part 1

Formats and Functions

CHAPTER 1

The Mobile Age

Megan K. Fox
Web & Electronic Resources Librarian
Simmons College Library

As public and academic library patrons rely more and more on mobile tools such as personal digital assistants (PDAs) and cell phones for daily communication, entertainment, and commercial interactions, it is natural that they also turn to them for information. Patrons want answers at their moment of need—a price comparison while at the mall, the answer to a bar bet trivia question while watching a ball game, the history of a cultural landmark while standing in front of it. Patrons want the flexibility to choose among hundreds of audiobook files when stuck in traffic, rather than being limited to the handful of CDs they carry with them; they want to have a large selection of novels to read on a long flight or on a lunch break, not just the single bestseller they can lug around in hardback. They also want to be able to access these materials on their own devices—whether a home computer, a WiFi laptop they bring to the grassy space in front of the library, a cell phone they carry while browsing in the stacks, or an iPod they plug into during their daily workout.

While we will always see the need for in-depth, quiet library research, curling up with a leather-bound classic, and rambunctious story hours for toddlers clutching their favorite board books, we also see an increasing market and demand for mobile access to facts and information—gratification anytime, anywhere, on one's handheld device. It's exciting that recent and forthcoming technological developments facilitate our ability to respond to these patron demands—and even to move ahead of their expectations, becoming leaders in demonstrating and implementing the most effective means of information access, evaluation, and use.

The Handheld Market

A quick look at handheld market penetration and forecasts provides clear proof of the trend toward ubiquitous mobile devices. For example, 58 percent of teens, 70 percent of adults,[1] and almost 90 percent of college students have cell phones, twice the number as just five years ago.[2] The Mobile Marketing Association (MMA) reports that worldwide mobile phone subscribers have reached 1.4 billion, surpassing landline subscribers, and mobile devices are not just being used to make voice calls. MMA also reports that nearly 95 percent of active U.S. mobile phones support text messaging, and 62 percent of subscribers use it. U.S. mobile subscribers are exchanging almost 7 billion text messages a month, compared to 2.5 billion in 2005. U.S. usage will continue to explode as infrastructure, devices, and adoption of mobile communications in the U.S. catch up with Asian and European trailblazers. Users worldwide exchange 350 billion text messages every month![3]

The Tools

PDAs such as Palm Pilots and Pocket PCs have been visible in our libraries since 2000, but these days our patrons carry a much broader variety of handheld devices. We see iPods, tablets, personal gaming devices, global positioning devices, and other new devices that shrink technology into smaller, more powerful pieces of multifunctional equipment. Increasingly, we see smartphones as patrons' handheld device of choice. Smartphones are mobile devices that provide many more features than just voice call abilities, most commonly text messaging and/or Web browsing. These devices, labeled "integrated," "converged," or "multifunctional," often provide a camera, MP3 player, calendar, address book, calculator, picture viewing capabilities, and more.

Some of the most popular models come from Palm's line of Treos (www.palm.com/us/products/smartphones). Nokia and Samsung are particularly strong leaders in developing innovative and smaller, but still usable, smartphone styles. A scan of their latest product pages reveals newer "clamshells," which look like the conventional "candy bar" design but open to allow a wide-format screen (640 x 200). You can also find small flip phones that open on two sides to reveal a thumb pad on each side of the screen, providing more accessible keyboard input buttons than usually found on a mobile device (www.nokiausa.com/A4409001 and www.samsung.com/products/wirelessphones). The latest models we see in the U.S. consumer market tend to run five to seven years behind those currently in use in Asia, where smartphones commonly provide mobile video downloads, live TV, video calling, and interactive gaming—which are just beginning to appear in the U.S. Many of the most exciting new phone devices are still only ready for European and Asian markets, because they rely on a 3G infrastructure—the next and third generation of mobile networks that provides the speed and bandwidth to support sophisticated multimedia.

Microsoft recently announced the launch of the Ultra Mobile Personal Computer (UMPC)—a less expensive, lighter, and more functional mobile computer than a traditional laptop. Slightly larger than a PDA, UMPCs have full PC and Internet capabilities. They offer anytime connectivity, with access to e-mail, IM, and Voice over IP (VoIP). The screen is optimized for finger touch of scroll bars and launch buttons, and a special on-screen keyboard appears as two semi-circles in the bottom corners of the screen, providing easy thumb input while gripping the device. The greatest criticism of the UMPC devices is that the battery life is much too short (only two to three hours), which prevents the device from being the ideal mobile solution. But the very fact that a major player like Microsoft is focusing on this market further shows its potential and demonstrates how critical it is for libraries to consider the implications for our services.

There also are a number of promising new ebook readers that take advantage of new, super thin, reflective E Ink screens. These provide crisp, readable displays that consume very little power (www.eink.com). Newer readers are comparable to a typical paperback or hardback in size—large enough to be legible, but small and light enough to carry and manipulate with one hand. Because their purpose is to serve as dedicated ebook readers, they provide functionality such as remembering the last page you were on and opening right to it when you turn the machine on, single-button page turning and font enlarging, built-in access to dictionaries and encyclopedias, and tools such as annotations and bookmarking. New models include the Sony Reader (products.sel.sony.com/pa/prs/index.html), which weighs less than nine ounces, can store about 80 books on its internal memory, and allows for about 7,500 page turns on one battery charge. Another similar new device is the iRex Illiad (www.irextechnologies.com/shop/products/iliad.htm). This hardware is much more promising than failed first-generation readers of the late 1990s, presaging a resurgence in portable ebooks.

Consumers are bringing this wide variety of mobile handheld devices, such as smartphones, minicomputers, and ebook readers, into the library as part of their communication and entertainment portfolio. We have a great opportunity to capitalize on these devices as platforms for delivery of library information and services. If we fail to do so, this clear weakness and gap in our services will threaten libraries' ability to remain competitive players in the world of information delivery.

The Mobile Optimized Web

One of the most logical uses of these mobile devices is accessing content delivered over the Web. A large number of handheld devices can use WiFi or other means to provide direct access to the Internet through a mobile form of Internet Explorer, Opera, or other Web browsers. Just as we saw in the early days of Web development, the wide variety of machines and browsers makes formatting content a challenge. Many Web sites are intended for large screens and are busy, long, wide, and full of images, Java, Flash, or other programming that many small devices can't handle. This has led to a market for the mobile optimized Web.

"Mobile device optimized" means that designers limit graphical content, forms, data entry, and Java, keep text small, and enable word wrapping. Webmasters are using simplified HTML, XHTML, XHTML MP, WAP, or WML to create versions of their regular Web pages formatted to display clearly on small PDA and mobile device screens. A general rule of thumb is that ADA-compliant Web pages will also be accessible on a PDA. Flash Lite is currently being developed to assist in creating content specifically for mobile devices and small screens, and there are plenty of primers on creating or optimizing Web content for PDAs and other small screens.[4] A new .mobi Internet domain is intended to designate those sites especially compatible with mobile devices. The company behind this, dotMobi (mtld.mobi), created special mobile-optimized style guides, mandatory for users of a dotMobi domain.

Many sites will automatically detect the kind of device and browser you are on, and serve up an appropriate version of content to you. Handheld users also have access to a growing selection of services that will translate, on the fly, any Web content into a version that can display on a small screen. These include Skweezer (www.skweezer.com) and Iyhy (www.iyhy.com). AOL converts pages on the fly by an algorithm created by InfoGin, which strips out JavaScript, resizes graphics, and pulls the most important content to the top of the page to reduce scrolling. Also, just as sites often have an option to reformat for printing or e-mailing, some sites have added an "IM to a friend" option (every book from www.harperteen.com) or a "send 2 phone" feature (every listing at cityguides.msn.com/default.aspx?where=bostonma).

In addition to shoehorning existing Web content onto mobile screens, some services also facilitate the creation of native mobile content—content "born mobile." SplashBlog (www.splashblog.com) streamlines the process of mobile photoblogging, allowing users to capture an image from their camera phone and publish it to an online photoblog. Mob5 (mob5.com) is a content management system for mobile Internet pages, providing easy forms and templates for individuals to create their own hosted mobile Web sites. You can create a mobile blog, or "moblog," through a service such as Blogger Mobile (www.blogger.com/mobile-start.g), the WINK site (winksite.com), or Rabble (www.rabble.com). Services like these contribute to the ever increasing amount of readily available content for mobile handheld users.

Sites as diverse as the National Weather Service (mobile.srh. weather.gov), Hoover's (mobile.hoovers.com), and PubMed (pub medhh.nlm.nih.gov/nlm) all have mobile interfaces. Polls of top mobile Internet categories and sites show what our users are seeking on their handheld devices: e-mail, weather, search, sports, news, entertainment, and maps, from sites including ESPN, CNN, Yahoo!, and Google.[5] Many content providers, including libraries, are adapting their regular information pages to be PDA-friendly. Content that is useful on a handheld includes information that changes often or is referenced frequently. For example, the Lincoln Trail Library System provides library hours, contact information, upcoming events, and directions for more than 140 of its member and affiliate libraries in a format that patrons can download and store on their handheld, using Avantgo (www.ltls.org/pda.html).

Mobile Access to the Catalog

As more patrons are carrying cell phones, PDAs, and other small handhelds, the major Integrated Library System (ILS) vendors have realized the need to provide an interface for these devices. Innovative Interfaces (III), Endeavor, SirsiDynix, and Talis have all developed new interfaces for the traditional catalog that can be accessed on a mobile device. III's product is called AirPac, and 89 libraries have purchased and installed AirPac as of June 2007. If you have created a personal library catalog using LibraryThing, you'll be pleased to know it is now available in a mobile version as well (librarything.com/m). As mobile interfaces become a standard expectation, librarians will be responsible for becoming proficient in assisting patrons in accessing our resources through a small screen and becoming familiar with using a phone key pad to type text or an iPod scroll wheel to navigate through menus, in order to connect patrons with library resources.

Ready Reference Content *On the Go*

Librarians are facilitating access to all kinds of dictionaries, encyclopedias, and other reference books that are being formatted for small screen mobile wireless devices. Information that patrons traditionally found at the reference desk, in the reference collection, is now often available for their handheld, accessible to them at the point of need, whether at their book group or out with friends at the ballgame. Take a look at Handango (www.handango.com), Handmark (www.handmark.com), or Tucows (www.tucows.com) for content that can be downloaded to a handheld, such as the *Baseball Encyclopedia*, *Zagat's*, *Kaplan Test Preps*, *Rand McNally Atlas*, and much more. In most cases, patrons can select the model of their exact device to get compatible downloads.

Point of Need Answers

People increasingly use their mobile devices for all kinds of quick answers outside of the library as well. In many cases, this means turning to traditional search engines such as Google, Yahoo!, AOL, and MSN. Rather than using them for searching, though, they use them for pointed, specific answers. This most often includes ready-reference answers such as definitions, phone numbers, stock prices, and sports scores, as well as geographically contextual information, such as nearby movie theaters and show times.

Companies to watch include 4INFO (www.4info.net), Medio (www.mediosystems.com), and UpSnap (www.upsnap.com), which all return answers instead of lists of links. Most claim to improve search results by making assumptions based on a user's previous searches. Most also allow you to save time by presetting searching shortcuts on your desktop to then use on your mobile device, such as presetting "M1" to translate to a look-up for movies in Boston. Answers.com has also released a similar mobile interface for their instant answers on more than 3 million topics. The site has a special informational section just for librarians in which it's explained that the site does not intend to compete with libraries for the research market. Instead, Answers.com sees itself as being in the *presearch* market, or the initial investigation of topics you need before you delve into the deeper research process—the quick, short answer niche (librarians.answers.com/main/answers_librarians_presearch.jsp).

Mobile Ebooks

In addition to content that answers ready-reference questions, users can also find popular monographs in ebook format for small screens. We still face the challenge that Teleread (www.teleread.org/blog) calls the "Tower of eBabel," that is, the 20-plus competing formats in which an ebook may currently be delivered. Luckily, a very promising standards effort is being driven by a nonprofit organization that plans to launch a nonproprietary open format standard, based on XML and CSS. OpenReader (www.openreader.org) is a powerful and thoughtful format for electronic books, articles, and other textual digital publications, which will work across most devices. If adopted by enough major players, OpenReader should introduce much greater flexibility and ease of use into the ebook industry.

Overdrive, EBL, ebrary, Fictionwise, and NetLibrary, among others, have hundreds of libraries up and running systems for circulating electronic books, including audio materials for PDAs, iPods, and other devices. Loads of books are available for free from Project Gutenberg (www.gutenberg.org), and for both fee and free from Manybooks (manybooks.net). Some libraries are promoting handheld usage by providing instructions on how to use existing ebooks on handheld devices.

The Aggregators Go Mobile

Driven by the adoption of small screen devices in the professional arena, medical, health, and legal database vendors have been the first to develop simplified interfaces for accessing their traditional databases. OVID, the well-known provider of health and medical information, provides OVID@Hand. The National Institute for Medicine provides Medline Databases on Tap for mobile professionals. EBSCO recently announced PDA access for their *DynaMed* product—an evidence-based reference tool. In the legal and news arena, LexisNexis and Factiva have both teamed up with BlackBerry to provide access to their content, and Westlaw provides Westlaw Wireless for handhelds. The other major vendors are sure to follow soon. If not, it is up to librarians, in our crucial role as advocates, to push our vendors to respond to developments in the commercial and consumer marketplace—helping to ensure the library and information world does not fall behind.

SMS Text and Alerts

Many of the services just described are designed for live Web browser searching. Even though many mobile devices are equipped with this capability, WiFi hot spots are still erratic—and data plans on a cell phone can cost two to five times the price of a regular mobile phone bill. Consequently, only about 4 percent of North American households report using the mobile Web regularly.[6] In contrast, more than 62 percent use text messaging from their phones and other mobile devices. A number of exciting informational texting services have been launched in this market. For example, even if you don't have or use Internet on your phone, you can still text Google at 46645 ("Google" without the final "e") and get an answer, such as a movie time. Send the word "shortcuts" to 46645 to receive a summary of texting search tips, such as *d* for definition or *t* for translate. A very useful free feature of many of the text services of Google, Yahoo!, 4INFO, and others is the ability to set up free Text Alerts—to automatically have sports scores, weather, horoscopes, stock quotes, and more scheduled to be texted to you on a one-time or regular basis. As major player Synfonic (www.synfonic.com) articulates, mobile users don't want a miniature version of a Web site; they want just the key nuggets of content from the full Web site in a format that's easy to access on their mobile device.

Communicating with Your Mobile Patrons

As opposed to instant messaging, which is generally computer-to-computer and already starting to be widely adopted in libraries (see the Library Success Wiki, www.libsuccess.org/index.php?title= Libraries_Using_IM_Reference), texting or SMS (short message services) are generally between two phones or handheld devices. We've all seen the unfortunate signs in libraries banning cell phones (for examples, see www.flickr.com/search/?q=cell+ phone+library). While no one disputes the fact that loud conversations (both on the phone and between two people physically in the library) are disruptive, most phones are now truly multifunctional. Some patrons, especially teens, are more comfortable texting than speaking on a cell phone. It is important that we do not alienate possible users by careless banning of a device, as opposed to providing more thoughtful suggestions for proper behavior modification.

Librarians are extending traditional reference services to respond to these new mobile communication options. Altarama (www. altarama.com.au) has formed a virtual SMS reference service for libraries. Through their service, a text message sent by a mobile patron is translated into an e-mail message, which is sent to the library's regular e-mail account. A librarian then sends an e-mail answer, which is translated back into a text message for the patron. The service can also be used to send other short messages, such as overdue notices. The Library of Curtin University of Technology in Bentley, Australia, provides lots of information on their implementation of the service, including initial usage, lessons learned, and more (conferences.alia.org.au/online2005/pres/a12.pps). Another example can be found at Sims Memorial Library at Southeastern Louisiana University (www2.selu.edu/Library/ServicesDept/referenc/texta librarian.html).

Text messages or texted RSS feeds are being used in libraries to inform users of new resources and upcoming events, and to monitor patron accounts. ILS vendors Dokimas (www.dokimas.co.uk) and Talis (www.talis.com) offer patron account alerts that send notification to a mobile device about items that are due or holds that have arrived. Other vendors, such as SirsiDynix and III, are not far behind, with plans to offer the ability for libraries to text circulation notices to patrons' cell phones in upcoming releases. Other tools that enable librarians to deliver content how mobile users want it, via a text message, include Teleflip (www.teleflip.com), which lets you send e-mail to (cellphonenumber)@teleflip.com, which then gets translated into a text message. Vazu (www.vazu.com) lets you fill out a simple Web form that also gets converted into a text message for the recipient.

Smartphones Services

Many colleges and universities are further pushing the boundaries of services that can be delivered on smartphones. Wake Forest has a MobileU (mobileu.wfu.edu) pilot program focusing on mobile messaging, mobile access to information such as calendars, campus announcements, and real-time location of the campus shuttle bus. It also provides some control over the device—including features such as turning off the ringer during a student's scheduled class times. The library at Wake Forest has created a MobileU-friendly version of its Web site using a mobile style sheet, providing library hours, style citation guides, and a stack guide, and allowing users to search the library catalog and selected journals. Additionally, they have an RSS feed for new materials, which students can access using the RSS reader on the MobileU device. Baruch College of the City University of New York (www.baruch.cuny.edu) provides "Air Baruch," which allows students to use their cell phones to check on class assignments (through Blackboard), check on PC loans available at the library, and reserve study rooms. Southern Illinois University (www.siu.edu) and Montclair State University (www.montclair.edu) are additional folks doing cutting edge pilots in this area.

Audio Content in Your Hand

Audio content is now extremely easy to make mobile and handheld. iPods and other digital audio players are so common these days that librarians and patrons are experimenting with ways they can be of use in libraries. South Huntington Public Library in New York was one of the first to get iPod shuffles, preload them with audio books purchased via iTunes, and check out the entire device. The Thomas Ford Memorial Library has trialed book and movie review podcasts, by teens, for teens. The Duke Divinity School Library has put audio instructions for using reference tools and databases up as a podcast so students can help themselves when the library is open but unstaffed. The Crouch Fine Arts Library at Baylor University has

40GB iPods with every listening reserve for every class loaded on each device. Even Thomson Gale announced last November they were offering podcasts with some of their databases. Creative uses of iPods are especially prevalent in higher education—and there is much for libraries to investigate and learn from projects at institutions such as Georgia College & State University, at which students download 39 films to their video-capable iPods for a history class, and a psychology professor podcasts the week's most frequently asked questions to supplement his office hours.

The Audible Air service (www.audible.com) even lets you download recordings wirelessly directly into your phone, without having to sync with a desktop workstation. Los Angeles Public Library has launched an e-audiobook service that allows patrons to download hundreds of fiction and nonfiction titles to a supported MP3 player, PDA, or Smartphone.

Museums and cultural attractions are employing companies such as Guide by Cell and Museum 411 to create self-guided audio tours accessible through cell phones. To access the audio guides, visitors call in using their own cell phone, and then enter the number of the item they want to hear. Simmons College Library designed a tour of its new building using this technology and integrated the tour on Guide by Cell and via iPods to be checked out from the Circulation Desk as part of the First Year Orientation for Fall 2006. Given the increasing prevalence of devices that can easily access, store, and play audio, and of patrons who are inclined to use audio, what else could libraries be offering? Instruction sessions? Story hours?

Video on the Move

Mobile video is poised to explode as well. The U.S. mobile video user base is expected to grow to more than 20 million by the end of 2007, up from less than 1 million today, says American Technology Research.[7] South Korea and Japan are the early adopters, but European and North American markets are not far behind, with three contenders planning to introduce mobile video broadcast services in the U.S. over the next 12 to 18 months. You may have heard of mobisodes—mobile episodes—or television specially shot and edited for the small screen. CNN, ESPN, music videos, even the jokes from last night's *Daily Show with Jon Stewart* are available for mobile devices. Mobitv (www.mobitv.com) provides MSNBC, Fox, and other live television for your mobile phone. Sony's LocationFree (www.learningcenter.sony.us/HomeAudioandVideo/LocationFree/ Research1/LocationFreeFeatures) is available on a variety of Sony wireless devices. By 2011, forecasts predict 514 million mobile TV service subscribers worldwide, up from 6.4 million at the end of 2005.[8]

Handheld Devices to Help Library Staff

Library staff are discovering ways to use mobile handheld devices to make our daily work easier as well. In addition to the same functionality our patrons find useful, from portable calendars to ebooks, many library tasks can be improved by using a mobile device. One common use is in gathering statistics, such as physical head counts, reference inquiries, and stack inventory. SirsiDynix has a PocketCirc product, which provides a handheld PDA for wireless circulation management—you can check out from anywhere, increasing efficiency without being tied to the desk. Similarly, Wireless Workstation is III's product for performing real-time, at-the-shelf inventory and remote circulation. These products allow you to go to where the work is. Wireless Workstation is still pretty new—about 20 libraries had it up and running as of June 2007. In planning for the future, could we combine new self-checkout options with handheld devices to allow patrons to check out their materials on their own mobile devices?

On the Verge

While mobile devices of one kind or another are quickly becoming ubiquitous, their effective use is still hampered by the difficulty in quickly inputting text. Using your thumbs on a numeric phone pad on which you have to click three times to get to certain letters will never be natural or comfortable for the majority of users. Many creative solutions are under development to alleviate this process. These include communicating with your device, not by entering text by hand, but through using a camera feature to start a query with an image, or using voice activation, or even using a GPS physical recognition of a location to initiate a request for more information.

According to Mobot (www.mobot.com), cartons of milk in Europe will soon have images of CD cover art printed on them. Accompanying each image will be a message urging people to take a picture of the art with a cameraphone; users who send in the electronic picture will be sent a free MP3 song in return. In the U.S., people will be able to use their cell phones to take a picture of a movie billboard, and then send the image to a special database that returns a preview, locates a theater showing the movie advertised on the billboard, or allows the user to buy tickets to the movie. This is called "mobile visual search." How could we use something like this in libraries? Could patrons browse the shelves at Barnes & Noble, take a picture of the cover of an interesting book, and send it in to get the catalog entry for it from their local library, see whether it is available, put a hold on it, and get reviews, author bios, and literary criticism?

We also have a lot of ground to explore in the area of voice recognition—a logical step on cell phones, which were originally voice-centric. Wake Forest MobileU participants use smartphones to perform voice-activated interaction. As Line 56 reports, you say "*laundry* to the phone browser, it comes back and says *what dorm*? You say *Smith dorm* and it says *what floor*?" This works all the way down to the individual washer and dryer level, letting you know when your wash is done or where it is in the cycle. As the folks over at Line 56 have already envisioned, "what if you could simply say the word 'catalog' to your mobile device and have it open the corresponding browser window?"[9] We already do voice-initiated speed dialing on our mobile devices; applications such as "turn the page" or "save this document" can't be far behind.

Companies are also creating handheld devices that take advantage of global positioning systems. This is sometimes called point and click: You could, for example, stand in front of a historical landmark, point your device at it, and click the search button. The device will use your physical location to know you are asking for more information about, say, Fenway Park. Similarly, you could enter a library, and when you turn on your mobile smartphone, it automatically opens the library's Web page or the online catalog. Some of these services, such as MSN's "Near-Me" search, take advantage of "geo-tagging," that is, the inclusions of location information as part of the metadata that is indexed for content. Companies in this field include Intelligent Spatial Technologies, Inc. (www.i-spatialtech.com/iPointer.htm) and GeoVector (www.geovector.com).

Always On

Mobile handheld devices have the advantage—and challenge—of being virtually always on and accessible. Since they truly are personal devices, search histories and physical locations can be harnessed to produce more accurate, individualized information and services. As storing, searching, accessing, and manipulating information on the go becomes more expected by our patrons and staff members, it is increasingly important for librarians to understand the kinds of content and services that we can and cannot provide for small-screen mobile devices, and plan our time and resources accordingly.

The electronic version of the *Bonita Daily News*, recently honored with the Newspaper Association of America's Most Innovative Multimedia Storytelling award for its coverage of high school sports, provides a good glimpse of where information delivery is going. Its Web site is simple and straightforward, so that it displays properly and is accessible on a small screen. It provides short message service with free scoring alerts of high school football games sent to subscriber cell phones. Sports fans also can watch video highlights of games on a computer, iPod, or handheld Sony PlayStation device. This is a new breed of information delivery, allowing users to access content when they want it, how they want it. This is how our patrons are going to expect and demand their information from libraries as well.

As we shift from limited hot spots on campuses and in libraries to enterprise-wide and city-wide deployments, and always-on connectivity becomes an expected utility in the near future, we have to keep pace with our most advanced patrons' requirements, as well as lead those who may not have the tools or natural inclination to go down this path on their own. Just as information delivery was transformed from its roots in oral traditions, to the written word, to printed texts, to electronic, the next monumental frontier is mobile. Now is the perfect time for libraries to think about how to take advantage of the trails being blazed by consumer markets and to leverage the widespread prevalence of personal handheld mobile devices to increase access to information and our responsiveness to patrons.

Recommended Reading

In the area of technology, there are new developments almost every day. Some of the best places to stay informed on mobile handheld developments and implications for libraries and to connect with colleagues grappling with these same issues include:

- Engadget Mobile, www.engadgetmobile.com

- Gizmodo: The Gadgets Weblog, www.gizmodo.com

- GottaBeMobile, www.gottabemobile.com

- Handheld and Mobile Computing Constituent Group, EDUCAUSE, www.educause.edu/handheldandmobile computingconstituentgroup/7098

- The Handheld Librarian, www.handheldlib.blogspot.com

- MobileRead, www.mobileread.com

- LIBRARY-PDAs Listserv: Library Support for Palmtops, www.lsoft.com/scripts/wl.exe?SL1=LIBRARY-PDAS&H= LISTSERV.ARIZONA.EDU

- PDA-ebook: Users of Electronic Books on PDA devices group, tech.groups.yahoo.com/group/pda-ebook/

- PDAlibraries group at Yahoo!, groups.yahoo.com/group/ pdalibraries

- PDAs in education, www.jiscmail.ac.uk/pda-edu

- TeleRead: Bring the E-Books Home, www.teleread.org/ blog

- Textually, www.textually.org

- Wireless Librarian (Bill Drew), wirelesslibraries.blogspot. com

Endnotes

1. ZDNet Research, Top mobile phone brands in U.S.: Sanyo, LG, Samsung, posting to IT Facts Weblog, May 9, 2006, blogs.zdnet.com/ITFacts/ index.php?cat=4&paged=2 (accessed July 1, 2006).
2. Student Monitor LLC, "Study Finds Record Number of Student Cell Phone Owners," Student Monitor LLC, January 21, 2005, www.studentmonitor. com/press/02.pdf (accessed July 1, 2006).

3. Michael Becker, "Research Update: Unfolding of the Mobile Marketing Ecosystem: A Growing Strategic Network," Global Mobile Marketing Association, October 11, 2005, mmaglobal.com/modules/wfsection/article.php?articleid=74 (accessed July 1, 2006).

4. Colleen Cuddy, "How to Serve Content to PDA Users on-the-Go," *Computers in Libraries*, 26:4 (April 2006): 10–12, 14–15, PDF: vnweb.hwwilsonweb.com/hww/jumpstart.jhtml?recid=0bc05f7a67b1790 e0df0e5347ba8f6b21d0b207df8174eedfb5a95e4cab82cc9cf5c385cd2d92a cc&fmt=P.

5. Maria Bumatay, "Email, Weather, and Search Sites Are Most Popular Categories for Mobile Internet Use, According to Telephia," Telephia, June 2005, www.telephia.com/documents/InternetPressRelease090705FINAL REVISED.pdf (accessed July 1, 2006).

6. Alexa Raad, "Making the Mobile Web a Reality in North America (dotMobi)," Global Mobile Marketing Association, May 21, 2006, mma global.com/modules/wfsection/article.php?articleid=423 (accessed July 1, 2006).

7. Olga Kharif, "The Coming Mobile-Video Deluge," Wall Street Journal Online, October 11, 2005, www.businessweek.com/technology/content/ oct2005/tc20051011_9768_tc024.htm (accessed July 1, 2006).

8. ZDNet Research, Digital camera market shares: Canon - 17.1%, Sony - 16.7%, Kodak - 11.8%, posting to IT Facts Weblog, April 30, 2005, blogs.zdnet.com/ITFacts/?p=1123 (accessed July 1, 2006).

9. Demir Barlas, "Wireless Wonderland," Line 56, February 24, 2006, www.line56.com/articles/default.asp?ArticleID=7365 (accessed July 1, 2006).

CHAPTER 2

The Future of FLOSS in Libraries

Daniel Chudnov
Information Technology Specialist
Office of Strategic Initiatives, Library of Congress

Free/Libre/Open Source Software, or FLOSS, describes both a philosophy of software freedom and a widely accepted set of best practices for the development of software by distributed communities, often made up of volunteers. The core philosophy of software freedom is that software should be free to use, study, copy, modify, and redistribute. These freedoms have been enshrined in licenses designed to preserve copyright and to ensure the persistence of these freedoms as software is shared among users. Several FLOSS licenses have proven widely successful worldwide, and, with these licenses, FLOSS is dramatically changing the international software marketplace.

Librarians already both benefit from and contribute to FLOSS. The following sections talk about the impact of FLOSS, both in general and on libraries in particular, how FLOSS is helping to drive changes in libraries today, how FLOSS echoes the history of large-scale library philanthropy in English-speaking countries, and where some of these changes might lead libraries and librarianship.

A Brief History of FLOSS

The early history of FLOSS has been written in many forms.[1] The rise of proprietary software, or software sold with explicit restrictions on the same rights that are specified as freedoms under FLOSS, occurred alongside the rise of the personal computer (PC) in the 1970s and 1980s. Prior to this, operating systems were often given away for free, and most software applications were custom-built, simply because such a substantial portion of revenues were earned on the sales of hardware and hardware support services (and because the number of customers for computing equipment was so small). As the advent of the PC made computing a low-cost, mainstream commodity, companies like Microsoft saw the potential marketplace for computer software and anticipated what it would become: an opportunity to sell multiple products for every computer, on every desktop, anywhere in the world.

Moguls like Bill Gates created the billion-dollar global software marketplace in part by privatizing software products under a legal notion of intellectual property. Although this created great economic wealth, it effectively criminalized the previously common practices of sharing software at little or no cost. Some computer science researchers immediately recognized this dilemma when proprietary software reached their laboratories. The influx of software restricting their rights conflicted with their need to share and study other software—which supported the very core of their research activities.

The rise of the Internet facilitated the development of the GNU Project (gnu.org), a free operating system initiative, the Free Software Foundation (fsf.org), a tax-exempt, nonprofit institution advocating for software freedoms, and the GNU General Public License, or GNU GPL (gnu.org/copyleft/gpl.html), a software license using copyright to enshrine software freedoms for all developers and users. Software developers realized that they could easily find peers around the world with whom to collaborate, and the tools provided by the GNU Project and the GNU GPL, along with the Berkeley Software Distribution, or BSD (see bsd.org) and the BSD License, provided an increasingly potent combination for preparing, refining, and distributing software worldwide without sacrificing the potential for additional collaboration in the future.

By the 1990s, FLOSS had a number of major successes, including the Linux operating system kernel, the Sendmail e-mail server, the Bind package for domain name services, and the Apache Web server. One or more of these likely touched most Web and e-mail transactions on the worldwide Internet. By the early 21st century, high-quality FLOSS options for more common applications—Firefox for Web browsing, MySQL and PostgreSQL for databases, Perl, PHP, Python, and Ruby for programming, and Ubuntu and other distributions of the GNU/Linux operating system, to name just a few—are commonplace. Indeed, they are so commonplace that few computers are entirely devoid of FLOSS components, from those inside large-scale computing infrastructures like those powering Google and Amazon.com to those on the desktops of normal people like you and me.

FLOSS in Libraries

All of these factors affecting the success and importance of FLOSS in both infrastructure-level and application support tools hold true in libraries today. Although we might not always be conscious of it, our Internet Service Providers use FLOSS, the supporting institutions housing our libraries use FLOSS, and major library software vendors use both FLOSS tools to develop their products and FLOSS components inside their products.

The benefits of this last change—that library software vendors use FLOSS—might not be obvious, but they are important. In the mid-1990s, for example, one vendor shipped an early Web-based OPAC, which depended upon a bundled, obscure, proprietary Web server. This raised two important issues. First, few individuals apart from those employed by the vendor could diagnose and troubleshoot problems in the server, because nobody knew anything about it. Secondly, libraries supporting this product could not learn more about how it worked, even if they wished to. The first problem could have been solved in part by switching to a proprietary but commonly used Web server like Microsoft's. Even in that case, though, library staff would still be stuck with a "black box" of sorts, unable to diagnose or troubleshoot anything about the server beyond what a manual or book about the Microsoft server might explain. Similar issues apply to the proprietary Web OPAC application.

Over the past 10 years, this situation has improved somewhat, as libraries and library vendors alike have realized the benefits of choosing FLOSS options. Many newer products in our market now use FLOSS—Web OPACs can run on Apache, for instance, and some common OpenURL resolvers are written in Perl and PHP. Many of these kinds of products ship in versions that can run in diverse configurations using Windows or Linux, and with either a proprietary database like Oracle or a FLOSS database like MySQL. This change means that libraries that invest staff time in learning Apache, Perl, or MySQL can not only apply knowledge gained to in-house software development, but can also apply all of this knowledge to otherwise proprietary vendor products. Additionally, because knowledge and experience with these common tools is widespread, a library invested in these components might be able to hire new staff with appropriate experience more easily.

Library-Specific FLOSS

The use of FLOSS in libraries as infrastructure and within vendor products is only part of the story. In the past 15 years, a wide variety of complete library-specific applications have been released under FLOSS licenses. Well more than 100 of these have been announced at oss4lib.org (Open Source Systems for Libraries) and on popular library technology e-mail lists. As of 2006, FLOSS library software covers a wide range of product categories, including:

- *Bibliographic management* – FLOSS tools supporting bibliographic management have been widely available for many years, and have recently improved in usability and the variety of supported formats.

- *Information retrieval* – A diverse array of information retrieval software is widely available, with a wide range of implementations in various languages. SWISH-E, Zebra, Lucene, Nutch, Solr, and Xapian can support a wide range of potential applications.

- *Metadata tools* – Includes the widely used Perl modules for manipulating MARC data, MARC.pm, and MARC::Record, as well as similar tools MARC4j, pymarc, and ruby-marc (in Java, Python, and Ruby, respectively).

- *OPAC/ILS* – Koha use is growing in smaller libraries, and the Evergreen project from the state of Georgia looks to serve a state-wide library system. PHPMyLibrary and PMB are also finding use and support, and FLOSS support tools for ISIS are in wide use all over the world.

- *Protocols* – Library protocols such as OAI-PMH and Z39.50/SRU have too many FLOSS implementations in various languages to name. Tools also exist for ISO ILL (OpenRequest) and NISO OpenURL (CUFTS and OLinks), and are forthcoming for NCIP.

- *Public services* – ReservesDirect provides a sophisticated online reserves tool; several FLOSS remote access proxy solutions are available; many workstation administration toolkits have long been available.

- *Repositories* – The growing product niche of repository software includes Greenstone, the first sophisticated FLOSS collection management system, and EPrints, FEDORA, DSpace, and aDORe. Each of these has had a significant impact in digital library research and development as well as in a growing number of implementations.

It is difficult to provide a more substantial listing of these applications, simply because so many exist. To learn more about today's market for FLOSS in libraries, visit the oss4lib site and associated mailing list and follow the popular Web4Lib (lists.webjunction.org/web4lib) and code4lib (www.code4lib.org) e-mail lists; discussion of FLOSS tools often occurs on each of these sites.

How FLOSS Succeeds

The first widely successful FLOSS applications in libraries were standards and protocol implementations. These mirror the areas where FLOSS first succeeded more broadly worldwide, primarily in infrastructure support, such as in implementations of standards and protocols (managing Internet traffic, e-mail servers, and Web servers, all of which follow longstanding standards). As with e-mail or Web traffic, many tools for manipulating MARC records exist because so many libraries have MARC data to manipulate. We know MARC well, and we can easily determine when a tool is handling MARC correctly, or explain why it is not. This same logic applies for other standards and protocols, such as the OAI-PMH standard, which can be easily tested for standards conformance.

This leaves a gap in more esoteric library application areas, such as virtual reference or serials check-in modules. The power of choosing to use FLOSS components, however, can have a major payoff even in these domains. A key consideration in software development is whether a problem can be described in terms of one problem a wide number of people have, or in terms of a variety of smaller problems lots of people have. The implementation itself of widespread standards and protocols prescribes solutions to widely understood problems. Similarly, the more easily any software application can be broken into well-understood pieces, the more likely a piece of a complete solution might be filled by existing FLOSS components.

In virtual reference software, for example, any number of widely popular FLOSS Web programming toolkits—such as Perl and Catalyst, PHP, or Ruby and Rails—might be used. For communications between machines, a well-known instant messaging protocol like Jabber/XMPP could be very useful, and many FLOSS implementations of Jabber/XMPP already exist. Because of this, anyone developing a virtual reference application in 2007, should they choose to use these already available components, would have a leg up on a software developer building a whole application from scratch. Add to this the benefits described earlier from using well-known tools for which experience is widespread, and libraries and library vendors are well positioned to develop, deploy, and release new FLOSS solutions for even seemingly obscure library problems.

Another major benefit of FLOSS options in both library and non-library applications is that libraries can choose to experiment with FLOSS tools at little or no cost. This allows a librarian to download, install, study, and test a software package with very little risk. Should such a package fit a need well, the library is free to deploy the package as a supported service. Librarians may even choose to modify and redistribute the tool themselves if the need arises, as long as they adhere to the license attached to the software they first received. These options are all available because of software freedom.

The learning process itself can similarly be enhanced with FLOSS tools. When I was a library school student, we learned the basics of information retrieval by creating an inverted file from a small text using index cards and then physically sorting them in a large room. This useful exercise is not necessarily passé, but consider how well it might be extended by then teaching students to implement the same index file with easy-to-use software built on FLOSS information retrieval components, and to have those students then vary the indexing strategy in various ways to see how those strategies must change as larger and more diverse information sources are indexed. These kinds of teaching opportunities were unavailable or cost-prohibitive when I was a student.

At their best, good FLOSS applications invite users to share in the development and support process. Much like usability testing of software allows users to help programmers improve that software, a healthy feedback cycle involving both FLOSS implementers and developers benefits all involved. The best FLOSS tools in most application domains are typically well documented and are managed by communities of developers and users, who in many cases provide support as sophisticated and responsive as that available from proprietary vendors—or even better. Similarly, the sharing of FLOSS-based solutions can quickly lead to enhanced communications with peer institutions, proving another collaborative opportunity for libraries with a long tradition of resource sharing in other forms.

Getting Started with FLOSS

The first places for a librarian interested in FLOSS to visit are fsf.org and opensource.org, the anchor sites for the organized FLOSS community. Next, visit oss4lib.org, home of information about FLOSS in libraries since 1999; it comprises hundreds of blog entries about library-specific FLOSS. These sites will orient you to the formal definitions of FLOSS, why it matters, where to go for more information, and how FLOSS has progressed in libraries.

In your library, when you next come to a decision about software-based services, ask yourself these questions:

- Are there FLOSS alternatives?

- Do products you're considering use FLOSS components?

- Does your vendor contribute to FLOSS?

- Does your license have a "FLOSS clause"?

A FLOSS-compatible license is best, but, realistically, the library software marketplace will have proprietary products and restrictive licensing for years to come. Sometimes, however, you might still be able to negotiate the addition of a "FLOSS clause" in an otherwise restrictive license. A FLOSS clause might provide your institution with one or more of the freedoms to use, study, copy, modify, or redistribute the purchased code. It might also limit the "triggering" of any of these freedoms to certain agreed-upon conditions or renegotiations. Even in a situation where FLOSS is not an option, some software freedom is better than none.

The best way to get up to speed with FLOSS is to try it where you are. Find a small project where your staff might use a FLOSS language or database instead of a proprietary option, or find, download, and experiment with one of the many library FLOSS applications listed at oss4lib.org. If you and your staff find something you like, consider joining its project community through a mailing list, or helping with documentation or with bug testing. Most of all, if it works for you, tell your colleagues all about it.

The Future of FLOSS in Libraries

As in the rest of the software industry, the growth of FLOSS in libraries has a cumulative effect. FLOSS servers can be built upon FLOSS network infrastructure, then FLOSS software components can be built upon FLOSS servers, and then FLOSS applications can be built upon FLOSS components. These kinds of shifts lead to several outcomes that are likely to define the directions taken by FLOSS in libraries.

Shifting Markets

As FLOSS pieces are added at each layer, commercial opportunities around each piece and each layer can shift dramatically. For example, consider the market for e-mail and Web servers. Several well-known and reliable FLOSS options exist in each category; these options fit the needs of a wide range of enterprises, from individuals and small businesses to Fortune 500 companies. When FLOSS options this good are available, the commercial opportunities shift from competing directly with the FLOSS options to offering high-quality support for the FLOSS options, or to offering significant added value to the FLOSS options, such as site-specific customization, integration, and tools for administration and analysis. Proprietary products can only compete successfully if they are as reliable as the FLOSS options and if they offer other significant benefits such as integration with other widely used tools. The library community is starting to see this pattern play out around library FLOSS applications, with vendors offering support for and integrated services around FLOSS repository and OPAC tools.

Opportunities for Collaboration

The tradition of resource sharing among libraries dates back centuries. In the past, resource sharing largely consisted of cooperative collection development, shared cataloging, and loan programs, typically organized by regions or the types of communities served by participating libraries. The history of automation in libraries similarly includes milestones where groups of libraries found new ways to improve services by pooling resources and sharing the cost of research and development.

Many new resource-sharing opportunities are afforded by FLOSS and the low-cost, low-barrier marketplace in which FLOSS has grown. Because participation can be easier, and geographical distance matters less, any two or more institutions can use the techniques common to FLOSS development to address problems together. New partnerships can easily involve combinations of small public libraries, medium-sized academic libraries, library system vendors, individual professionals, students, and even library patrons. When you begin to think of the potential range of partners as encompassing *everybody*, and when you begin to act on this opportunity by finding and engaging anyone willing to help—regardless of their affiliation or location—you realize that the whole world can be your systems office, or your vendor. You might also find yourself becoming a vendor to the rest of the world, by posting a message on an e-mail list and/or by publishing your code to a Web site.

This realization might come slowly. Until you experience it yourself, it is hard to believe that, even without promotion incentives or contracts or local peer pressure, you can easily grow to trust and depend upon total strangers working in environments wholly unlike your own to help make services in your library better. Having experienced this myself many times over, and having observed many colleagues going through the same realization in recent years, it is clear to me that, once the FLOSS bug bites you, its effects can be permanent. You may never define your "workplace" in the same way again.

Easier Searching Then, Easier Software Now

We can hope that most librarians are over the traumatic shift from being "expert searchers," using complicated and difficult search command sets, to the present world, where everybody believes they can find everything through one simple search box. If this trend can be deemed "democratizing search," then we can imagine the onset of FLOSS (among other factors, including those that made FLOSS possible) as a trend toward "democratizing software." Over the past 20 years, the search services that came to dominate worldwide access to information won because they are simpler, more accessible, more usable, and good enough. During this same period, while it became easier for more and more people to search and find information, it has become easier for more and more people to develop and deploy software. This is due to many factors, including better software tools, cheaper computing power, and the prevalence of FLOSS.

Because it is easier now to employ computing power with better software distributed as FLOSS, it is also easier now to develop and deploy library services. Those inexperienced with FLOSS might at first dismiss FLOSS options for operating systems, database engines, programming languages, and applications as "immature," "not as powerful as what we're used to," or "not serious enough." If these sound familiar, remember that these were the same critiques heard in libraries for years as searching for and finding information became democratized. Just as with search, software is now becoming quickly democratized, and librarians would be fools to fail to take advantage of the new power in our hands. The software freedoms FLOSS provides ensure that this power can stay in our hands.

Grinding Down the Library Software Marketplace

Libraries are well positioned to benefit from the massive amount of innovation, commoditization, and freedom present in today's software marketplace. When we need a database—relational, hierarchical, XML, embedded, or object-based—we have well-known FLOSS options to choose from. When we need to implement search interfaces, terrific FLOSS information retrieval libraries are available. FLOSS Web application frameworks are at the leading edge of tools for building usable, dynamic Web interfaces. Standards and FLOSS reference implementations of a plethora of information packaging, transformation, and communications techniques are ready and waiting for us to use.

The mental switch we need to flip is to learn to think of what many of us still consider "library problems" as less unique to our own domain. The more we see solutions developed in the broader software marketplace as solutions applicable to library services, the easier it becomes to choose FLOSS infrastructure. The more we can choose FLOSS for library service infrastructure, the more we can focus on what makes library services unique. The answer to the question: "What makes library services unique?" might be different for all of us, but FLOSS can move beyond some of the old answers—"our data is hierarchical," "we need good search interfaces," and "we focus on accessibility and usability"—allowing us to focus even more.

In this way, we can expect the "library-ness" of today's library software to fade somewhat, and for more solutions relevant to libraries to appear from nonlibrary software and service providers. The very notion of what has defined "library automation" for the past 30 years will shrink to mean primarily legacy operations; more and more of our critical systems, standards, and services will come to be supported by solutions developed outside of our community, and customized and optimized within it.

Carnegie Library, FLOSS Library

At the end of the 19th century, the program funded by Andrew Carnegie to support the construction of libraries in English-speaking countries left an indelible impact on our society, and changed libraries dramatically. It helped to bring new and improved services to previously unserved and underserved communities; it helped to increase literacy and to share culture and civic participation; it led to a rapid increase in the demand for librarians and training in librarianship. Millions were donated, but the grants did not come without conditions: They provided only capital support for construction (not books), and they typically required a long-term commitment from municipalities to staff, fill, and sustain the libraries over time.[2]

In 1900, it was impossible to run a library without a building, but you could have a library without software. In 2007, it is impossible to run a library without software, but you can have a library without a building. If you consider FLOSS to be as massive a donation of time, energy, and useful products today as Carnegie-built libraries were 100 years ago, you might think twice before ignoring FLOSS options for your next project or purchase.

As with Carnegie funds, FLOSS does not come without conditions. FLOSS components and applications are only tools, which you and your library must turn into supported, useful services. FLOSS is not "free" of licensing or copyright; FLOSS licenses and the copyright system promulgate and enforce software freedom. FLOSS options might ask more of you than you might otherwise choose to agree to, but in many circumstances, the trade-off can be more than worthwhile.

On the other hand, it is easy to imagine the potential benefits: FLOSS can help to bring new and improved services to our communities, to help us increase literacy, share culture, and encourage civic participation. It might lead to a dramatic change in how we staff and partner among libraries, depending on the marketplace shifts and new collaborative opportunities FLOSS can offer. Although the ultimate commitment to create and sustain libraries must still come from the institutions and communities that our libraries serve, FLOSS can bring the talents and achievements of the rest of the worldwide software community into our libraries and our communities, more rapidly, inexpensively, and usefully than ever before.

Endnotes

1. Various, *Open Sources: Voices from the Open Source Revolution*, Sebastopol, CA: O'Reilly, 1999, www.oreilly.com/catalog/opensources/book/toc.html (accessed 31 July 2006).
2. G. S. Bobinski, *Carnegie Libraries: Their History and Impact on American Public Library Development*, Chicago: ALA, 1967.

CHAPTER 3

Mouse Bites Cat: Taking Back the 21st-Century ILS

John Blyberg
Head of Technology and Digital Initiatives
Darien Library

Buying a library automation system is much like buying a family home, with one major difference. Imagine if you could neither visit the house you were buying nor send in an inspector. Instead, you could only rely on the description given to you by the seller's real estate agent. She would, like any good agent, play up the best features of the house. She would fail to mention that the furnace needs to be replaced, that the roof leaks, and that there are no windows in the master bedroom. Sure, you could ask questions. You could even ask: "Is there a nice view from the master bedroom?" The answer you might get is: "You can see many trees from the master bedroom." What the agent fails to mention, however, is that to see these trees, you have to stand in the doorway and look down the hall at a mirror set up at a 45-degree angle to reflect the hideous tree-patterned wallpaper lining the stairway. This summarizes the current RFP (Request for Proposal) process.

The inherent problems with the current vendor–library relationship only begin at the RFP process. Before I proceed, though, let me be clear that my goal is not to vilify ILS vendors. They are for-profit companies in a world where profit is a necessary cog in the perpetuation of civilized society. Library automation systems are critical tools—valuable pieces of software that facilitate a fluid and dynamic library experience. Without them, libraries would be forced to rely on the imprecise, paper-based systems of the past. Our ILSs have enabled us to cut administrative overhead significantly over the years, leading to vastly larger collections and impressive circulation numbers. There is no doubt that our vendors, despite our sometimes tempestuous mutual history, have chosen to create complex and worthy products. It's important, therefore, to separate the software itself from its associated relationships. Our relationship has evolved over time and is a summation of the actions of both vendors and libraries. No blame can be placed in either camp. (Or, if you are inclined to place blame, it should go in equal parts to both parties.) Pragmatically, it is what it is. The goal of this chapter is to acknowledge a flawed partnership system and suggest a set of rules or standards to serve as parameters for the vendor–library interconnect.

The Balance of Power

The first step in understanding this complex relationship is to analyze the nature of its power structures and how they have shifted dramatically, creating an unbalanced condition. Unlike most software products, library automation systems are not influenced by natural market forces in the way one might expect. While the sales process does rely upon reputation to an extent, when the entire product pool has been soured by a perceived and ongoing enmity between client and seller (whether earned or not), the variables that factor into purchase decisions tend to deviate from traditional factors. Reputation, quality, price, and so on, become less meaningful; the overwhelming din of dissatisfaction drowns out any voice of approval. When this happens, buyers often become numb to criticism of the products they may purchase. The unfortunate irony lies in the fact that the loudest critics are often the most irrational, while those who have both criticism and praise to offer (and whose voices simply get lost in the row) are worth listening to. The end result is that reputation and quality lose their relevance. While cathartic, "vendor-bashing" is a zero-sum game that alienates vendors and inhibits our ability to make sound, reasoned purchase decisions.

From what I've observed, libraries often default to looking at how other fiscally comparable libraries are choosing their ILSs instead of making the decision for themselves. As a result, libraries often commit to a new system without truly knowing the ramifications of that choice. These are lost opportunities—during the selection process, libraries have significant power with respect to their potential vendor. Once the purchase has been made, the library will never again have the same level of influence.

The Sphere of Influence

Vendors are cognizant of the fact that once libraries have committed to a new automation system, their sphere of influence diminishes almost completely. This is simply because libraries can no longer produce sufficient leverage when trying to settle disputes. Once a library has purchased an automation system, it can't just be returned if it doesn't perform as expected. This is the first, and possibly biggest, power inequity between the vendor and the library. Often, several years of planning and hundreds of thousands of dollars go into a migration. After a sale, the vendor is no longer in a position where it benefits from offering incentives to the library. In fact, at this point, the library becomes a support liability; the vendor's main priority becomes to minimize the cost associated with that customer. Because the big profit has already been made, the vendor can only expect annual maintenance fees from then on out (not exactly pocket change, but certainly a fraction of the initial outlay).

Vendors have developed a support process that ensures that they maximize even that revenue stream. Remember, vendors are companies. Structurally, they are no different from any other software company. The sales team is a highly motivated, well-connected group of people that stands to make an incredible amount of money off of a sale. The most egregious ones will often tell you *anything* to close the deal, if you let them. The sales team is typically separated from support and implementation and can be out of touch with some basic realities of the company they represent. As customers, we need to be aware that we may not be getting straight answers.

Technical Complacency

Another significant power bias stems from the fact that many (if not most) libraries are simply not staffed with people who have the expertise and experience to evaluate, with any perspicuity, the many technical aspects of the software or contractual agreement. On one hand, vendors have been very helpful in this regard—they often provide turnkey solutions that simply *work*. That's fine, and even in some cases desirable, but the price for that luxury has been the loss of vendor accountability. Lack of internal technical expertise has left libraries extremely vulnerable in many ways. On my Weblog (www.blyberg.net), I talk about the need for libraries to shore up that liability by hiring coders or highly technical people, training existing employees, and conducting technology audits. Libraries place themselves in a precarious situation by not doing everything they can to stay on the face of an ever-cresting technological wave. Vendors are but one of the many rapacious creatures who know that technology is our Achilles heel. They conceal their appetite in tricky turnkey solutions that leave very little wiggle room for doing anything "unintended." Let's be realistic, though—it's in their nature. We may just as soon pass judgment on a cat for hunting down a field mouse.

A good example of the type of behavior that technical complacency leads to is the common practice of hardware price gouging. While it is not uncommon for vendors in many different markets to be involved with computer equipment resale, the margins seen in our industry are staggering. I have little issue with mandating hardware profiles, as long as they can be requisitioned by the customer. It is not uncommon for a vendor to lock us in to buying $12,000 worth of hardware for $40,000, and to deny libraries the option of maintaining it themselves. The popularity of turnkey solutions has resulted in many companies mandating hardware profiles that can only be purchased through them. Then, costly support contracts often involve one or more third parties for hardware maintenance—by the time a server reaches your rack, there may be four or five fingers in that pot. The reason for the outrageously inflated cost quickly becomes clear: profit sharing. Again, this is fine, if you're willing to pay for it *and* if you have the option of supporting and buying the equipment yourself. More often than not, however, this is not the case.

There are some very serious implications of letting this fleecing continue. One RFID system vendor, for example, sells a self-check system that consists of a mid-range Dell Dimension desktop (about $600 from the Dell Web site), a touch screen LCD (about $600), a barcode scanner ($130), a receipt printer ($200 for a nice one), and their RFID pad (RFID tag readers are typically about $80, but the same company will sell you the reader by itself for $1,200, so let's go with that number). I'm being generous when I put the total street value for the self-check hardware at $2,730. Bundled with their software, however, the company charges $17,000 per unit. The fact that libraries continue to pay such extortionate prices amounts to little more than a subsidy for these companies—a misuse of public funds, at the very least. I often wonder what the public response might be if the amount of money spent on these systems was disclosed. How many books, CDs, or DVDs can $17,000 buy? Two of these self-checks could pay for a full-time employee for an entire year. It's almost as though we see these numbers and agree to pay them because such high prices indicate complexity beyond our comprehension. The truth is, though, that it's entirely possible to create a self-check of our own for just the cost of the hardware. We pay these prices because we are unaware of our options. The same can be said about many of the features we purchase for our ILS.

Rights and Relationships

After emerging from an automation system migration in 2005 and witnessing much of what I've described here, I felt that the library industry, as a whole, had "purchased" itself into a relationship that is unhealthy, unproductive, and—worse—stifling to innovation. We had decided to launch a new Web site in tandem with our new automation system. While I was working on integrating our site with the system, I saw, first-hand, the type of inadequate, inflexible mediocrity being foisted upon us. Integrating the Web site with the automation system at a level that would provide a seamless experience between the two proved to be an extremely difficult project, and brought us well outside the bounds of "intended use." It occurred to me that the likelihood of another library doing what we had done was, unfortunately, very slim because there was no mechanism within our new system to facilitate such a project—no meaningful API, no access to the database, and much of the system's output seemed hard-coded. We were in uncharted territory. In fact, I began to wonder if we had violated a number of contractual agreements by, literally, hacking into our own system to tap in to various data sources.

As I thought about the unfortunate circumstances many of us seem to be mired in, I began to think about what it was we truly needed from our vendors. The old, "give a man a fish, and he'll eat for a day. Teach a man to fish ..." line comes to mind. Obviously, I'm interested in the latter. It seemed that the most subversive thing I could do would be to propose several extremely simple demands that, to almost everyone, would sound completely reasonable—because, in principle, they are. This very short list of equitable requirements would address the problem directly.

As I formed the list in my mind, I thought that its impact might be greater if I were to present them as a manifesto and call them a "Bill of Rights." Thus, the *ILS Customer Bill of Rights* was born (www.blyberg.net/2005/11/20/ils-customer-bill-of-rights). I sat down for about 20 minutes and blogged four basic, inalienable rights. These were, and continue to be, my demands:

1. A full-blown, W3C standards-based API to all read–write functions

2. Open, read-only, direct access to the database

3. The option to run the ILS on hardware of our choosing, on servers that we administer

4. High security standards[1]

That's it. It's worth noting that this list is tech-centric. It does not attempt to address the functionality of the system, the interface, the circulation, acquisition, or collection components—those key elements are already under scrutiny by libraries. Instead, I wanted the "Bill of Rights" to serve as a starting point for libraries to begin thinking differently about the entire purchase and migration process, moving us away from one that enables the current vendor–library relationship. I think the most common misinterpretation people make of this post is that it's intended for vendors, when in fact, it is first and foremost a manifesto for libraries.

APIs

The first item in the list calls for a "W3C standards-based API (Application Program Interface) to all read–write functions." W3C refers to the World Wide Web Consortium. According to its site (www.w3.org/Consortium), "W3C primarily pursues its mission through the creation of Web standards and guidelines. Since 1994, W3C has published more than ninety such standards, called W3C Recommendations."[2] In other words, this is the group of people who, in essence, decide how the Web works.

When they say "recommendations," they are being modest. One of the "recommendations" they developed is XML—a ubiquitous standard used by developers to transmit complex data. XML's strength is in its ability to encode three-dimensional data objects in a textual syntax that is easily transmitted via the Web. The use of XML has evolved over time into a number of implementations called "Web services." While Web service technologies like SOAP (Simple Object Access Protocol) are W3C-sanctioned, others, like REST (Representational State Transfer), have been developed outside the auspices of the W3C yet have gained enough popularity to be considered "standard." Amazon's API, for example, involves a REST implementation. The W3C is currently planning a new specification for what they call the Semantic Web, an evolved version of the current Web, where programs can interact, with dynamic intelligence, with each other—not just with people.

If you're not familiar with Web services, the most important concept to understand is that they are a universally agreed-upon set of tools that allow systems to interact with other systems and software. This is what is commonly referred to as an API.

Modern programming convention heavily recommends that software products provide an API to their major functions. Microsoft's .NET platform, for example, is an extremely rich API to the MS Windows operating system. It allows software developers to reuse code already written by Microsoft. This provides three major benefits. First, it facilitates very rapid development. Second, it ensures a higher quality product, because as Microsoft releases updates and fixes, any dependent software benefits from those patches as well. Third, and most importantly, if there were no API, software developers would not be able to write software for the Microsoft operating system unless they were privy to the Windows source code.

Traditionally, librarians have not been concerned with the ability to program for their ILSs because libraries didn't employ programmers. Several factors are slowly changing this. One major reason for the newfound interest in library programming is due, in large part, to the unacceptably slow pace of innovation among vendors. Quite frankly, librarians are getting tired of waiting around on the possibility that their vendor will someday produce a requested feature. Unless potential customers are requesting that feature, vendors have very little incentive to produce and innovate. Another reason is that when a new feature is released vendors typically charge exorbitant amounts for a subpar product that could have been developed easily in-house, given the right tools. Yet another reason for the emergence of the "library coder" is Web 2.0—the Read/Write Web. Web 2.0, which favors constant and consistent change and innovation, is at odds with the rigid, monolithic structure of the 20th-century ILS. Where Web 2.0 exists in a state of "perpetual beta," our vendors favor highly controlled upgrade paths. This may be an arrangement that works for them, but it does little to benefit libraries.

Inside the Box

Folks in Maine have a saying: *You can't get there from here.* I think that is the sentiment many library techies have when it comes to trying to do something with their system. The problem with complete reliance on a vendor for new features and functionality is that you can only do as much as the system allows. There is no room for thinking outside the box; the box is closed so tightly, and we have the constant fear that if we fiddle with it, it might pop open like Lemarchand's box, bringing with it a slew of demonic ILS-slayers who are just itching to take down the system.

That reality might not be too far off if vendors allowed write access to their back-end databases, which is why I conditioned my second request as "read-only." Being able to run custom queries against our databases allows us to provision for any eventuality. Programming, by nature, is a creative endeavor. As such, we can expect that new, exciting, and creative uses for our own data will be found and exploited by coders in the future. It gives us the ability to harness *our* data—that is, the data that we own, that we have grown, harvested, cataloged, and pruned over the years. It seems to me that unfettered access to this data should be among the most basic rights afforded to libraries by their vendors. At the very least, it would ensure that we could always "get there from here."

Serve Yourself

My third request has met with the most resistance from vendors who are afraid, rightly, of the possible support ramifications associated with allowing their customers to manage their own servers. I'm fairly specific when I say I'd like the "option to run the ILS on hardware of our choosing, on servers that we administer." What I do not say, however, is that vendors should not provide the customer with very specific hardware requirements. To me, that is a perfectly reasonable practice. Libraries should have the option of speccing and purchasing their own hardware, then doing the install in a manner that is consistent with the rest of their enterprise environment. Of course, this is my systems administrator side talking, but one of the problems many organizations suffer is that they fail to acknowledge the need for unity between infrastructure and function. They purchase many disparate, standalone, appliance-like solutions that operate independently. The result is a hodge-podge of servers and systems that create a cacophonous array of independent and completely isolated data sources.

A good systems administrator will know how to evaluate software and systems in the context of their network and server infrastructure in a way that will help facilitate ubiquitous access to an institution's data. It's important to allow customers the option of determining for themselves whether they want to be responsible for the integration of new systems into their enterprise.

Security

Lastly, I mention security because, quite frankly, I'm ashamed at the level of information security maintained in libraries. We are solely and ultimately responsible for the well-being of our networks and our data. More importantly, we have a solemn duty to protect the privacy of our patrons. As libraries, we've maintained a unified front against government intrusion into patron records, but that means very little when the back door is left wide open.

Shortly before I wrote the Bill of Rights post, our interlibrary loan cooperative was hacked and left in an irreparable state. What made the hack so significant was not the fact that the intruder brought the system to its knees, but the fact that the cooperative was not able to recover from it in a timely fashion. They failed to maintain a viable disaster recovery plan, and have not, to this date, recovered fully.

The ILL hack prompted me to do a little experiment. I identified five other libraries running the same automation system as ours and attempted to log in to their systems using the default passwords provided by our vendor. I was shocked when I was able to gain access to three of them. Using these login credentials, I had complete access to their patron records. I immediately logged out and notified each library. While I believe that it is the responsibility of each library to change its own passwords, given the fact that vendors know about, and take advantage of, the lack of technical expertise in libraries, it seems to me that if they want to sell turnkey systems, they are somewhat culpable for this type of vulnerability. At the very least, their best practices should be modified to address the "default password" convention—an unnecessary and risky method of transferring access to customers.

It is virtually impossible to secure a network completely. There are myriad ways to gain access to, disrupt, or damage systems for those who are so inclined. Ultimately, network security comes down to prioritizing sensitive areas on the network and hardening them as much as possible. When sensitive patron information is involved, we need to know what types of systems are in place to protect it. We need the ability to control security levels, detailed audit trails, and robust disaster recovery options. Security is not one of the areas libraries or vendors tend to focus on when discussing their systems. Visit a vendor booth at any major conference and actively observe what the sales associates focus on and the types of questions they are asked. Look at their literature and pay attention to what is *not* there. Very little attention is paid to security. As customers, we need to be made aware of vulnerabilities as they are discovered. The dissemination of this information should be a priority. In addition, we ought to be provided with a comprehensive third-party security audit of the system itself.

None of this means anything, however, if there is nobody at your library who can understand it and, more importantly, act upon it.

The Wind of Change

A steady wind of change is blowing through the library industry, and it seems to be galvanizing a group of passionate people around what many call Library 2.0, or L2. L2 encompasses everything from physical space, to technology, to library policy. Its inception can be traced back to the vibrations sent out by the radical and evolutionary nature of Web 2.0, which merges technological networks with social ones. A growing number of people in the library industry recognize that the tenets of Web 2.0 are fundamentally compatible with library philosophy; several of them are contributing chapters to this book. The discussions and ideas surrounding L2 are resulting in a number of radical changes in libraries throughout the world—successful changes that will clearly be with us for years to come.

What is not so clear, however, is how prepared we are as an industry to maneuver in a technological marketplace with the same speed and agility as our commercial counterparts. We have most of the tools at our disposal to do so now; what we lack is a recognition of the cost of complacency. We need to become technology centers in our communities and unify our entire organizations around what we do best: teaching, inspiring, and enriching. We will be well on our way if we can create a robust, data-centric environment that includes an equal partnership with our ILS vendors. This dream will go unrealized, however, unless our broken systems are challenged and fixed. Whether we encounter institutional inertia or a deep-rooted codependency with our vendors, it must be addressed. A curse is simply a truth about ourselves we have not yet acknowledged. Acknowledgment is the blessing. We can bless our future now and take back what is rightfully ours—creativity and vision.

Endnotes

1. Blyberg.net, ILS Customer Bill-of-Rights: A Collection of "Must-Have's" for Doing Business in a Web 2.0 World, www.blyberg.net/2005/11/20/ils-customer-bill-of-rights (accessed July 14, 2006).
2. World Wide Web Consortium, About W3C, www.w3.org/Consortium (accessed July 14, 2006).

CHAPTER 4

Six Years Too Late: Chasing Our Destiny in the Electronic Publishing Age

Jill Emery
Head of Acquisitions
University of Texas at Austin

It is a harder task than first expected, this gazing into the distance and trying to describe what signifies the intersection of horizon and ground. Hearing an elegant, thought-provoking lecture or reading an inspiring passage in a book can fill us with ideas about our future, but few of us take the time to jot down our thoughts, research the possibilities, and work on making these germinal ideas our new reality. Over the past 10 years, though, we've seen electronic publishing move from a fad to a trend: It is now our new reality, both in the scholarly publishing markets and in the realities of library budgets. The evolution of digital publishing, further, continues at an extremely rapid pace.

This evolution is now focused on the disintegration of our current vessels of information delivery. In the next 10 years, the scholarly journal as we now recognize and deliver it will cease to exist. The future of the journal is mixed, as in mixed media, new subject silos of mixed content delivery, and new distributed models of delivery. Scholarship is disintegrating and re-integrating itself into new collections, new learning tools, and new ways of being. Libraries are just at the cusp of considering how, why, and to what extent we will be capturing and preserving these new types of scholarship. We want to hold on to what has come before; we feel the desperate need, now more than ever, to capture the historic record. This, however, denies the fact that libraries have been voraciously capturing the historic record for centuries now. Libraries are not going to walk away from everything that's been collected, housed, and stored; this material will continue to be warehoused, albeit in lesser quantities than before. In addition, there is a movement afoot to digitize these unique print collections and make them more broadly accessible through both local repositories and the Google Book Search project. We just need to shift our focus, putting an emphasis on the stuff coming at us in the here and now, and worrying a little less about what has come before.

The new destiny of libraries is made manifest by our end-users. Libraries must learn to collect and disseminate the universe of knowledge in the ways our users want, not in the archaic traditions of ideological incoherence that have evolved with print resource management. Libraries can do this in three simple ways.

1. We must learn to broaden our focus beyond the bibliographic universe. Libraries must relinquish the past to the past, and trust in our previous foundations of knowledge, collections, and development.

2. We must accept that the scholarly universe is now technology driven, and recognize that technology changes frequently. Technology demands constant change for those attempting to manage information delivered through and by technological means.

3. We must accept that our future is driven by our users, not by our collections. Libraries must develop better discovery and delivery tools for content, in order for that content to remain relevant to future generations.

Here are some thoughts on how these paths can be chosen.

Jackie Collins vs. *Journal of American History*

Jackie Collins novels are often used as an example of the type of material libraries, especially large academic research libraries, should avoid spending time, effort, and money on collecting and maintaining. This is not to belittle Ms. Collins' talents and abilities as a writer; she has obviously been very successful throughout her writing career, making the bestseller lists many times over. In fact, any university offering a popular culture cross-disciplinary degree or minor study program would be negligent if it failed to collect her novels, and her work provides scholars with fine examples of genre studies. However, it can be argued that these novels are not among the most academic work populating the scholarly bibliographic universe.

On the other hand, the *Journal of American History* is one of those venerable collection staples that buffers up at least one, if not two, subject area accreditations in an academic library collection. It is ranked number eight by the 2005 ISI Journal Citation Reports in the History category and has an impact factor of .922. Few would argue against the necessity of collecting this title in an academic research library collection.

One thing to note about both Jackie Collins novels and the *Journal of American History*, though, is that both are readily available to the interested reader. WorldCat shows that 1,891 libraries worldwide own copies of the *Journal of American History;* it is also readily available from the History Cooperative in electronic form back to 1999, in JSTOR from 1964–2000, and in at least one aggregator collection. Jackie Collins novels can be found in as many as 1,734 libraries world-wide, in any used bookstore—both local and online—as well as in audiobook versions. It can be argued that the *Journal of American History* is as ubiquitously available as a Jackie Collins novel—in which case, if it is a waste of time, effort, and money to acquire and preserve Jackie Collins novels, it is also a waste of time, effort, and money to acquire and preserve a print version of the *Journal of American History*.

The historical commitment that many academic research libraries made to collect as much of the scholarly bibliographic universe as possible was based on the concept of information scarcity. The lack of universal availability of a scholarly journal such as the *Journal of American History* made it a prime collection target. As Rick Anderson points out in an article in *Serials*, though, "Today, however, most of the information that most people need most of the time is almost literally lying around on the ground for them to pick up whenever and wherever they want it."[1] In today's world of information glut and prime real estate costs, libraries need to seriously consider, and reconsider, each and every title brought in and processed for inclusion into their collections. Comparing the circulation statistics of the online versions of the *Journal of American History* with the print circulation and use of the title, one would find roughly a two-to-one, or in some cases three-to-one, ratio. The World Wide Web allows us the freedom to share content across vast boundaries and distances, obviating the need for duplicate archival copies of print materials within a given geographical area. As Paul Virilio notes in *The Information Bomb*: "We are not seeing an 'end to history' but we are seeing an end of geography."[2]

Some Are Bigger Than Others

So, then, why do libraries continue to invest our time, money, and effort into maintaining these cumbersome and unwieldy print collections? Academic research libraries have always resembled a group of young boys in a gym locker room, judging themselves against one another by the size of their collections. However, it is well past time to create a new metric for the academic research library community, letting them compare themselves on the services they offer their end-users, as opposed to the number of books and journal subscriptions they scrimp and squirrel away. We would be better served by developing dark archives of these titles at each participating institution, to help remove the concern about the need for duplicate copies. It is as though libraries cannot fathom that titles could exist separately from their walls … as if the fallen tree, which has been processed, pulped, and turned into a journal, will suddenly disappear from being completely. There is also this strange notion that, if collection stops at this point, then all the collections of the past will suddenly disappear as well.

This is exactly why various libraries have agreed to partner with private enterprise entities on digitization projects such as Google Book Search and Yahoo!'s Open Content Alliance. The University of Michigan's Mark Sandler was recently quoted in the *New York Review of Books*, saying: "In the past, these works [the books UM and Google have digitized] were accessible to a base population of 40,000 students, faculty, and staff. That's about four readers for each book included in the project. When electronic versions of these works were made accessible to the entire world, suddenly 40,000 potential readers became 4 billion, and the odds of consumer interest jumped from 4:1 to 400,000:1."[3]

In the end, this appears to be our greatest anxiety in regards to letting go. We have the notion that, if libraries stop collecting, then scholarship will stop being created, and it will all disappear completely. This is an extremely self-serving concept, and one that disallows for the growth, evolution, and change of our scholarship models. While libraries have been frantically grabbing up and warehousing the scholarly bibliographic universe, scholars have been investigating new ways of collaborating and of disseminating scholarly discourse.

Flashing Across the Screens

The first changes began in the late 1990s with collaborative preprint scholarly article distribution through a Web site, which has developed over time into an archival server hosting the service known as ArXiv. Around the same time, tools for collaborative teaching possibilities were also being developed, which resulted in electronic classroom models such as those provided by Blackboard, Inc. These tools allow for the dissemination, discussion, and contribution of information to scholars and students around the world. Furthermore, these tools and others like them have given rise to new sets and configurations of scholarly information that most libraries are not collecting or archiving, since most library operations are still focused and designed around print materials.

Just over a dozen libraries, large library consortia, and research institutes in North America have thrown themselves into the early fray of trying to capture, manage, and create a historic record of this and other "born-digital" scholarship. Born-digital refers to content that has only ever existed in digital format, a huge growth area for scholars and scholarship. The libraries at the forefront of this form of collection building do so in two main ways: first, via institutional repositories that allow for the direct deposit of scholarship by researchers, professors, and graduate students, and, second, via the creation of digital library collections to showcase local unique collections. (Some of these may actually currently be in print, but are presented in digital form to the world of scholars.) Given the limited number of libraries currently at work on these projects and the large amounts of money it takes to convert a library's operational model from print processing to digital processing, however, the library presence in this arena has been largely eclipsed by that of the commercial providers.

Libraries are still in the early years of capturing and trying to maintain digital content in an entirely digital realm. This is perhaps the largest growth area for libraries of the future, and is what will most likely supplant the majority of traditional library collections and collection building. As content becomes more aggregated, versioned into preprints, published works, and post-prints, disintegrated into subject-type silos, and mixed media, libraries will need to have mechanisms on hand to collect and disseminate these new forms of content. As electronically available content grows, libraries must abandon the large-scale management of the bibliographic universe; it will become relegated to smaller and more discrete communities. The print medium will continue to serve as the main information conduit for various groups of scholars. However, these communities will continue to shrink, become more specialized, and become more marginalized.

Publishers' Next Top Model

The rise of electronic publishing has required publishers to re-evaluate their publishing models and to develop dual systems for print and electronic dissemination of their content. Libraries often fail to recognize that the rise of technology and technological processing has had as major an impact on print publishing as in the development of online publishing. The rising costs that libraries began to see almost 30 years ago stemmed in part from the technological impact on article receipt, peer review, and the other value-added services a publisher brings to a high-impact, peer-reviewed paper. As online publication began to grow and develop alongside print publication, many publishers found themselves hiring more technical staff and adding a new infrastructure to provide the services their readers expected. Now, many publishers consider the electronic versions of their titles to be the definitive works, treating print publication as the archival or secondary line of publication for a given article or journal title.

During this evolution in the publication process, the pricing model for how libraries pay for a subscription (or access to a subscription) evolved as well. Initially, most pricing schemes were based on a database model of access, or on the purchasing of large sets of titles and what is commonly referred to as the "big deal." In "big deals," a single library (or group of libraries) purchases all the subscriptions for any given publisher, based on the subscriptions these libraries hold, plus a surcharge for the additional content access. The big deal has some favorable attributes, such as a price inflation cap, usually guaranteed for three or five years. The downside to the big deals is usually a cancellation cap, which disallows libraries' dropping below a certain percentage of their total spending. Initially, libraries found these deals to be quite worth their disadvantages in providing their students and faculty with access to the greatest number of titles. However, after a couple of renewals, the amount libraries were paying started to seem excessive when compared to the amount each title was used within the big deals. Today, many libraries prefer to pay on a title-by-title basis for electronic access to journals (although some do feel that purchasing a big deal or package works better for the community they serve). As Adam Chesler recently noted in his article on core issues in regards to pricing models in *Learned Publishing*: "There is unlikely to be any one model that makes all parties happy, but the aim should be to find one that makes key stakeholders comfortable, and that is perceived by the vast majority as clear and fair (if not always affordable—an inevitable problem at some level that may be alleviated by customized pricing for selected customers or groups, depending on the interests of the publisher)."[4]

Some of the most interesting areas to watch develop are the electronic access pricing models for reference materials and the various electronic book offers. Right now, the business models for electronic books are all over the map, and have been for the past couple of years; there's no accepted model that really works for most libraries. Models libraries can choose from range from a subscription model or prepaid approval plan for electronic book collections, to title-by-title choice, to the database model of electronic books incorporated with electronic journals and grey literature.

When It All Falls Apart

The other interesting developments in electronic publication lie in the changing nature of information delivery. Many believe that the journal as content delivery mechanism is outdated, and that it needs to be abandoned in order to provide quicker access to scholarly research. Carol Tenopir recently pointed out in *Library Journal*: "When the entire text is digitized and searchable through various search engines, traditional containers might not matter anymore."[5] Libraries are investing quite a bit of money in developing new access modes to content and trying to make information discovery as seamless as possible. The purchase of article collections and more discrete amounts of information may become more sensible and cost-effective than the purchasing of entire titles and pre-packaged information. If a new model of peer-review is developed and impact factors of individual articles created, then the purchase of individual articles may become a more viable and attractive option to libraries in the near future.

Best Things in Life Aren't Free

The "open-access" electronic publishing movement is also growing. Open access publishing inverts the costs involved in publishing a scholarly article; an author pays for the publication of his or her research article, which is then made freely available to readers. There are various models in regard to open-access publishing currently underway. In one model, a library or institution pays for membership to the open-access provider, which underwrites the work of that institution's researchers and scholars in the open-access journals. Both BioMed Central and the Public Library of Science (PLoS) work in this manner, and they have developed electronic journals with relatively high-impact factors. Another model involves publisher-based initiatives, such as Oxford Open from Oxford University Press, where an author pays a fee to have his or her article published freely in one of the publisher's publications. Presently, just a few publishers offer this model of open access.

Some of the early adopters of institutional repositories in libraries are also investigating open-source publication as a way to help capture their institutional scholarly record. Most recently, Rice University announced an initiative to re-open their university press as an open-source publishing model. Material will be produced digitally, with an on-demand print option available for a fee. This option provides the purchaser with a bound copy of the research produced. It will be interesting to watch the Rice University model develop, and to see how the cost structures for institutions and libraries that take on the role of publishers develop over time.

Open-access models are continuing to grow and prosper, presenting high-quality research "for free." Libraries, however, still face underlying costs when acquiring open-access materials, which may require the library to pay author fees or membership fees. Even if acquisition of open-access titles is not underwritten by the library, processing and maintaining access to these titles still has associated costs. Libraries also need to consider archiving issues; those that lack institutional repositories can find maintaining a copy of an open-access article problematic. Rick Anderson writes: "The second thing I feel fully confident in predicting is that the percentage of high-quality information available at no charge to the public will never reach 100."[6]

Business In vs. Business Out

Libraries still insist on maintaining their print-purchasing models, allowing themselves to remain trapped into particular purchasing modes by their campus purchasing offices. We need to look at ways to renegotiate our business practices with our own internal purchasing offices. Libraries are very quick to point their fingers at publishers, proclaiming that publishers are forcing them into unsustainable or restrictive purchasing schemes. At the same time, though, libraries fail to make an argument within their own organizational structures to change the traditional content-purchasing models that have been in place for the past 50 years. When we fail to examine our own practices, we have little room to argue that any publisher is recalcitrant and resistant to change when it comes to purchasing material and access to material. Libraries need to become better advocates and change agents within their organizations in order to stay up with the content demands of their end-users—and the sooner, the better. This is a primary factor in holding libraries back from becoming truly service oriented in an on-demand society.

Options, Options, Options

The library serials budget of the future should be broken into three main areas of funding. The first area of funding would be designated for unique and specialized material that will be collected in print format only. These types of material include highly visually oriented titles such as those used in art and architecture, specialized collections such as foreign language-based collections, and material for some of the specialized sciences where Web versions of the titles cannot provide the quality of graphics needed. The second area of funding would be earmarked for electronic subscriptions. These could be selected and collected in the same way as print publications, with funds set aside for the purchase of backfiles, where necessary. The last area of funding would be to underwrite open-access publishing and to subsidize pay-per-view access to temporary-use research materials and to materials where the cost of a subscription is too high. There would be an annual evaluation of these three provision methods. Libraries should re-evaluate the balance, moving titles from print to electronic, or from electronic to pay-per-view, or from pay-per-view back to subscription (if the cost per use is found to be equal to or at the same level as that of a subscription).

Service, Please

Along with these changes to library purchasing and budgeting models, the library of the 21st century has to become indispensable to the greater organization it serves. As many businesses have learned, the broader the spectrum of resources we can make readily available via the World Wide Web, the broader the demand for those resources and our services. Libraries today are no longer seen as pantheons or hallowed halls of materials. To be viable in any given scenario, libraries must be integrated service providers, helping students, faculty, and other staff select wisely from the vast array of the universe of knowledge for any given subject area or research emphasis.

The only way this can be achieved is for subject librarians/bibliographers to become integral to every subject area on campus. This means attending faculty meetings, spending time in faculty offices, and existing in the minds of all the department members to which you serve as a liaison. One colleague at a small liberal arts college in San Antonio, Texas, has become such a valued member of his subject area that, when a prospective graduate student visits campus, he or she is always introduced to this subject librarian. In essence, he has become a selling point for the university. He has gained this respect by always being available to teach information-oriented classes for any professor, by providing them with customized new book lists of items that may interest faculty working on particular research, by attending all public lectures given by his faculty and their students, and by his willingness to have "office hours" for graduate students to call on him in person or virtually with their research needs.

Other successful librarians have established subject Weblogs for their faculty. These Weblogs incorporate RSS feeds for the tables of contents of library-provided subscriptions, as well as for podcasts from publishers and from professors within their online courseware. Collection development and collection management in the 21st century requires bibliographer/subject librarians who understand the array of options available to their constituencies and find new ways of presenting this information that is both contextually viable and indispensable to the patrons they serve on a daily basis.

Destiny Manifest

Libraries have fallen behind in information delivery and options in the 21st century. We have let caution and traditions take precedence over our service orientation, and we have allowed business offices and content providers to dictate the terms under which resources are provided and offered. However, all of these trends can be reversed and re-conceptualized as library services of the future. In order to remain sustainable, libraries must listen closely to their end users, moving to provide the resources and services that will make them an integral part of their information community. We have a vital role to play in the information dissemination of the future if we are willing to take the risk of letting go of the older, traditional means of resource acquisition and commit to new ways of doing business in the future. The question is whether libraries can fulfill their manifest destiny.

Endnotes

1. Rick Anderson, "What Will Become Of Us? Looking Into The Crystal Ball Of Serials Work," *Serials* 19 (2006): 88.
2. Paul Virilio, *The Information Bomb*, trans. Christ Turner, London: Verso Radical Thinkers, 2005: 9.
3. Jason Epstein, "Books@Google," *The New York Review of Books* 53:16 (Oct. 19, 2006), www.nybooks.com/articles/19436 (accessed June 27, 2007).
4. Adam Chesler, "Core Issues In Pricing Models For Scholarly Journals: A Qualitative Overview," *Learned Publishing* 19 (2006): 146.
5. Carol Tenopir, "The Value of the Container," *Library Journal* 131 (2006): 32.
6. Anderson, 90.

CHAPTER 5

Academic Libraries as Scholarly Publishers

Dorothea Salo
Digital Repository Librarian
University of Wisconsin

I amar prestar aen: han mathon ne nen, han mathon ne chae, a han noston ned 'wilith.

—JRR Tolkien,
The Return of the King
(translated from English by David Salo[1])

Academic librarians have historically been the scholarly literature's collectors and preservers, its major purchasers and ultimate disseminators. What happens between author manuscripts and the ink (or, increasingly, pixels) on journal pages has rarely been our concern. The world, however, is changing. We are moving (willingly or not) toward more and earlier intervention in the scholarly publishing process, in order to maintain acceptable levels of access in the face of both unendurable serials price increases and shifts in the ways researchers communicate results to each other.

Fuel for Change

University presses and scholarly societies managed functional, affordable publishing models for quite some time. What happened?

Many scholarly societies, especially in the hard sciences and medicine, sold their journals outright to large for-profit publishers who contributed back a cut of the proceeds; others came to depend on journal subscription revenue to fund other society activities. For-profit publishers grew, merged, and came to control large swaths of the scholarly record, allowing them to squeeze profit from low-readership, low-profit journals by bundling them with crucially necessary ones. The resulting "big deal"[2] has broken library budgets, even consortium budgets; ripple effects have decimated the ranks of university presses, causing publication difficulties for humanities and social-science scholars whose tenure and promotion rests on the publication of scholarly monographs.

Times have not been easy for publishers, either. The advent of electronic publishing and distribution meant expensive experimentation and workflow retooling for publishers who suddenly had to produce two or more versions of journal content. Keeping electronic content from unauthorized eyes required additional investments in staff and technology. The sheer amount of research skyrocketed, causing special problems for well-read, high-impact journals whose submissions overwhelmed available staff and peer reviewers. Finally, as some researchers moved toward accessing journals electronically through library e-resource subscriptions rather than in print, individual subscriptions to journals began to decline, pinching journals' profits.

Many stakeholders, academic librarians hardly least among them, are now saying louder than a whisper that the current situation is unsustainable; access to the scholarly and research record is in decline, and cannot be allowed to decline further. A broad-umbrella movement gaining influence and currency is the "open-access" movement, in which scholarly publication occurs electronically without charging readers for access, either directly or indirectly (as through library subscriptions).

In the U.S., whose commitment to open access is lagging considerably behind that of other countries (notably the U.K.), the federal government has just begun to address access issues surrounding taxpayer-funded research. The National Institutes of Health (NIH) started a voluntary open-access policy in 2005, requesting (but not mandating) that funded researchers deposit some form of their final report in the NIH's PubMed Central digital repository. The policy's dismal showing in its first six months of operation, in which only 3.8 percent of eligible research was actually archived, caused an ongoing re-evaluation of the policy that is likely to lead to mandated deposit of NIH-funded research in PubMed Central. Congress also responded, introducing the CURES Act and the Federal Research Public Access Act (FRPAA), both aimed at increasing open access to federally funded research.

One form of open access to research bypasses journals altogether, and for that reason is often excluded from definitions of open access that focus entirely on peer-reviewed literature. Frustrated by the slow pace and difficulty of journal publication, some researchers have turned to less formal but more open methods of disseminating their results and data. "Grey literature" is burgeoning on the Web, including pre-prints, technical reports, conference slide-decks, working-papers series, and more. Although they lack peer review—which has in any case come under attack lately for bias and error—these materials are achieving considerable penetration into the scholarly conversation. Libraries are beginning to ask what role they should adopt in hosting, disseminating, recommending, filtering, and preserving grey literature.

Without peer-review or editorial-board imprimatur, without publisher marketing or librarian support, how are researchers finding grey literature, and why do they read and cite it? Scholars, it turns out, are hardly more immune to the attractions of Web search engines than undergraduates, and grey literature is present to search-engine crawlers in much higher density than peer-reviewed work.

Indeed, evidence is mounting that research material made available online without barriers to access is more easily found, more often read, and more often and more quickly cited.[3] This means that toll-access publishers and researchers are working somewhat at cross-purposes. Researchers desire the widest possible dissemination of their findings; the more they are read and cited, and the more demonstrably influential their work, the better for their careers. Publishers whose business model relies on content ownership, on the other hand, must restrict access to the content they own to those who pay for that access. Researchers are not generally aware of this disconnect; most have as much access as they believe they need, and when they do not, they tend to blame library budgets rather than publishers. Moreover, the research demonstrating open-access citation advantages has not yet garnered widespread attention.

In an allied development, "impact factors" that purport (however sloppily or erroneously) to gauge an article or journal's importance by counting the number of times it has been cited have been gaining influence in retention and tenure hearings. Standard Web metrics such as number of downloads are also gaining attention. Notably, impact factors and download numbers are calculated *post-dissemination*, shifting quality measurement to some extent from traditional pre-publication measures such as peer-review and acquisitions editing. A piece of grey literature can count its downloads and citations without having to undergo peer review.

How will journals be funded, if not through subscriptions? John Willinsky's excellent book, *The Access Principle*, suggests 10 economic models for open access,[4] countering the myth that the only economic model is that in which the author pays a fee to the publisher to consider or publish the article. Subsidies, grants (either to the journal or to authors), and in-kind support from libraries and other stakeholders may also help defray costs. Most intriguing among Willinsky's suggestions is that of a publishing "cooperative,"[5] in which libraries, university presses, scholarly associations, and other stakeholders contribute money, expertise, and in-kind support to the publishing enterprise.

Most advocates divide open access to the peer-reviewed (as opposed to grey) literature into two modes, the "green" road and the "gold" road. The "green" road is self-archiving, in which researchers deposit copies of their work on the World Wide Web. Widespread and time-honored in computer science, physics, and engineering, thanks to efforts such as arXiv.org, this approach has yet to find numerous adherents in other fields. Self-archiving venues range from individually hosted author Web pages, through discipline-specific repositories such as library science's E-LIS (eprints.rclis.org) and dLIST (dlist.sir.arizona.edu), to institutional repositories, which are usually managed by the institution's library. The FRPAA bill is of particular interest because (unlike under the CURES Act, which mandates deposit in PubMed Central) institutional repositories may be acceptable deposit venues, depending on how each agency interprets the open-access mandate.

Self-archiving depends on publisher willingness to permit it, or author willingness to flout copyright after signing it over to a publisher. An uneasy and unstable compromise reigns at present. More than 80 percent of publishers require authors to sign over copyright.[6] Most researchers do not understand that publishers own legal rights to their work, although foresighted universities such as MIT are beginning to issue calls for their faculty to amend or cease signing copyright-transfer agreements. Nonetheless, toll-access publishers do not care to alienate their authors by forbidding permission to self-archive or by challenging institutional repositories or e-reserves systems. Some publishers do forbid deposit into disciplinary repositories; although, curiously, not in fields where disciplinary repositories are well-established.

The "gold" road to open access involves publishing journals—with the normal trappings thereof, such as editing and (crucially) peer review—without charging access fees to either readers or libraries. Some of these journals, notably those under the auspices of the Public Library of Science (plos.org), recoup some or all of their costs by charging authors processing fees, which authors may then charge back to their funders. The sustainability of this model has been questioned, but at this early date it is difficult to distinguish problems specific to open access from the problems common to all new journals, which typically take seven or more years to become solvent.

Of those journals offering open-access content, not all offer open access to the entire journal, in hopes that the embargoed "extra" content will support subscriptions while still offering authors the benefits of open access. Willinsky cites "partial" open access, in which some articles are made available freely while others are reserved for subscribers; other modes of partial open access include reserving editorial material such as book reviews for subscribers, or reserving access to certain file formats to those who pay, as the American Physical Society does with XML-encoded versions of its journal articles. "Hybrid" journals offer authors the choice between traditional toll-access publishing—free to them, not free to readers—or open access supported by an author fee.

Technology

Several technological developments have fostered interest in new publishing models and workflows. Obviously, the World Wide Web reigns supreme; reducing dissemination costs to near zero is the *sine qua non* of open access. Other developments should receive due credit also. The steady decline in electronic-storage costs allows cost-effective maintenance of substantial electronic archives, while the rise in networking speeds permits easy and effective dissemination of multimedia and datasets as well as formal papers. Data curation is now a growth area in digital libraries research and experimentation.

Software and services supporting lower-cost electronic publishing and archiving have seen rapid development since the turn of the millennium. Institutional and disciplinary repositories can choose to install open-source software packages such as DSpace (dspace.org), Fedora (fedora.info), and EPrints (www.eprints.org/software), or buy hosting services such as OCLC's CONTENTdm (www.oclc.org/contentdm) or BioMed Central's Open Repository (openrepository.com). Journal publishers can reduce overhead costs significantly by moving to an all-electronic workflow for manuscript submission, editing, and peer review, using the Public Knowledge Project's open-source Open Journal Systems (pkp.sfu.ca/ojs). Cornell University Library is currently testing DPubS (dpubs.org), journal-management software that is designed to integrate with DSpace or Fedora repository software; DPubS underlies Cornell's Project Euclid suite of mathematics journals (projecteuclid.org).

New technical and certification standards for data-modeling, metadata exchange, and archiving also underlie the open-access movement. The Open Archives Initiative created the Protocol for Metadata Harvesting (OAI-PMH; www.openarchives.org/OAI/open archivesprotocol.html), through which data providers such as repositories expose metadata in a straightforward XML format for harvest by Web crawlers and search engines. OAI-PMH requires that data providers expose Dublin Core metadata, but allows richer metadata of any format (including MARC) as well. The most important OAI-PMH harvesters at present are Google Scholar (scholar.google.com) and the University of Michigan's OAIster search engine (oaister.umdl.umich.edu). The National Archives and Records Administration collaborated with the Research Libraries Group (now part of OCLC) in 2005 to publish a draft report, the "RLG-Nara Audit Checklist for Certifying Digital Repositories" (www.rlg.org/en/page.php?Page_ID=20769). The report outlines policy, technical, staffing, and content-management decisions a digital repository must make in order to be considered "trusted." Although actual certification based on this checklist is some years off, the checklist itself remains useful for repository planners and managers.

One piece of technology that might be thought to impact dissemination and use of electronic materials, the ebook, has proven to be a red herring—if by "ebook" is meant a handheld electronic device specifically designed for storing and presenting reading materials. Even during the boomlet of the late 1990s, ebook devices were never designed for or marketed to an academic audience, and current research into "e-ink" has likewise ignored academia. Progress in this realm appears unlikely to impact scholarly publishing within the next decade.

Experiments

Experiments in open access have mushroomed both inside and outside libraries since the Association for Research Libraries founded the Scholarly Publishing and Academic Resources Coalition (SPARC; www.arl.org/sparc) in 1998. SPARC partners with publishers experimenting with more sustainable business models, and creates advocacy and educational materials such as the recently revamped Create Change Web site (www.createchange.org).

New open-access journal publishers dot the scene, particularly in fields where journal pricing has become particularly egregious. The United Kingdom's BioMed Central (biomedcentral.com), the first open-access journal publisher, manages a large stable of journals in biology and medicine, supporting itself with for-pay services such as image archiving. The Public Library of Science (PLoS), which is supported by grants, memberships, and author fees, has launched a small stable of fully open-access journals in biology and medicine. Although a June 2006 hike in author fees caused consternation among some authors and finger-pointing by toll-access publishers, impressively high-impact factors for the new journals continue to attract high-quality submissions.

Traditional toll-access publishers are experimenting with open-access business models as well. Shortly after Springer-Verlag hired former BioMed Central head Jan Velterop as its Director of Open Access, it instituted an "Open Choice" program, which charges authors publication fees in return for allowing open access to the resulting article. Elsevier, the Royal Society of the United Kingdom, and other publishers have similar programs.

Several academic libraries now sponsor open-access journals by managing an installation of Open Journal Systems. A few university libraries have gone beyond journals, however. The University of Tennessee has launched Newfound Press (www.lib.utk.edu/newfound press), which hopes to publish open-access monographs as well as journals. At Rice University, the Digital Library Initiative is one sponsor of Connexions (www.cnx.org), which will host the university's relaunched university press as an all-digital open-access operation.

Other, generally longer-running, library initiatives offer support for publishing without actually managing the entire endeavor. The University of Michigan Library's Scholarly Publishing Office (spo.umdl.umich.edu) supports online journal and monograph publication through software development, hosting, and conversion and printing services. Cornell's Digital Consulting and Production Services (dcaps.library.cornell.edu) offers a similar service menu, but also includes copyright services such as permissions-seeking and ownership-tracking.

Experimentation with post-publication peer-review is legion. BioMed Central offers the post-publication peer-review service Faculty of 1000 (facultyof1000.com), in which experts recommend individual papers. Open Journal Systems allows journals to accept commentary on individual articles, archiving the comments along with the article. Naboj (www.naboj.com) represents a review overlay atop the arXiv disciplinary repository; this model demonstrates how open access enables new services and new communication structures.

The longest-running experiment thus far, however, is the institutional repository. Many academic libraries opened these without fanfare and without solid planning for librarian support, assuming that the gathering momentum behind open access would drive faculty to deposit materials. Reality has proven harsher; faculty are only slowly becoming aware of open access, and have proven unwilling to expend effort to deposit their materials without an external demand (such as a department or university mandate) or an obvious return on the investment of their time. Libraries have responded with marketing programs and development of such extras as download statistics and "researcher pages" that behave like mini-CVs. Those with the most successful repositories, however, have found library-internal uses for the repository (such as digitized special collections material or electronic theses and dissertations) rather than relying wholly on faculty for materials.

Why Should Libraries Be Publishers?

Once we accept that scholarly publishing must change, we have a duty to ask why we should shape its future. Is this in our mission? Are we best suited to do it? Can we afford to do it? What's in it for us?

I believe academic libraries are uniquely situated to redress the systemic imbalances and infelicities in the scholarly publishing system.

Unlike scholarly societies, academic libraries do not expect to fund their other activities via publishing. Unlike for-profit journal publishers, academic libraries have no shareholder obligations; we exist to serve research and researchers. Unlike university presses, academic libraries are not expected to be financially self-supporting. Indeed, open access fits quite neatly into our core mission of disseminating quality information; we should have little trouble justifying publishing expenditures to cost-conscious university administrators.

Moreover, we academic librarians have skills that transfer well to publishing. Our experience with digitization projects has created a fairly large pool of Web-savvy digital librarians. We indubitably understand far more about digital preservation than do publishers. As researchers ourselves and as liaison and reference librarians, we understand the scholarly process and work closely with researchers. We even know all about citation formatting, abstract construction, and indexing!

The production skills we lack should not worry us unduly; many necessary links in the publishing chain are filled by the very faculty we are closest to, and most production tasks were outsourced by publishers long ago. Acquisitions editing, editorial-board work, and peer review are faculty tasks. Copyediting, file conversion, typesetting—all are done by freelancers or service bureaus, at commodity prices so low that even volume discounts hardly matter.

We can also offer new publishing-related services that at best would be loss leaders for for-profit or society publishers. Data curation is likely the best lever, particularly in the sciences; integrating it with existing research-data services and institutional repository workflows should draw faculty interest. We can come up with post-publication review services of our own. In the humanities, we can offer production and archival support for innovative digital projects that faculty may not be able to manage on their own. Even the Modern Language Association is beginning to admit that digital scholarship should be valued on its merits, just as print scholarship is.[7]

Scholarly publishing makes or breaks academic careers. Since publication record is crucial to hiring, retention, and tenure decisions, librarians involved in publishing will find that they have real, if subtle, power. Naturally, we welcome relevance, but power that differentiates between patron and patron will require some adjustment to our normally patron-neutral outlook. The trust institutions place in their libraries should prove helpful as new publishing projects negotiate the treacherous waters of academic prestige.

Less controversially, involving libraries in the publication process will aid in the long-term preservation of electronic materials, since the methods by which electronic resources are produced are so closely tied to their suitability for preservation. Leaving preservation of electronic journals to their publishers is an untested and uncertain preservation model. In a toll-access environment, journal backfiles may pay for themselves through library subscription or pay-per-article access models. Deadweight (from a publisher's point of view) is mounting, however, from licenses that quite properly insist upon library access to backfiles even after journal cancellation. When providing access (and associated services such as usage metrics) costs money instead of making it, how long will publishers remain in the preservation business? Should they leave it, what will happen to the scholarly record? Libraries must answer this question for the electronic scholarly record, just as we have answered it for print; experiments such as the collaborative archival program LOCKSS (Lots of Copies Keeps Stuff Safe; www.lockss.org) and the member-supported archiving service Portico (www.portico.org) point to possible futures.

Though considerable attention has been paid to possible subscription savings via gold-road open access, libraries should factor in other potential cost savings as well. An open-access article (whether in an open-access journal or self-archived) can be linked to in an electronic-reserve system without royalty cost or copyright liability. Indeed, this is such a benefit that libraries might well consider asking e-reserves staff to contact authors of often-used articles to ask that those articles be self-archived.

The barriers we face in moving toward open access are generally not technological; they are social and organizational. Librarians are still hashing out libraries' proper role in judging, acquiring, and preserving electronic content. Faculty and administrations have been slow to respond to librarian appeals. Publishers and scholarly societies that own revenue-positive journals spread fear, uncertainty, and doubt. Finding and preserving the grey literature now scattered all over the open Web is a tremendous challenge. New open-access journals face the same marketing, revenue, and prestige issues as any other new journal—except that detractors tend to attribute any difficulties purely to the open access model. Still, the tide is turning; although a purely open-access scenario is no more than a chimera, open access makes too much sense not to command a larger piece of the scholarly communication pie.

Brave New Open-Access World

Open access is already changing academic libraries, to judge from the increasing job opportunities for repository librarians and scholarly communication experts.

Open access is not, however, "free" access, because publishing is not free, even considering unremunerated labor from faculty and the savings in overhead made possible by all-electronic workflows and dissemination. Research funders and institutions are unlikely to accept all the costs of gold-road open access, even in the well-funded fields at the root of the serials crisis. Over time, libraries will have to pick up some costs as well, by joining organizations such as SPARC and PLoS, by offering a pool of funds for faculty publishing in open-access journals, or by offering in-kind services such as journal hosting and archival. At present library budgets are squeezed from both directions, since it is impractical to drop journal subscriptions in favor of support for open-access publications. Eventually, however, open-access experiments, both by libraries and publishers, should cause subscription price pressures to ease, freeing up money to support open access (as well as languishing monograph budgets).

Many libraries opening institutional repositories have found to their considerable dismay that faculty are not flocking to the new service. Some have responded by allocating staff time specifically to the repository, both for marketing and for services such as batch file import, metadata creation, faculty training, and copyright clearance. Others may decide to close repositories to new deposits while they rethink their planning. In the long term, however, I expect many libraries will decide that not every institution needs its own repository. Consortial repositories such as the Washington Research Library Consortium's Aladin-RC (aladinrc.wrlc.org) conserve scarce technical staff, allowing each individual library to focus on outreach and services.

To some extent, whether faculty embrace open access is out of libraries' hands, dependent as it is on decisions by government, private research funders, scholarly organizations, and college and university administrations. Some faculty will have no choice, owing to mandates from research funders or institutions; we should stand ready to explain what is happening and assist faculty as they start to comply with these mandates. Other faculty will find open access on their own, enticed by hopes of additional professional impact or librarian curation for their work; we should encourage, support, and recognize them for their efforts. Skeptics are legion and will remain so; we must express our positions firmly but respectfully, and be transparent about our role in the open access movement and what we hope to gain from it.

Certainly libraries, library consortia, and library professional organizations should try to influence decisions by funders, institutions, and governments in favor of open access. Less-well-funded libraries have a particular interest in speaking up, as their access to research literature will improve most. Their experience also counters the unfortunate refrain from short-sighted large research institutions that open access is unnecessary because *their* faculty have all the access they need. Immediate results are unlikely, however; wide-ranging changes in a longstanding publication system take considerable time. Self-archiving mandates are probably out of reach of most institutions at this juncture. Asking (or even requiring) faculty to retain some rights in their journal articles, a strategy pursued at such universities as MIT[8] and the University of California system,[9] has met with more success and lays important groundwork for further progress.

Libraries can expect software for journal management and archival to improve significantly. DSpace, for example, is less than five years old. Repository and journal-management software, with its emphasis on preservation and workflow, is a natural complement to digital-library software such as Greenstone (greenstone.org), which emphasizes attractive and functional user interfaces. I expect these different types of software to interoperate better in the short term; strawman proposals are already being floated for new interoperability layers.[10] In the long term, they may merge, become modular enough to give rise to mix-and-match systems tailored to specific needs, or adopt so many features from one another as to be nearly indistinguishable. Either way, we can expect more finished, flexible, reliable, and capable software than we currently have.

We can also expect further experimentation with shared data and metadata. The rather crude search-and-discovery systems OAI-PMH enables point the way toward much more refined systems that mingle advanced text-mining techniques with the collection developer's keen eye for value and the cataloger's and indexer's long-honed subject-assignment skill. Easy availability of datasets will likewise jumpstart innovative and necessary meta-research in the sciences.

Not all harvesting experiments with OAI-PMH have been rosy, of course. The National Science Digital Library discovered that considerable technical support was necessary for data providers to reach even a minimal level of technical efficacy and metadata adequacy.[11] Clearly, academic libraries will have to bear metadata-training and metadata-revision burdens; we cannot possibly expect to keep up with the volume of metadata creation all by ourselves. Together with Indiana University, the University of Illinois at Urbana-Champaign secured an IMLS grant to do low-cost training across the country in 2007 and 2008 on creating "shareable metadata." Their experiences will doubtless inform further training programs.

The greatest advantage of open access is that it will inevitably awaken researchers to the economic consequences of their own publishing decisions. The current model separates researchers' decisions about where to publish from libraries' decisions about what to buy. Arguably, this has exacerbated the serials crisis, as researchers with eyes on their own career advancement ignored or blamed librarians for overburdened library budgets. My hope is that the next stage of open-access growth and development will intertwine libraries further with the research process as publication partners, co-creators, and disseminators of information, as well as its collectors, describers, and preservers.

Endnotes

1. "For the world is changing: I feel it in the water, I feel it in the earth, and I smell it in the air."
2. Ken Frazier, "The Librarians' Dilemma: Contemplating the Costs of the Big Deal," *D-Lib Magazine* 7:3 (March 2001), www.dlib.org/dlib/march01/frazier/03frazier.html (accessed June 22, 2006).
3. Steve Hitchcock, "The Effect Of Open Access And Downloads ('Hits') On Citation Impact: A Bibliography Of Studies," opcit.eprints.org/oacitation-biblio.html (accessed June 27, 2006).
4. John Willinsky, *The Access Principle*, Cambridge, MA: MIT Press (2006): 212–213.
5. Willinsky, 227–232.
6. John Cox and Laura Cox, "Scholarly Publishing Practice: Academic Journal Publishers' Policies And Practices In Online Publishing," Second survey, 2005, Association of Learned and Professional Society Publishers, 2006.

7. Scott Jaschik, "A Tenure Reform Plan With Legs," *Inside Higher Education*, 2006, insidehighered.com/news/2006/01/05/tenure/ (accessed July 5, 2006).

8. See the new MIT Copyright Amendment Form, libraries.mit.edu/about/scholarly/copyright-form.html (accessed July 6, 2006).

9. See the University of California Academic Senate's white papers and policy proposal at www.universityofcalifornia.edu/senate/committees/scsc/reports.html (accessed July 6, 2006).

10. Bekaert et al., "Pathways Core: A Data Model for Cross-Repository Services," *Proceedings of the 2006 Joint Conference on Digital Libraries*: 368.

11. Carl Lagoze et al., "Metadata Aggregation and 'Automated Digital Libraries:' A Retrospective on the NSDL Experience," *Proceedings of the 2006 Joint Conference on Digital Libraries*: 230–239.

Part 2

Change and Challenges

CHAPTER 6

Game On!
Meeting the Needs of
Gamers in the Library

Beth Gallaway
Library Trainer/Consultant

Why do libraries need to pay attention to video games? Because library patrons play them! Gaming has grown from its roots in miniature and dice table games, through electronic arcade boxes, into a nearly $11 billion industry. Gaming is the medium of choice for the Millennial generation—or gamers, digital natives, 'net gen—call them what you will. No matter the label, they share an affinity for technology, multitasking, and making social connections. They are globally oriented, team-oriented, and "me"-oriented.[1] Researchers John Beck and Mitchell Wade believe that these characteristics are a direct result of growing up playing games in which they are the center of universe, complete concurrent ongoing tasks, benefit from working in groups, and are rewarded for innovation, practice, and creativity. Their book, *Got Game*, recently updated in paperback under the title *The Kids Are Alright: How the Gamer Generation Is Changing the Workplace* (HBS Press, 2006), defines gamer generation characteristics and attitudes in contrast with those of the baby boomer generation. This is a must-have title for library managers who want not only to understand their patrons, but to learn what the new breed of younger librarians emerging from library schools value.

What Are Games Good For?

Not just young people play video games, though; the demographics may surprise you. According to the Entertainment Software Association, gamers' average age is 33.[2] Twenty-five percent of adults over age 50 play,[3] and more than 45 percent of gamers are women.[4] The Pew Internet & American Life Project's report on Teens and Technology reveals findings that 81 percent of teens surveyed in early 2005 said they played games online.[5] (Note that "online games" doesn't even account for handheld, mobile, console, or PC gaming.) When something has captured the hearts, minds, and interests of so many people, we need to investigate how this phenomenon fits into libraries. Libraries continue to choose the role of providing popular materials in their long-range planning sessions, and many public library mission statements include the concept of serving the educational *and* recreational needs of the community. Video gaming is popular, educational, and recreational, and thus fulfills libraries' mission.

Educational? That's right! James Paul Gee's *What Video Games Have to Teach Us About Learning and Literacy* (Palgrave McMillan, 2003) defines 32 learning principles found in games, including risk-tasking in a "safe" environment, rewarding of practice, use of affinity groups, probing cycles, situated meaning, self-knowledge, and identity formation.[6] Additionally, gaming reinforces the new literacies established by educator David Warlich: specifically, exposing knowledge, employing information, expressing ideas compellingly, and ethics on the Internet.[7]

How do these new literacies relate to the game environment? Information gathering in a game goes beyond just locating information, including the ability to understand and explain found information regardless of its format. The environment must be constantly monitored and evaluated, as the player makes split-second judgments of what to attend to and what to ignore. Game information, whether stats, quests, or inventory items, must be analyzed and organized before implementation.

Employing information includes going beyond simple math computation and measurement, extending to the analysis and application of numbers. Game spaces with robust virtual economies such as Everquest (Verant Interactive, 1999) and World of Warcraft (Blizzard, 2003) even require gamers to employ a currency conversion rate. In many games, numbers have a great deal of meaning, for levels of difficulty, experience, durability, and more.

Expressing ideas compellingly means the ability to take information gathered and employed and convey that information to someone else. This happens within the game, with mentoring relationships and the teamwork of guilds, and also outside of the game, through a rich and complex web of fan sites. Mechanics matter, and creativity and efficiency are highly rated. The expression of ideas can be in one format or several, including text, images, audio, and/or video. The practice of expressing ideas of a game may come in the form of modding (re-creating game content), fan fiction (writing stories about characters created/owned by someone else), or machinima (films/videos created through recording video game play).

If all you know about games comes from watching kids monopolize the Internet for Runescape after school or reading news stories about pornographic modifications for games, a little background information may be in order. The term "video game" encompasses arcade games, games played on a console, such as Microsoft's Xbox 360 or Nintendo's Wii, games played on a personal computer or laptop, games played on a handheld device or mobile phone, and games played on the Internet. Video games require a piece of software that holds the coding for the game, a unit to decipher the code and render it into multimedia text, audio, and graphics, a screen for display, and some manner of controller to manipulate the characters and objects in the game.

The trend in controllers is moving away from the sedentary and toward physical activity, meeting just one of the seven developmental needs established by the National Middle School Association.[8] Rhythm games such as Donkey Konga (Namco, 2004), Guitar Hero (Red Octane, 2005), and Dance Dance Revolution Ultramix 4 (Konami, 2006) require movement with a specially shaped controller (drums, guitar, dance pad) to execute gameplay. In 2003, Sony pioneered the EyeToy, a light-sensitive camera that reads bodily motion for a series of games that emulate sports and other activities. The Wii, Nintendo's next-generation console, debuted with a motion-sensitive wand-style controller shaped like a remote control. The versatile controller might pivot one way to be used as a steering wheel for driving games, swing like a tennis racket for sports games, or pair with a second piece, a nunchuck, to simulate a fishing rod and reel.

Professor Arlette C. Perry, chairwoman of the exercise and sports-sciences department for the University of Miami School of Education, conducted a study that found that playing video games provides a slight physical workout that burns more calories than passive television viewing. The fighting game Tekken 3 (Namco, 1998) is "equal to walking about two miles per hour metabolically."[9] Dance Dance Revolution gets players' heart rate up to 140 beats per minute—constituting aerobic activity.

Many cite hand-eye coordination as a benefit of frequent game-play. New York City's Beth Israel Medical Center, in conjunction with the National Institute on Media and the Family, recently completed a study of 303 surgeons participating in a medical training course focused on laparoscopic surgical procedures that included video games. The researchers found that surgeons who played video games immediately before the drill completed it an average of 11 seconds faster than those who did not.[10] Errors committed during the training lengthened the time it took to complete the task—indicating that faster finishers made fewer mistakes. The results supported findings from a small study conducted by Dr. James C. Rosser in 2003, which showed that doctors who grew up playing video games tended to be more efficient and less error-prone in laparoscopic training drills.[11]

Gaming in Libraries

In addition to improving hand-eye coordination, gaming programs have the potential to meet the developmental needs of young adults, historically the most underserved group in libraries—and a large game-playing demographic:

- Treating a question about a game soundtrack, release date, or cheat code as a serious reference query creates a positive social interaction with adults and peers.

- Enforcing general library behavior guidelines while youths play games enforces structures and clear limits.

- Games that include physical activity or creative expression meet developmental needs.

- The very act of game playing, competing against oneself or someone else, develops competence and achievement.

- Meeting demand for gaming services, collections, and programs may fulfill a need for meaningful participation in the community.

- Playing games allows the player to define him- or herself in terms related to the game.

Still need convincing? Gaming meets the developmental assets for adolescents defined by the Midwest research organization the Search Institute (www.search-institute.org). (In addition to their adolescent asset list, the Search Institute has developed asset lists for infants, toddlers, preschoolers, and elementary-aged children; no matter what age group you want to serve with games, you can use a Search Institute asset list to gauge their developmental appropriateness.) Of the eight asset categories, video gaming supports all eight! Here's how:

Support: The family that plays together, stays together! Families join World of Warcraft guilds together, compete in intergenerational Dance Dance Revolution (DDR) Tournaments at the Ann Arbor (MI) District Library, and go head-to-head with their handhelds and pass off traditional controllers to one another in games like Katamari Damacy (Namco, 2004) and Super Smash Brothers (Hal Laboratory, 1999). When a parent or guardian drops off a participant at one of my programs, the teen has a signed permission slip in hand—indicating that an adult family member has signed off on the program, and knows where that teen is. Support for adolescents also comes in the form of building other adult relationships with adults the teen is not related to. This may be one of the most important and unrecognized roles of the young adult librarian: to be a mentor and coach to teens. When librarians play along with the kids or demonstrate the game, they model behavior and establish affinity.

Boundaries and Expectations: Boundaries are set by informing participants of the rules, and holding them accountable when these rules are broken. Designers and coders preset the rules of any game. Often, a brief instruction manual that sets the premise accompanies the game. Contents include diagrams to show what the controller buttons and knobs do, as well as definition of the basic gameplay and rules. Not all the rules may be given—often, the game requires testing through an abbreviated scientific method: hypothesize, experiment, analyze, and repeat. Of video games, Stephen Johnson says, "It's as if you were to sit down to play chess and different rules applied but no one told you how the pieces moved: You would have to figure it out on your own."[12]

In addition to game-specific rules, young adults in a library-sponsored gaming program have to follow program rules (turn-taking, sportsmanship), as well as the library's code of behavior (respect for property and for each other). Clearly setting expectations and enforcing boundaries helps young adults discern the way the world works, teaches responsibility and socialization skills, and more.

Empowerment: Young adults gain a sense of purpose from the feeling that the things they do have an impact. When their ideas and suggestions are not only listened to, but are implemented, this validates their voice and interests. A community that responds to youth recommendations for services, collections, programs, and spaces shows it values youth and views youth as a resource. Ignoring the medium of choice for an entire generation may have disastrous results.

Constructive Use of Time: Simply put, time spent at the library participating in a program is time not spent on the streets or alone at home engaging in risky behaviors. Gaming programs offer social encounters in a constructive environment—with adult supervision. Critical thinking and problem-solving skills are engaged, physical activity is involved, and creativity can often be incorporated as well. At a recent DDR program, teens added personal flair to their synchronized steps with arm movement, facial expressions, lip synching, chanting, or clapping along, and even in the clothing they chose to wear.

Commitment to Learning: Anyone who thinks that video games do not involve reading has never played one. Nearly every game contains environmental text—ads on a race car and speedway, dialogue in a fantasy role-playing game, maps, letters, and more. At the 2005 Games, Learning and Libraries Symposium sponsored by the Metropolitan Library System in Chicago, researcher and assistant professor Constance Steinkuehler, an expert in literacy and cognition, said that gamers involved in massively multiplayer online role-playing games spend nearly four times as much time creating game content as they do actually playing. So, not only are they reading but they are: conveying game knowledge in the form of walkthroughs and tips; telling the stories of their clans and guilds by writing fan fiction; building Web sites; creating machinima videos; creating modifications for the game, such as new equipment, costumes, and objects; and becoming active in the politics, legislation, and community-building of the game world through forums, trials, and previews.

Social Competencies: The stereotype of a trench coat-clad gamer sitting alone in a dark basement surrounded by empty soda cans and pizza boxes is a myth of the past. Today's gamers are social creatures. In the Entertainment Software Association's 2005 survey, 50 percent of gamers stated they played games with someone else, and 25 percent reported playing online against a live opponent.[13] In the gaming programs I've run, I've observed that even kids who are competing against one another in Dance Dance Revolution, Guitar Hero, and EyeToy help their opponents by offering tips and constructive criticism. They naturally figure out how to set up the game play so everyone has a chance to try. There are social aspects to this planning and decision making, including turn taking, selecting games, practicing peaceful conflict resolution, and working as a team.

Positive Values: Will Wright, designer of the Sims, is very interested in games that create empathy and emotions. It is still the act of game playing, rather than the games themselves, that develops feelings such as caring. In games, mentoring and teamwork led youth to placing high value on helping other people, even those they are competing with. Encouraging teens to use games ethically (e.g., adhering to end-user license agreements, not pirating software) develops integrity and responsibility. Time spent playing games is time spent avoiding sexual activity and alcohol/drugs—games can induce restraint through appeal alone. The growing social impact of the games movement has also led to the development of games that promote equality and social justice through political and health simulations, such as Outbreak at Water's Edge or 3rd World Farmer (www.socialimpactgames.com).

Positive Identity: The formative teen years are all about identity: figuring out oneself and one's place in the world. It's a time of experimentation and of trying on new personas at the drop of a hat. Games create a safe space for teens to try new things and to express themselves in ways that might not be acceptable in the real world. It can be fun—and cathartic!—to role play or to step outside of one's own character in a game like The Sims or Halo. Playing in a first-person perspective is a very powerful thing. Gamers literally control the action of the game environment, so the player feels he or she has control over the "things that happen to me." Imagine growing up with this can-do, take charge attitude! The result is a degree of self-centeredness, but also high self-esteem. Youth learn through game play that their actions have consequences and they are responsible for the choices they make; they have impact. They also learn that it's OK to make mistakes, because that is the only way to learn.

Get in the Game

Once one has made the decision to support gaming, where to begin? Not every community (or administrator!) will be open to starting video game collections or programs. Start small and meet the needs of gamers by:

- Using games to conduct reader's advisory
- Being a strategy guide when instructing
- Embracing your inner technogeek
- Being flexible
- Immersing yourself in pop culture—especially video game culture!
- Trying some games yourself

Reader's Advisory for Gamers

The best reader's advisory interactions are really reference interviews. We are used to asking, "What authors do you like to read?" or "What are the last three books you read and enjoyed?" and "What did you like about them?" From there, we try to line readers up with new titles or authors that contain elements similar to the names and titles they mention to us. Instead of asking about books, try asking your readers under the age of 30, "What games do you play?" If your patron mentions a title you are unfamiliar with, simply say "Tell me more!" or ask "What do you like about it?" Games, like books, have genres. From a short interview, one can determine what makes a favorite game appealing, and offer some read-alike suggestions. For example, a fan of The Sims might enjoy the drama of the relationships in the game, the saga of following generations of a family, or the architectural and interior design mode. The Library 2.0 spin would be to invite your gaming patrons to come up with a game-related booklist, a display, or a review blog.

Guides, Not Bosses

Librarians are generally helpful people; most of us were drawn to the profession because we wanted to help, to teach, and to empower. When delivering bibliographic instruction, it can be very tempting for us to do all of the talking. This, however, doesn't appeal to those who have grown up playing games—where the person in charge is an adversary to be beaten. Avoid being a "level boss" by, for example, making your lessons on using library databases interactive. Instead of telling the students where to click, give them an assignment (or "quest") that allows small groups to search different terms, and have a free-for-all. Let them play and make mistakes. Ask each group to share results. Invite a demo of expertise. Then, be a strategy guide by offering some searching tips, or suggesting a different Web site to search. Instead of telling students or patrons to avoid Wikipedia like the plague, *start* with Wikipedia. Explore its merits and drawbacks before showing off some great resources that might a better choice, depending on the topic at hand.

Become a Technogeek

Make sure that regular upgrades are part of the library's long-range plan. Recognize that being in a beta stage is now the norm; you'll never catch up, so stop stressing over it! Roll out pilot projects such as making part of your Web site readable on cell phones and PDAs. Start a Runescape club and allow comments on the library's blog. If something doesn't work, hit the imaginary "reset button" and try again. Embrace Web 2.0 technologies that encourage user feedback and participation, mobility, and content creation. Get a screen name. Start a wiki. Think like a gamer—approach everything with a scientific method by testing, pushing, and trying to break it. Finally, keep up with technology news. The library community contains a number of blogs on all types of technogeekery that will help you stay on top of your patrons' interests, needs, and desires, as well as providing stories about best practices to help you employ pilot projects in your own institution.

Bend Over Backward

Most people fear change, especially change they are not in control of. Gamers not only expect change, they anticipate it. Remember the concept of sticky content for your Web site, or something that changes frequently in order to draw visitors back because they want to see what's new? Extend this idea to your physical building; an unpredictably changing display, flower arrangement, or bulletin board turns figuring out what's different into a game. Flexible furnishings such as stacking cushions, wheeled ottomans, and video rockers can easily be moved, creating a customized seating area. Also, make your facility's Web site appealing to gamers by allowing them to customize it; let them change the way your Web page looks with CSS, for example.

Demonstrate your own flexibility by finding ways to say *yes* to patron requests. Keep a "No Log"—a simple list of things patrons ask for that is against policy or against the rules, like drinking in the computer area, or downloading to a portable USB hard drive, or connecting a digital camera to a library computer. Review these *no*'s at regular management meetings to find ways to accommodate the needs of your patrons. Finally, plan for change. Write it into the long-range plan, and stick to it!

Pay Attention

Immersing yourself in pop culture and reading the newspaper every day will make you a better librarian, no matter what population you serve. Know what's hot (and what's not), so that you can keep up with patron requests. Read Steven Berlin Johnson's *Everything Bad Is Good For You: How Today's Pop Culture Is Making Us Smarter* (Riverhead, 2005) for a convincing case of how the complexity of story arcs on television shows like *ER* and *Lost* keep our synapses firing. Especially, keep up with crossovers. Remember, the new literacy is cross-format; chances are that if a new *Spiderman* movie comes out, novelizations, comic books, graphic novels, movie soundtracks, and video games will be among the related merchandise its fans will want to borrow. Some series take the crossover concept to the next level, such as the Japanese series *.hack//Sign*, which requires the consumer to read, view, and play anime, manga, films, and video games in a specific order to make sense of the whole story. The storyline centers around the protagonist Tsukasa, who struggles to cope with his inner self, his past, and his inability to log out of the MMORPG World.[14]

Begin to pay attention to gaming culture. Watch machinima, such as the Halo 2 based *Red vs. Blue* sitcom, or the talk show *This Spartan Life*. Read a video game-focused Web comic such as Penny Arcade or PvP. View PBS's Culture Shock You Decide: Video Games, an interactive exercise designed to help you determine your level of acceptance of violence in video games. Skim gaming magazines while shelving, paying attention to the ads for new releases. Pay attention to gaming news by reading the Game On! Video Games in Libraries blog (libgaming.blogspot.com) or join the LibGaming Google Group (groups.google.com/group/libgaming) to follow gaming in the library world. If you are a young adult librarian, participate in the

YALSA Gaming Interest group (communities.ala.org) and look at events like YALSA's 2007 Teens & Technology Midwinter Institute.

Play!

At some point, try some games yourself. Just as we are trained not to judge books by their covers, we should remain similarly open-minded about the video game medium. Some simple games to try might include:

- Penguin Baseball (fury.com/mirror/penguin.html) – Perfect your hand-eye coordination by bunting a penguin

- Chicktionary (Blockdot) (www.shockwave.com/gamelanding/chicktionary.jsp) – A word game for fans of word searches and Scrabble

- Diner Dash (Playfirst) (www.shockwave.com/gamelanding/dinerdash.jsp) – A waitressing game that will make you appreciate even busy days on the reference desk

A list of additional games is available online at home.comcast.net/~begallaway/gamelist.html. Once you've tried a game or two, pass a link on to a colleague, incorporate gaming as a team-building exercise at your staff development day, and equate video gaming to such leisure activities as board gaming, chess, bridge, and the newly popular Sudoku.

Collections

Librarians unfamiliar with games may be more comfortable relating them to an older immersive technology we know and love: books. Like books, games can be grouped by audience (children, teen, adult), genre (sports, action/adventure, puzzle, role-playing, first-person shooter), and format (CD or cartridge). Just as book authors (Clancy), series (*Harry Potter*), and genres (mystery) develop a following, game fandoms are created around designers like Sid Meier, Will Wright, and American McGee, around series such as Final Fantasy or WarCraft, and around platforms such as Nintendo and Playstation. Games can be assessed on some of the same evaluative criteria we use for books and multimedia: by examining details such as plot, setting, tone, character, line, color, transitions, and design.

Like films, and now graphic novels, video games are voluntarily rated. The seven-tier ratings system established by the Entertainment Software Association in 1994 examines video games against a checklist of some 40 elements, through both sample footage and actual gameplay. The mass media would have us believe that all games are violent first-person shooters, but M-rated ("Mature") games accounted for just 15 percent of all video game sales in 2005.[15] This means that 85 percent of all games sold are rated either E for Everyone, E+10 for ages 10 and up, or T for teen (13–17). Additionally, organizations for educational gaming and social change games are springing up, as the number of serious and religious games increase.

Both *Voice of Youth Advocates* and *School Library Journal* now produce regular columns featuring video game reviews. Other good sources are the periodicals *Electronic Gaming Monthly* and *Game Informer*. The Library Success Best Practices wiki (www.libsuccess.org) is another great resource for both programs and collections. Our collections should be based on what patrons are requesting. Focus on console games that don't require registration or activation codes, and use DVD or CD security cases to deter theft.

Here to Stay

Gaming is not a passing fad; industry data suggests that video games will generate $21.9 billion in hardware and software revenue by 2008.[16] Given these figures, what does the future of gaming in libraries look like? Not only will libraries come to accept games, but we will embrace them as a new form of storytelling. As games become increasingly realistic, the technology will continue to decrease in size and increase in speed. Educational and serious gaming will continue to increase. And social and economic activity will migrate to virtual worlds such as Second Life (Linden Lab, 2002), an online 3D community built entirely by its users, which as of July 2006 was growing at the rate of 3,000 new registrants a day. Philip Rosedale, the founder and CEO of Linden Lab, told *Wired* in 2004: "I'm not building a game … I'm building a new country."[17]

This country apparently has space for a library. In April 2006, the Alliance Library System (ALS) in Illinois purchased a plot of land to build a virtual library, intending to attract Illinois residents within the community and act as a referral to local physical libraries. The project was a "response to a shift in people of all ages from media consumers to media creators. … they want to create and contribute, not just consume."[18] The project has grown by leaps and bounds, with a virtual reference desk staffed several nights a week by volunteer reference librarians from all over the world, and programs and events that include bibliographic instruction, professional development for librarians, book discussions, and virtual author visits. EBSCO and OCLC have offered trials to databases and WorldCat, and partners include in-world newspapers, writing groups, ebook creators, and artists, as well as organizations like Tech Soup. With more than three dozen dedicated volunteers and more than 140 e-mail list members, ALS has invited participation from other libraries to ascertain what digital residents want in a 21st-century virtual library—and then build it. (Read about the Second Life Library in detail in Chapter 12.)

The Second Life Library is a perfect example of the culmination of delivering services to patrons who live online, of meeting users where they are, of trying pilot projects, of adapting to change, and of adopting content creation technologies. Although not a game with goals and objectives, Second Life shares many characteristics with video games. The challenge to create an avatar as a representation of oneself, the social networking and building of affinity groups, and the tendency to create and modify content in and around the world all pay tribute to video games. The interface and the ability to zoom in and out are designed for—and by—a generation that has grown up focusing on a screen while their hands manipulate a character.

Resources

BoingBoing, www.boingboing.net
Electronic Gaming Monthly, egm.1up.com
Entertainment Software Association, www.theesa.com
Game Informer, www.gameinformer.com
Library Success: A Best Practices Wiki, www.libsuccess.org
Penny Arcade, www.penny-arcade.com
Pop Goes the Library, www.popgoesthelibrary.com
PvP, www.pvponline.com
This Spartan Life, www.thisspartanlife.com
VOYA Teen Pop Culture Quiz, www.voya.com

Endnotes

1. John C. Beck and Mitchell Wade, *Got Game? How the Gamer Generation Is Reshaping Business Forever*, Cambridge, MA: Harvard Business School, 2004.

2. ESA, Essential Facts About the Computer and Game Industry, 2006, www.theesa.com/archives/files/Essentialpercent20Factspercent202006.pdf (accessed July 1, 2006).

3. ESA, *Essential Facts About the Computer and Game Industry*, 2006.

4. ESA, *Essential Facts About the Computer and Game Industry*, 2006.

5. Amanda Lenhart et al., "Teens and Technology: Youth Are Leading the Transition to a Fully Wired and Mobile Nation," Family, Friends & Community, Pew Internet & American Life Project, July 2005, www.pewinternet.org/PPF/r/162/report_display.asp (accessed July 1, 2006).

6. James Paul Gee, *What Video Games Have to Teach Us About Learning and Literacy*, Palgrave McMillan, 2003.

7. David Warlick, "The New Literacies," Scholastic Administrator, Mar–Apr 2005, www.scholastic.com/administrator/marapr05/articles.asp?article=newlit (accessed July 1, 2006).

8. NMSA, NMSA Research Summaries, Young Adolescents Developmental Needs (1996), www.nmsa.org/Research/ResearchSummaries/Summary5/tabid/257/Default.aspx.

9. Michael Park, "Study: Kids Get Slight Work-Out Playing Video Games," Fox News Sunday, May 07, 2006, www.foxnews.com/story/0,2933,194605,00.html (accessed July 1, 2006).

10. "Study: Video Games Can Help Cut Surgical Errors," Reuters, May 24, 2006, abcnews.go.com/Health/wireStory?id=1997480 (accessed July 1, 2006).

11. Verena Dobnik, "Surgeons May Err Less by Playing Video Games," MSNBC April 7, 2004, www.msnbc.msn.com/id/4685909 (accessed July 1, 2006).

12. "Everything Bad Is Good for You," NPR Morning Edition, May 24, 2005, www.npr.org/templates/story/story.php?storyId=4663852 (accessed July 1, 2006).

13. ESA, *Essential Facts*.

14. ".hack//Sign," Wikipedia, en.wikipedia.org/wiki/.Hack//Sign (accessed July 1, 2006).

15. ESA, *Essential Facts*.

16. Data Monitor, "Next Generation Video Game Consoles," October 12, 2005, datamonitor-market-research.com/Merchant2/merchant.mvc?

Screen=PROD&Product_Code=BFTC1208&Category_Code= (accessed July 1, 2006).

17. Daniel Terdiman, "Fun in Following the Money," *Wired*, May 8, 2004, www.wired.com/news/games/0,2101,63363,00.html (accessed July 1, 2006).

18. Lori Bell, Tom Peters, and Kitty Pope, "Enjoying Your First Life? Why Not Add a Second? Developing Library Services in Second Life," Serious Games Source, June 30, 2006, seriousgamessource.com/features/feature_063006_second_life_library.php (accessed July 1, 2006).

CHAPTER 7

Thriving in the Age of Google

Joseph Janes
Associate Professor and Associate Dean
for Academics, The Information School
University of Washington

What is Google? It may seem fatuous, in 2007, to even ask, as though there were any way to escape its reach and dominance, as though it hadn't already become a household name—and a verb. It's now enshrined forever in the language by the *Oxford English Dictionary*, which somewhat charmingly lists the searching sense (with a first usage in 1999 from a posting in the Usenet newsgroup alt.fan.british-accent—how much has the world changed?) second to a cricketing use from the turn of the 20th century.

This is worth exploring briefly, though, merely to establish the terms of our discussion. Google is a search engine, yes. While we're plumbing the depths of the *OED*, it defines a search engine as: "*Computing*, a piece of hardware or software designed for searching, *esp.* a program that searches for and identifies items in a database that correspond to one or more keywords specified by the user; *spec.* such a program used to search for information available over the Internet, using its own previously compiled database of Internet files and documents."

Fair enough; that's a reasonable technical definition. For most people, however, I'd imagine that the rough definition of Google, or any search engine, would run something along the lines of "the little box in the computer that searches the Internet." And, for most people in most situations, that definition will do just fine. The technical underpinnings and algorithms and complexities that lie beneath the workings of a search are of very little interest to your average searcher.

Google is, indeed, the most successful search engine by any useful measure: usage, corporate market capitalization, advertising revenue, and so on. Surely, though, there's more to it than this. It's common at times like this to refer to Google's corporate mission, now familiar to those who want to understand it better, or tell scary stories around librarian campfires: "Google's mission is to organize the world's information and make it universally accessible and useful."[1]

Google's nothing if not ambitious. Casual readers of that sentence can be forgiven for thinking that Google's mission sounds a whole lot like what libraries, museums, archives, and other cultural heritage institutions have been trying to do for centuries.

But of course, that's really *not* what those institutions have been trying to do. Read the sentence again, carefully. No institution, no matter how grand, not even the Library of Congress or the British Museum or the Bibliotheque Nationale or the Smithsonian, has tried to organize the *world's* information. At least, nobody's seriously tried that for centuries. And as far as making it universally accessible goes, any heritage institution worth its salt would rather go down with the ship than let anybody paw over its deeply held treasures, for obvious and appropriate reasons of conservation and preservation. We have tried to help make such resources useful, but taken in whole, Google's mission is actually much grander and more encompassing than that of most libraries and similar organizations.

But soft, there is more. That mission statement has been thrown about quite a bit, but I find the sentence that follows, from their corporate overview page, to be even more instructive: "As a first step to fulfilling that mission, Google's founders Larry Page and Sergey Brin developed a new approach to online search that took root in a Stanford University dorm room and quickly spread to information seekers around the globe." *As a first step*. This is a striking indication that the founders' ambition is not limited to building the world's most successful search engine. Clearly, they see that more is possible and is on the way, which has been borne out by a large number of ancillary features, products, and services that have been introduced over the last several years.

I first began to grasp this idea a few years ago, when I discovered the Google calculator feature. It's one of many little tidbits buried on the Web Search Features page,[2] along with the phone book search and stock quotes and currency conversion. Simply put, if you type a mathematical expression (575+956, say, or my favorite, half a cup in teaspoons), you'll get an answer (1,531, and 24, respectively), along with a link in case you wanted to actually search those expressions.

This is a simple little thing, kind of fun, kind of cute, quite possibly the product of a Google programmer's late-night languor, and easily overlooked. For me, though, it was my first indication that Google had ideas. It seems clear it is not, and will not, be content with simply being a great search engine.

Not that there's anything wrong with that. Search engines, in general, are conduits to information. They fulfill functions similar to those of library catalogs, serials databases, and other familiar finding tools. Those more traditional tools have stand-alone uses as well, to verify citations, research an author's repertoire, trace a publication's history, determine a publication date, and so on. In general, however, they were designed as a means to the end of locating and accessing other works. Search engines do much the same sort of thing.

When you begin adding features, though, they cease being primarily means to an end, becoming ends unto themselves as well. The Google calculator, along with Google Maps and Google Earth, Blogger, Google Finance, Google Talk, Google Calendar, Froogle, and allied services such as Picasa and Gmail—and on and on—make it fairly plain that Google is not content to simply point people elsewhere. And yet, they've avoided the trap that AOL, Yahoo!, and MSN fell into: Each of these search engines tried to be a destination for original content, which can make a site continually fresh and interesting, but also carries a substantial burden of creation. Google's resident services are generally very low-impact, at least from Google's perspective, requiring considerably less overhead on its part.

Google has also been very canny in recognizing the range of information resources it could (and couldn't) cover. A few years ago, it would have been possible to legitimately say that Google covered a relatively small slice of the information pie. It did a reasonable job of indexing and providing access to the freely available Web. As with any search engine, though, it could only index a certain subset of that freely available Web—some pages aren't linked, so they can't be found by a spider, some sections of the Web are less accessible, and so on. Even with many billions of pages in its indexes, it could only hope to have a chunk of what was there.

This left a lot of stuff. Beyond the "rest" of the free Web, there was the invisible Web, sites behind password or other authorization controls, and Web pages created on the fly by databases and inaccessible to spidering programs. Moreover, any digital information not on the free Web (such as, for example, abstracting and indexing databases, fee-based information services, and non-Web-based resources) wasn't available, nor was anything, of course, not in digital format, such as books.

So, as massive and encompassing as Google appeared in, say, 2003, there were lots of areas where it had very little or simply nothing to offer. In the intervening years, however, it has moved into new areas and significantly broadened its reach. In particular, the introduction of Google Scholar and Google Book Search (formerly Google Print) addresses two very large missing pieces of the pie, those of digital journals and printed books. Marginal success by either or both of those projects would represent a hefty expansion in the areas in which it could justifiably claim to be a contender for the eyes and searches of the public, positioning it even more centrally as a competitor to libraries and their services.

What Can Google Do?

There are a number of things that Google can do very well, which are worthy of attention here. First, and probably most apparently, it allows *searching for specific words or phrases*. In the last few days, I've searched on words and phrases such as <Jewish holidays 2006>, <circe>, <strait australia new guinea>, <jackson square>, particular ZIP codes, and so on. If I wanted to get really fancy, I'd use some *semi-sophisticated search technique* such as restricting results to a particular file type or domain or using the Boolean OR. While Google does permit (or even, arguably, encourage) mindless chimpanzee-level searching, there are some relatively useful techniques available under the hood for the small minority of searchers willing to unearth and use them.

Searches such as these are often of the momentary, fill-in-the-missing-piece variety. Most of my searches can be explained by working on crossword puzzles, writing, and planning my courses for the coming year. While none of these was a particularly deep or defining information need for me, each was an impediment that I quickly and easily removed with a few keystrokes. (If you see a parallel to the traditional notion of ready reference here, you get a gold star.)

Which is not to say, of course, that a Google search or its results can't be life-transforming. This must undoubtedly happen on a regular basis, for information needs that are meaningful and important and that can be met using this kind of searching and these kinds of resources.

I find that many people use Google, though, as an *orientation* device. When a word or phrase is unfamiliar, google it and you'll at least get an idea of what it is and, perhaps, where to learn more. Because of the nature and scope of the free Web that underlies Google, it has a certain advantage of *breadth*. It is increasingly difficult to run across topics, concepts, ideas, or names that aren't somewhere represented or discussed on the Web and that can be found in a Google search. And, as a freely available Web tool, Google is *ubiquitous*, available, and ready all the time, from anywhere you can get to a Web browser (with certain national and network limitations, of course).

Google is *free*, *quick*, *easy*, and, in general, *good enough*. In a good-enough world (which it has always been; Zipf's Law of Least Effort dates back to 1949, so this isn't an overnight phenomenon[3]), good enough is good enough, and generally wins over other alternatives.

There are other, subtler, effects of Google and its ilk. Searching used to be hard. It used to require work and thought and effort, and, often, physical movement to get to whatever it was you needed to search. Now, of course, with the proliferation of search boxes, search is easy and even fun.

That shift, I believe, helps to *change the way people think about searching*. As the opportunities to search expand and the act of searching becomes more commonplace, it will seem closer to people, more a part of their regular lives. This could, as a result, *change the way people think about information*. It, too, will no longer be something remote, or needing exertion to identify and use, it will be simply there, ready and waiting to be found and incorporated into whatever people are trying to do.

I once asked a group of students to watch themselves searching Google for a few days and consider how they might have found the same information previously, before Web searching. I expected them, naturally, to say that they would go to or call the library, or some other professional-type response. To a person, they said they more than likely simply wouldn't have searched. One student said that it would have been one of those "I guess we'll never know" kind of experiences; another said that Google meant you no longer had an excuse to be ignorant. Sobering.

It's not a huge leap from that to a shift in *the way people think*. If people are surrounded by information and ways to get at it, suffused with and encircled by it, it is difficult to imagine that this won't have an effect on their thinking and creative processes. I wouldn't argue that their creations and thoughts would be better informed, merely that they would think and create differently, at least partially as a result of the availability and perceived presence of information in their work and personal environments.

That's a fairly grandiose leap, and I have no evidence other than supposition to offer in its defense. Technologies often shape the way we perceive and act upon the world around us, so it's not out of the question that the use of search engines and increased availability of information could have these kinds of effects.

What Can't Google Do?

Before we just turn out the lights and cede the field to the search engines of the world, let's examine the other side of the equation. Despite its considerable strengths, Google is not without its shortcomings, to wit:

Organization systems of all types perform two vital, related, but quite different functions: searching and gathering. While Google is a fine tool for searching for the specific, it's substantially weaker at the *gathering* function, at bringing together groups of like things. So while I would easily think of Google first, say, to identify a song from a lyric I heard on the radio, I wouldn't use it to collect a set of Web sites around song lyrics. Google could be used to achieve that, but I'd prefer to use a tool that had some sort of explicit directory function, such as Yahoo! or the Librarian's Internet Index, where categories facilitate gathering.

Because of the largely indiscriminate nature of spidering programs, Google is not in a position to *select* or *evaluate* or *decide upon* the pages that are added to its index. Links are followed, files are read and indexed, and that's about it. Thus, any notion of the coherence or purpose of a collection of resources is missing, in favor of breadth and reach. It goes without saying, therefore, that Google is not in a position to make any claims on the *accuracy* or *authority* (or quality, reliability, timeliness, usefulness …) of the pages it indexes.

A number of functions we similarly take for granted in human-mediated information services are absent in search engines. There is no easy way for searchers to receive *assistance* in search technique, evaluation and understanding of results, or use of the information they find—or, for that matter *an understanding of the nature of their information need* as one would hope would be the result of, say, a reference interview.

The Google "secret sauce," the algorithms it uses to produce the ranked retrievals in response to search queries, is extremely complicated and very powerful. It produces, in general, very good results, and there are, as we've seen, a number of techniques available to a searcher to refine or improve the precision of results. Yet those *advanced search techniques are still quite limited*, in comparison to those available in library-oriented systems with extensive metadata in highly structured records, as contrasted with metadata-light HTML documents. To be sure, some of those more powerful techniques are often confusing to users (and sometimes even to professionals), but they can be of great use when necessary. Moreover, *Google can only search one thing*, the Web, while libraries have access to a wide number of different kinds of information sources and resources.

As a global, or at least transnational, service, Google is a one-size-fits-all tool. Obviously, this works in a large number of cases, and their local service seeks to mitigate that by focusing searches on a particular geographic area. But try as they might, they are *unable to be tightly connected in any meaningful way, to any community* in the same way one thinks libraries are.

Finally, while Google has the advantage of breadth as a result of the nature of resources available on the free Web, it suffers from the concomitant *lack of depth* of those same resources. It is certainly true that there are a large number of comprehensive resources on the free Web, and that in some cases an extensive research or information need could be well satisfied there. That likely pales in comparison to the depth to be expected in works such as books, research reports, journal articles, conference proceedings, and so on. It's worth remarking that this may well be a temporary situation as time goes on and the Web evolves (see the end of the previous discussion).

So Where Does That Leave Libraries?

The most obvious answer to the challenge that Google poses to the library world is to exploit its shortcomings. That may seem a little mercenary or crass, and as proceeding from a position of weakness. However, if one examines those shortcomings a little more closely, one sees that they map well to areas of traditional soundness for libraries, allowing us to proceed from a position of strength—and even confidence. These go hand in glove, then, to provide a set of ideas for ways to position libraries in a Googlified world:

Advocate for quality. Not to mention authority, timeliness, etc. It is a good-enough world, and no amount of effort on our part is likely to change that. However, when the need is sufficiently important, people will want and value the high-quality stuff, and we can be there to provide it.

Provide help and understanding. The human touch is, still, remarkably powerful. To be sure, there are people and information needs (private, embarrassing questions, for example, or people too ashamed of their own inability to find what they're looking for) where that touch is decidedly unwelcome. For others, though, having some-one available to help them understand and think through their infor-mation needs, what sources might be available, how to search them, how to use the results, and so on, can be just what the doctor ordered, and can literally change their lives.

Help doesn't always have to be person-to-person, either. It's great when it can be, but it doesn't scale well to a massive audience. There are ways to help potentially large numbers of people without per-sonal interaction or intervention; quite simple ones such as good sig-nage in buildings, good design and information architecture of library Web sites, and even great old chestnuts like pathfinders. If ever there was a tool designed for the Web, it's the pathfinder—links to good resources on somewhat general topics, ideas for further research, search terms and subject headings, authors and organiza-tions to consider, and so on—perfect for an on-the-go, 24/7 world.

Maintain strong collections. Most librarians don't need much of a nudge on that score, so I won't belabor this, other than to reinforce why it is of high importance. Those collections must represent a range of high-quality resources, beyond the superficial or transitory, and they must be designed and tended for the communities they are meant to serve. (I assume it goes without saying that I mean collec-tions of both digital and analog materials here.) The ability to consult and draw upon a range of different kinds, format, and genres of resources is a signature of the library world, and one worth building upon even further.

Use sophisticated search techniques, and love metadata. I've finally come to terms with the fact that Dialog isn't going to make an 11th-hour comeback, so all my years of learning and using and teaching and writing those arcane little commands have gone by the wayside. Much as I will miss the (3N)s and /DFs and their cousins, there still are many opportunities in systems we use today to go beyond the plunk-a-few-words-in-and-hope-for-the-best methods of search engines. Boolean and proximity operations, limiting by fields, taking advantage of special features of specific databases and systems, pearl growing using controlled vocabulary, and the like can yet be powerful methods of improving both the recall and precision of searches and yielding significantly better and more effective results.

Be where they are. That cryptic and pithy little maxim incorporates two ideas I think are vital to the future success of libraries. The first is to understand and really be a part of the community and clientele you serve, knowing the demographics and the people, the individuals, their needs and hopes and aspirations and creative impulses and what they want from their library. Keep in mind, it's really theirs; we just get to play there every day.

That kind of understanding will allow you to maintain the kind of collections I just described, yes. It will also allow you to be where they are when they need you. Because, by and large, when they need you, they likely won't know they need you, or at least not you specifically. This means being available and accessible, in the form of reasonable opening hours and days, buildings in the right places, bookmobiles, and Web sites that provide the kinds of resources and services people want in useful and usable ways. (For example, what do most people think a "database" is? Or a "catalog"? A "citation"? It ain't what you and I think, trust me. Use language that normal people understand.)

It also means being in their minds and thoughts when an information need arises that you can do something about. To be honest, if somebody in your community is trying to find out the capital of Bolivia and googles it, I'm all for that. Google will outperform any reference librarian in searches like that, flat out, even if you happened to be standing at the reference desk, poised with your hands over the *World Almanac*, ready to strike like a cobra. I don't mind, of course, if people ask those kinds of questions of libraries, but that seems an increasingly unlikely and unrealistic scenario.

However … if that same person is planning a trip to Bolivia, or wants to host a Bolivian exchange student, or write a paper on the history of Bolivia, or research a piece of Bolivian pottery or the details of how it got its name, or any of a hundred other in-depth, meaningful, interesting, chewy information needs like that, we all know they're going to get way better stuff from a library than from Google.

And I'd much rather have highly trained and experienced librarians working on those kinds of needs anyway; that's what we were truly meant to do.

The challenge, now, is to help *them* to understand that. When we achieve that, when libraries are central to the information lives of their communities, then we will not only have survived the challenges that Google presents, we will thrive in their midst.

Endnotes

1. www.google.com/corporate
2. www.google.com/help/features.html
3. George K. Zipf, *Human Behaviour and the Principle of Least-Effort,* Cambridge, MA: Addison-Wesley, 1949.

CHAPTER 8

Libraries and the Read/Write Web

Michael Stephens
Assistant Professor, Graduate School of
Library and Information Science
Dominican University

Remember your first glimpse of the World Wide Web? Remember surfing to various pages and finding text, images, and links? Remember building your own Web page with HTML? Maybe you were even the person who built that first page for your library! Oh, how we coded and planned for those pages: building resources, selecting and organizing our favorite sites, and uploading graphics and scanned images.

A New Landscape

That era has given way to a new incarnation of the Web that is changing the way libraries can interact with library users. Librarians should be paying close attention to the behaviors, uses, and communities growing in this new realm—and should seek every opportunity to participate and to share their human voice.

Tim Berners-Lee, the creator of the World Wide Web, was featured in the October 2005 issue of *Smithsonian* magazine as one of 35 people "Who Made a Difference." In his *Smithsonian* interview with Tom Standage, Berners-Lee said he sees the growing trend of Weblogs for communication and conversation directly with readers and wikis for collaboration among groups of people as the right way to go for the Web.[1] This statement points to one of the most important shifts in the online world: a user-centric focus. Berners-Lee sees the new platform as moving closer to his original concept: the Web as a pool of shared knowledge. Similarly, I see a Web where folks—anyone and everyone who can get access—can find others like them, a Web where connections are made and conversations play out online.

Libraries of all types have enhanced their services via the tools of the Read/Write Web, including blogs, wikis, RSS, instant messaging, and more, meeting library users where they live. Jenny Levine's discussion (Chapter 11) of the offshoot of Web 2.0, Library 2.0, explores user-centric libraries further.

Enter the Read/Write Web

This next "version" of the Web has been called many things: the Social Web, social software, the Read/Write Web, and Web 2.0. New digital tools allow users to create, change, and publish dynamic content of all kinds, creating our own information and entertainment channels; other Web 2.0 tools syndicate and aggregate this content.

"Web 2.0 is the network as platform, spanning all connected devices," writes Tim O'Reilly, founder and CEO of O'Reilly Media. "Web 2.0 applications are those that make the most of the intrinsic advantages of that platform: delivering software as a continually updated service that gets better the more people use it, consuming and remixing data from multiple sources, including individual users, while providing their own data and services in a form that allows remixing by others, creating network effects through an 'architecture of participation,' and going beyond the page metaphor of Web 1.0 to deliver rich user experiences."[2]

O'Reilly's take on the user echoes Michael Buckland, who almost 15 years ago urged librarians to consider their users and the tools they were using: "Since library services are provided for people to use, two relationships become important: How will changes in the provision of library services affect library users and what they do, and how should changes in the tasks and work habits of library users affect the provision of library services?"[3]

Trendspotting librarians have picked up on Web 2.0, finding their users actively living and playing online. Sites like Flickr, MySpace, and Blogger allow us to make connections, have conversations, and share our lives. Everyday folk have embraced the Read/Write Web as a way to put themselves out there.

Express Yourself

People are now able to "express themselves" by putting their lives online. This can truly rattle the cages of librarians, who are trained to protect the privacy of their users to the utmost degree. Librarians and libraries, though, should also find ways to put themselves and their services out there, where we can be found by library users. The Web is where people are interacting. A 2006 *Newsweek* cover story touted the insurgence of the new Web, made up of social connections and interactions centered around music, images, or other content. One interviewee simply defined this online shift as "the live Web"[4]—a great pool overflowing with self-expression!

It comes down to having presence. Primarily, presence for the library and its services, but I'd also urge librarians to consider using these tools to build presence for the profession. Do folks still expect to find the librarian stereotype? Making a "librarian trading card" like those found on Flickr (www.flickr.com/groups/librariancards/pool) lends a 21st-century view of our profession.

What better way to learn how these tools work—and see how we might improve library services to users with Web 2.0 applications— than to dive in and try them out? Read over the listing of tools, investigate some of the Web sites mentioned here, and try a few out. With experience, we are better able to educate our users, who are already experimenting with social tools.

What Does the Read/Write Web Let Us Do?

Before we examine social tools and how libraries have adopted their use, it is useful to examine the principles or affordances of the Read/Write Web. Paul Miller, Technology Evangelist for TALIS, a U.K.-based ILS vendor, explored Web 2.0 and libraries in an article for the online journal *Ariadne*. He writes that "Web 2.0 is about participation, communication, facilitating community, remixing content, and trust. And it's about the user!"[5] Bryan Alexander, Director for Research at the National Institute for Technology and Liberal Education, summarized the concepts of the Social Web as strands of microcontent and the beginnings of a new, seamless way to experience the Internet in an article for *Educause*: "Rather than following the notion of the Web as book, they are predicated on *microcontent*. Blogs are about posts, not pages. Wikis are streams of conversation, revision, amendment, and truncation. Podcasts are shuttled between

Web sites, RSS feeds, and diverse players. These content blocks can be saved, summarized, addressed, copied, quoted, and built into new projects."[6]

How do these principles and affordances of social software look when applied to libraries? What are we doing with this new Web?

- Communication – There is a willingness to share information and to be transparent, and user participation is welcomed. Libraries use Weblogs to create conversations.

- Facilitating Community – The library serves as a venue for community involvement and the sharing of ideas and knowledge. Conversations play out online.

- Harnessing the Collective Intelligence – New information is created via collaboration between librarians, or between librarians and library users. A locally focused wiki is created to share referrals and information. An academic library podcasts the recent speech and discussion of a noted professor.

- Participation – Everyone has a hand in the creation of content; ideas and knowledge flow freely and are available for remix and reuse. The library hosts a wiki for its long-range plan, inviting staff and users to participate and create a vision for the future.

- Remixing Content – Content is freely available for use and reuse. Content is "mashed-up" and new systems are created. A librarian creates a Google Maps mashup of the library's branches, each clickable to display contact information and hotlinks. A library feeds RSS content from various sources to other Web pages within its community or campus.

- Rich User Experience – People can have conversations and create together. Comment-enabled Weblogs allow library users to discuss plans and programs.

- Seamlessness – Users discover the library in the online spaces where they "live" and play. A library user installs a plugin for Amazon or the Internet Movie Database that lists library holdings. One click takes the user to the library catalog for a hold or pick up request.

- Self-Expression – Users can post about as much or as little of their lives as they care to. A library encourages users to post material reviews in the online catalog.

- Trust – New library systems must be based on trust: trust between library staff and trust with library users for participation and collaboration. Administrators and managers allow staff to create resources and post content. Librarians release control of their data and their Web presence. Librarians trust their users to interact, comment, and collaborate within their online presence. Darlene Fichter urges librarians in a 2.0 world to embrace "radical trust" when building resources—together.[7]

Librarians should also think about how their libraries encourage the hearts of users. Many of the Web 2.0 tools allow us to do just that: encourage our users to think, feel or remember, and to share those feelings via a blog, wiki, or other tool.

Tools of the Read/Write Web

It seems that a new social site or Web-based tool goes live almost every day. Sites that allow folks to make connections and to share and remix content populate the new Web. Librarians use a number of Web 2.0 tools to enhance or create services.

Blogs

One of the most talked about Web 2.0 applications lies in the use of Weblog (blog) software to create easily updated, content-rich Web sites. What began as a software tool for people to share their lives online, as with a public journal, is now changing the way many organizations and businesses create Web content. Weblogs can contain anything from diaries to news to links to book reviews; the software frees us to create and post any content we desire. Weblogs usually present content in reverse chronological order so the newest entries are at the top of the page where the user's eye falls first.

In *Naked Conversations: How Blogs Are Changing the Way Businesses Talk with Customers*, Scoble and Israel argue that blogs are better than traditional marketing venues, because they allow instant two-way communication with customers. They theorize that businesses who fail to provide a Weblog that allows customers to interact via comments may lose customers to a business that does allow two-way communication.[8]

Once configured, blog software automatically creates HTML pages, archives, links, and categories, via an easy to use Web-based interface that allows people to create and edit posts from practically anywhere. Popular software includes Movable Type (www.sixapart.com), a powerful for-fee business-oriented package, WordPress (www.wordpress.org), an open-source, free application, and Blogger (www.blogger.com), a solution that hosts blogs on a remote server for free.

How are libraries using Weblogs? Some, such as the Ann Arbor (MI) District Library (www.aadl.org), have rebuilt their entire Web presences around Weblogs and a feature-rich content management system. Others, such as the St. Joseph (IN) County Public Library (www.libraryforlife.org/blogs/lifeline/index.php), have added a blog to their current online presence. A library blog can be used to disseminate information about new materials, services, databases, and more; allowing librarians to focus more on content than coding.

"Biblioblogs," or all things libraries and Weblogs, include:

- Association & Organization Weblogs – Devoted to news and information about a library-related association or organization.

- Conference Weblogs – Could be related to associations or organizations; devoted to all things related to a conference or meeting.

- Internal Weblogs – Devoted to internal communication and news. Can replace the staff Intranet.

- Librarians' Weblogs – Opinions, insights, and information from librarians and library workers. Might be devoted to a specific topic or type of library work.

- Library News Weblogs – A straightforward catchall—all the news that's fit to blog, if you will!

- Marketing & Promotion Weblogs – Announce and promote activities and programming, might be tied to the library calendar.

- Materials/Resources Weblogs – Highlight certain parts of a library's collection. Might focus on fiction, electronic resources, new reference books, or newly-added DVDs.

- Project Weblogs – Chronicle a project: a new building, a long-range plan, a research study.

- Service-Oriented Weblogs – Devoted to a particular library service, such as gaming programs for teens or book clubs.

- User-Specific Weblogs – Focused on a particular user population—teens, faculty, seniors, graduate students—highlighting library services and news just for that group.[9]

Other ideas for library blogging include a Summer Reading blog, a One Book One Campus blog, and the library director's blog. Links to the various types of library blogs can be found at Amanda Etches-Johnson's "Blog Without a Library" (www.blogwithouta library.net).

Starting a Weblog may be the best way for a library to jump into the social software pool—don't miss the chance to communicate and create conversation directly with staff and users.

Podcasts

Podcasting, the syndication of audio content via blog posts or RSS, has also made great waves in the social Web. Some libraries are experimenting with sharing audio content, including book reviews for on-the-go listening, interviews with visiting authors, and general library news.

Libraries should explore this method of content delivery further, as more and more people come to expect various channels of content from the media, corporations, and service-oriented institutions. With video-casting or video-blogging on the horizon, media-rich content delivery via various formats will become both expected and necessary.

Future library users may also look to the library for a space to gather and create content. Podcasting stations, sound studios, video editing booths, and media labs are all important concerns for future library spaces.

RSS

RSS is an acronym for "Rich Site Summary" or "Really Simple Syndication." This XML format lets people syndicate Web content, from news stories to corporate information to blogs to podcasts. In lay terms, RSS is like the suitcase that transfers the content from your blog (or other syndicated content) to an aggregator such as Bloglines (www.bloglines.com) or Newsgator (www.newsgator.com). RSS contains directions for the data, so that other services can understand it and place all the parts in the right order; like a delivery service that brings Web content to your door. If you start a library blog, realize that most blogging software creates an RSS feed as part of the "back end" of the HTML Web pages.

A librarian who uses Bloglines or another aggregator to monitor feeds from various resources such as blogs, news sites, and current awareness services, will find it easier to stay in the know and "keep current," as discussed by Roy Tennant in *Library Journal.* Tennant reminds librarians that sites such as Feedster.com offer a way to search for news feeds related to any subject area or interest, and that adding current awareness pages by gathering many different feeds together can also add value to digital libraries.[10] Libraries can also place RSS feeds of content on their Web sites to build awareness and presence.

The Hennepin County Library in Minnesota (www.hclib.org) offers RSS feeds from almost every piece of its database-driven Web site. The page of library news, the subject guides, the HCL calendar of events all provide feeds. The Hennepin County ILS offers users the ability to customize catalog searches and "subscribe" to them, in order to monitor new catalog additions and news from the library.

Wikis

Wiki software allows groups to collaboratively edit a Web site. Wiki software tracks changes, builds tables of contents and headings automatically, and affords anyone with access the chance to contribute to the pages. Some sites, such as SeedWiki.com, offer free wiki space, or software such as the open source MediaWiki (www.mediawiki.org) can be loaded on a library's server. Wikis excel in encouraging collaboration, and often include useful features such as "versioning," which tracks the histories of documents.

The most famous example is, of course, Wikipedia (www.wikipedia.org), which is edited by people from all over the world. Some librarians have also embraced wikis to organize projects, build resources, and share information. The librarians at Butler University Library built the Reference Resources wiki (www.seedwiki.com/wiki/butler_wikiref) to annotate all of their online and print resources, allowing easy access by staff, students, and the librarians themselves.

Another wiki for students is Chad Boeninger's Biz Wiki at the Alden Library of Ohio University (www.library.ohiou.edu/subjects/bizwiki). Boeninger works as a bibliographer with faculty in the College of Business and the Department of Economics to develop the library's collections, and is also available to help students and faculty members with their research needs in person, via IM, a business resources blog, and via the wiki. In an interview at the ALA TechSource Blog, Boeninger describes the benefits of using a wiki:

> The ability to add content to the wiki is incredible. I never imagined that I would be updating and adding content as much as I have been. Whenever I find a new source, or discover how to use an old source in a different way, I can add that information to The Biz Wiki. I've been in the middle of class, IM transactions, and reference interviews, and I've been able to add content that would help the current Biz Wiki user(s) and future users as well.[11]

Librarians at the St. Joseph County Public Library created subject guides for their patrons (www.libraryforlife.org/subject guides/index.php/Main_Page), allowing them to discuss and suggest additions to such pages as Business and Health via the "discussion" tab, while the librarians edit the pages via the wiki interface.

The next step, of course, lies in creating a collaborative wiki space where librarians and library users work together. Boeninger offers this space, but has seen few edits from students or faculty: "I initially thought faculty and students would be more willing to add content to The Biz Wiki, but this has not been the case. I've come to realize that they just do not have the time, or the interest, to add content. However, should the time come when they want to contribute, the option is available for them to do so."[12]

Instant Messaging

Instant messaging enables real-time, synchronous conversation between two or more people using a messaging client. Messaging clients include AOL Instant Messenger, Yahoo! Messenger, Microsoft Messenger, and Google Talk. Their features include:

- Buddy List – A listing of your trusted friends, colleagues, and family

- Chat Window – A window that displays the ongoing conversation and an input box for text

- Status Indicator – A notation of location or current state of being, such as "In my office" or "Out to lunch" (also known as an "away message")

Other features might include file transfer and the capability for video chat or voice chat. Other applications, such as Trillian (www.ceruleanstudios.com), allow librarians to monitor multiple services through one login.

In *Library Journal*, Aaron Schmidt and I noted: "IM reference works in much the same way as do other flavors of reference—just think of it as a sped-up e-mail transaction. Questions generally begin with a cordial preamble, just like at the reference desk. Some introductory behavior, however, is unique to younger users. 'Are you real or are you a robot?' is commonly asked of IMing librarians."[13]

The Library Success Wiki lists more than 100 libraries offering a reference IM presence, and librarians have found it's a pretty easy service to start and sustain. IM is great for handling quick, ready reference questions, but don't be afraid to conduct an online reference interview. The give-and-take of IM enables better communication than other forms of online reference, such as e-mail.

Libraries of all sizes are trying IM. Adding IM presence to your one- or two-person reference desk really should not disrupt workflow; I have yet to hear of any library that was overwhelmed with IM questions. Establish a policy: in-person questions first, then phone, then IM, then e-mail (if you do it), then snail mail. If this is a part of the information services you provide, there's nothing wrong with looking up from the screen and saying to a patron: "I am just finishing up an IM reference question and then I'll be right with you." You can treat IM interruptions the same way; let the person you're chatting with know you have to handle another issue but that you'll be right back.

Embedding IM chat windows in Web pages is another way to meet users where they are. The Darien (CT) Library has an embedded IM presence via a service called MeeboMe on their "Contact Us" page www.darienlibrary.org/contact.php. The Web 2.0 site www.meebo me.com creates an IM widget from your library's IM information with just a few clicks.

IM is just one small step toward a new landscape of the way folks may ask questions of their librarians, including SMS (Short Message

Service, or texting). Be ready for the time that questions come in to the library from any number of devices and aggregate into one place—your reference desk computer. From what I can tell, it's coming!

Spaces and Places of the Read/Write Web

So, where are people hanging out to engage in their creating and remixing and interacting online? Currently talked about, hotly debated, and even ridiculed by some, tremendously popular social networking sites such as MySpace and Facebook offer users a chance to make connections, post pictures, create blog entries, IM, e-mail, and share as much—or as little—of their lives as they choose.

Libraries such as the Hennepin County Public Library and the Public Library of Charlotte and Mecklenburg County (PLCMC) in North Carolina have created MySpace pages to reach out to young people in the spaces where they are interacting. Content such as their 2006 Teen Summer Reading Program video goes up on both the PLCMC teen site, The Library Loft (www.libraryloft.org), and the library's MySpace page (www.myspace.com/libraryloft). Hennepin placed a search box for its online catalog right into its MySpace page (www.myspace. com/hennepincountylibrary).

At colleges and universities, Facebook offers students a similar way to make connections and meet and greet. Libraries and librarians are adding their presence here, too. Robert J. Lackie, Associate Professor/Librarian at Rider University in Lawrenceville, New Jersey, posted at the LibraryGarden blog about his use of Facebook:

> As a librarian and professor, I joined Facebook last year when I found out that the students in my public speaking class were communicating with each other via that tool, instead of our university's email system. It was amazing how much more open and willing the students were to sharing information about each other and their individual and group projects in our class, via Facebook. They were thrilled that I was willing to join Facebook, and they loved that I used it to find out and celebrate their birthdays, for instance, as they came up during the semester.[14]

Beyond these "big two" social sites, a number of others have increasing impact, including:

- Flickr (www.flickr.com) – Image hosting and community built around photos. Images can be tagged, commented, and linked. Librarians, and some libraries, use Flickr for images and outreach.

- Last.FM (www.lastfm.com) – Music site that makes connections between people. Plugins feed the songs that are played on a person's computer back up to the Last.FM site, which tracks statistics. Users can find new music, tag songs, and make connections with other users.

- YouTube (www.youtube.com) – Video sharing and hosting community, picked up by Google in 2006. Again, libraries and librarians have a presence here. Brian Matthews uses the site as a clearinghouse of videos for library instruction, as detailed at his blog the Ubiquitous Librarian.[15]

More Web 2.0 sites are added each week, and will continue to be created to enable connections between people, via their writing, images, music, and more.

Blocking Social Sites?

In summer 2006, the Deleting Online Predators Act (DOPA, H.R. 5319) attempted to prevent access by minors to "commercial social networking websites and chat rooms," defined as any site that "allows users to create web pages or profiles that provide information about themselves." Also included in the definition are site features such as IM, e-mail, and chat rooms. *School Library Journal* editor Brian Kenney was prompted by DOPA to editorialize:

> Yes, here we go again. A 'quick fix' that we're not asking for, which won't work, and which subverts the real purpose of schools and libraries: educating young people. No matter where you come down on the whole MySpace-in-libraries debate, do you really want your library locked in a 'tech-nobubble,' cut off from the evolving Internet?[16]

It's scary to think that federal legislation might cut schools and libraries off from access to the social Web, when librarians could be playing a valuable role of guide and educator to everyone curious about participating in creating content, conversation, and community.

We can't hide from social networks. The sites and services that replace MySpace—the ones that will probably combine the hottest features of the hottest Web sites today, such as music, video, blogs, IM, and more—will be very important to our users. We need to be there; we need libraries and librarians to have a presence. Librarians need to be experienced, strategic, engaged citizens of the social spaces in our future—both representing our institutions and serving as guides.

Learning 2.0

In August 2006, the Public Library of Charlotte and Mecklenburg County held a technology summit for library staff. Michael Casey, who coined "Library 2.0" and authors the LibraryCrunch blog (www.librarycrunch.com), and I opened with presentations about the 2.0 world. Then, the staff was introduced to a new program: "Learning 2.0." Conceived by Helene Blowers, Public Services Technology Director for PLCMC and blogger at LibraryBytes (www.librarybytes.com), the Learning 2.0 online course guided library staff through a set of "23 Things" they can do in the new Web:

> Learning 2.0 is an online learning program that encourages staff to learn more about emerging technologies on the web that are changing the way people, society and libraries access information and communicate with each other.
>
> Over the course of the next eight and a half weeks, this website will highlight '23 Things' and discovery exercises to help staff become familiar with blogging, RSS news feeds, tagging, wikis, podcasting, online applications, and video and image hosting sites.[17]

Any staff member who completed all 23 Things received an MP3 player and was entered in a drawing for a laptop and other prizes at the library's staff day. Blowers stressed that she wanted staff to take ownership of their own learning. No training sessions were given. Staff were to read the learning modules and then take time on their own to explore a site such as Flickr, YouTube, or a variety of other Web-based apps.

This model struck a chord with the library community, and Blowers reports other U.S. and Australian libraries and library systems utilizing this system to educate staff on the Read/Write Web. Organized technology training is giving way to exploration, experience, and play. In "Teaching People to be Savvy Travelers in a Technological World," in the May 2006 *Computers in Libraries*, librarian and trainer Brenda Hough presented tips for a new style of training, including:

> Stop trying to provide step-by-step directions. ... Try to approach the class as an opportunity to help participants leave with increased independence, increased confidence, and an increased awareness of the potential benefits and applications of the technology in their own lives.[18]

This is a step toward adopting a 2.0 philosophy for your library. The principles of the Read/Write Web, such as trust, experience, and collaboration, can also be useful for shifting your library staff to a newer view of learning, interaction with users, and service.

The User as Content Creator

The new landscape can be summed up by noting that people are able to create content easily online like never before. "Generation C" is growing up with the Internet, technology, and the ability to create content of all kinds and share it via the Web's great pool of knowledge. An article in the *Economist* reported on a telling Pew Internet & American Life Project study that found that 57 percent of American teenagers create content for the Internet—from text to pictures, music, and video. "In this new-media culture," says Paul Saffo, a director at the Institute for the Future in California, "people no longer passively 'consume' media (and thus advertising, its main revenue source) but actively participate in them, which usually means creating content, in whatever form and on whatever scale."[19]

How should librarians be handling this trend? If you are planning a renovation or new building, you will find yourself sadly behind the times if you don't incorporate some facility for group collaboration and digital creation. This doesn't have to be on a grand scale, but make some type of technology available. A study room could become a podcast studio, as needed. A small computer center could be changed into the "Digital Collaboratory." Pay attention, and align your technology classes with what people want to do online!

Watch this trend closely; it will surely color the way we interact with our users in the future: library as digital recording studio, as group performance space, as production house. The next wave of librarians will have to have command of information channels, context, and content—as will libraries. For the profession and our institutions to move forward, we must be very aware of the power of these new connections, conversations, and opportunities to collaborate. Librarians have the skills to understand the new channels of information, but must also embrace and understand the new methods of delivery and the online landscapes where interaction and expression play out. Technologies such as RSS, blogs, wikis, and podcasts—and whatever tools and syndication methods come next—will surely shape the way people, from all walks of life and all professions everywhere, will get their streams of information, entertainment, and content. Librarians need to make sure they are in the middle of it all: guiding, planning, and gaining experience using the systems to build a presence for information professionals and the users we serve.

Endnotes

1. Tom Standage, "Tim Berners-Lee," *Smithsonian* 36:8 (Nov. 2005).
2. Tim O'Reilly, "A Compact Definition of Web 2.0," 2005, radar.oreilly. com/archives/2005/10/web_20_compact_definition.html (accessed July 5, 2006).
3. Michael Buckland, "Redesigning Library Services: A Manifesto," 1992, sunsite.berkeley.edu/Literature/Library/Redesigning/html.html (accessed July 5, 2006).
4. Steven Levy and Brad Stone, "The New Wisdom of the Web—Next Frontiers," www.msnbc.msn.com/id/12015774/site/newsweek (accessed June 23, 2006).
5. Paul Miller, "Web 2.0: Building the New Library," 2005, www.ariadne.ac. uk/issue45/miller (accessed July 10, 2006).
6. Bryan Alexander, "Web 2.0: A New Wave of Innovation for Teaching and Learning?" 2006, www.educause.edu/apps/er/erm06/erm0621.asp? bhcp=1 (accessed July 10, 2006).
7. Darlene Fichter, "Web 2.0, Library 2.0 and Radical Trust: A First Take," library.usask.ca/~fichter/blog_on_the_side/2006/04/web-2.html (accessed July 2, 2006).
8. Robert Scobel and Shel Israel, *Naked Conversations: How Blogs Are Changing the Way Businesses Talk with Customers*, New York: Wiley, 2006.

9. For more on the different types of Weblogs, see: Michael Stephens, *Web 2.0 & Libraries: Best Practices for Social Software, Library Technology Report*. Chicago: American Library Association, 2006.

10. Roy Tennant, "Strategies for Keeping Current," *Library Journal* Sept. 15, 2003: 28.

11. Michael Stephens, "Wikis in the University Library," 2006, www.tech source.ala.org/blog/2006/05/wikis-in-the-university-library.html (accessed July 20, 2006).

12. Michael Stephens, "Wikis in the University Library."

13. Aaron Schmidt and Michael Stephens, "IM Me," *Library Journal* April 1, 2005, www.libraryjournal.com/article/CA512192.html (accessed July 20, 2006).

14. Robert J. Lackie, "MySpace and Social Networking Sites," librarygarden. blogspot.com/2006/04/myspace-and-social-networking-sites.html (accessed July 20, 2006).

15. Brian Matthews, "Do You YouTube?" theubiquitouslibrarian.typepad. com/the_ubiquitous_librarian/2006/07/do_you_youtube_.html (accessed July 26, 2006).

16. Brian Kenney, "We Don't Need No Tech Control," *School Library Journal* June 1, 2006, www.schoollibraryjournal.com/article/CA6337058.html (accessed July 23, 2006).

17. "Learning 2.0," plcmclearning.blogspot.com (accessed October 31, 2006).

18. Brenda Hough, "Teaching People To Be Savvy Travelers In A Technological World," *Computers in Libraries* May 2006: 8–12.

19. "Among the Audience," www.economist.com/surveys/displaystory. cfm?story_id=6794156 (accessed July 6, 2006).

CHAPTER 9

Libraries and Privacy

Robert Bocher
Technology Consultant
Wisconsin State Library

Privacy has been an essential principle of the library profession for many decades. This principle is strongly supported by the American Library Association (ALA), and library privacy protections are codified in most state statutes. Technology, meanwhile, continues to pose both challenges and opportunities for libraries in a variety of areas—including privacy. Our professional commitment to ensuring patron privacy must be part of any assessment of whether to implement technology to provide better library services.

Privacy and Its Constitutional Antecedents

It may surprise some that there are no specific privacy rights enumerated in the U.S. Constitution; the word itself is absent from the document. This absence notwithstanding, the Supreme Court has found ample room in the Constitution to establish several important privacy rights based on judicial interpretations of language found in the Bill of Rights.

Several key Supreme Court decisions establishing a basic right of privacy have been related to reproductive rights, or the intimate "private" relations between consenting adults. A landmark case in this regard was the 1965 decision in *Griswold v. Connecticut*.[1] In this case Connecticut law forbade anyone, including married couples, from using any drug or article to prevent conception. In overturning the lower court's conviction of the Planned Parenthood League of Connecticut, of which Estelle Griswold was the director, the Supreme Court found that clauses in several Amendments, when taken together, created a right of marital privacy. The Court cited language from the Fifth Amendment's clause against self-incrimination, which then "enables the citizen to create a zone of privacy which government may not force him to surrender."[2] Another Supreme Court case addressing reproductive rights was the *Roe v. Wade*[3] decision in 1973, which legalized abortion. What is less well-known about this still controversial decision is that the Court based much of its rationale on the right of privacy recognized previously in *Griswold*.

Privacy and Federal Statutes and Protections

While the federal courts have had to rely on interpretation to craft a basic right of privacy from the Constitution, many federal statutes do directly address privacy issues. For example, the Privacy Act of 1974 prohibits unauthorized release of personal information that federal agencies have on file; people also have the right to review their personal records and request corrections if errors are found.[4] The Family Educational Rights and Privacy Act (FERPA) protects the privacy of student education records for any school that receives funds under programs administered by the U.S. Department of Education.[5]

The Federal Trade Commission (FTC) is the major Executive-level agency responsible for a variety of consumer privacy protections, including oversight of the Privacy Act of 1974. The agency is also involved with the increasingly serious issue of identity theft—an obviously malicious invasion of your privacy, with potentially far-reaching consequences. On May 10, 2006, President Bush signed an Executive Order establishing an Identity Theft Task Force to enhance federal efforts to prevent and prosecute identity theft crimes.[6] The FTC is one of the federal agencies that will work with this task force. Unfortunately, technology has made it much easier for scam artists and nefarious individuals to engage in identity theft. For example, anyone with an e-mail address has certainly received bogus requests designed to get them to reveal personal information—which can then compromise privacy and lead to identity theft.

Privacy, Libraries, and Issues of National Security

The tragic events of September 11, 2001, brought to the fore the complex issues and interrelationships between technology, national security, and privacy. The library profession has been—and will continue to be—an important party in this evolving dynamic of balancing security and personal freedoms, including personal privacy rights and the privacy rights of library patrons.

Many librarians are aware that federal law enforcement's interest in libraries long predates 9/11. As far back as World War I, some libraries cooperated with the Department of War (now the Department of Defense) in reporting on patrons who requested information on explosives.[7] The Library Awareness Program, however, brought the issue of federal interest in patron activities into much sharper focus.[8] This program, conducted by the FBI from 1973 to the late 1980s, attempted to (1) restrict access by foreign nationals to unclassified scientific information, and (2) enlist librarians to report to federal authorities any "foreigners" who may be using unclassified scientific materials in libraries.[9]

To some in the library profession, the Library Awareness Program may seem almost quaint compared with more recent revelations about how far law enforcement authorities have gone in attempts to protect national security. These have, in turn, resulted in many questions related to the protection of privacy rights. Regardless of your position on this issue, there is little doubt that in the aftermath of September 11 an entirely different light is now being cast on the issue of library privacy, as well as on the broader issues of privacy in our daily lives.

From a library perspective, the most common and oft-stated privacy concerns in the post-9/11 world center around various sections of the USA PATRIOT Act. This act, passed just five weeks after 9/11, is a complex amalgam that amended more than 15 other existing federal statutes.[10] A key impact on libraries is that the Act makes it easier for law enforcement to obtain a warrant to request circulation data or any other information a library has regarding a patron's use of library services or resources. Furthermore, language in section 215 of the law prohibits library staff from notifying the patron (or anyone else) that an individual is under suspicion, that a warrant has been issued, or that the library has given information to law enforcement authorities.[11] In 2006, a group of Connecticut librarians successfully challenged the PATRIOT Act's "gag order."[12] This challenge resulted from the library receiving a formal letter from the FBI requesting any information related to use of a specific Internet workstation on a particular date.[13]

Reauthorization of the USA PATRIOT Act in early 2006 again elicited strong reactions from the library community. Revised language that eventually passed Congress did raise the standard by which the FBI can request library records. In the original act, the FBI had only to claim that information was sought from the library as part of an authorized investigation. Under the new revised language, it will now be necessary to define what information is sought with "sufficient particularity" to more accurately specify what is being requested.[14]

While the library community's attention has been focused on the PATRIOT Act, several other recent actions by federal law enforcement have very real privacy implications for libraries. In one such action, federal law enforcement has been trying since 2004 to get the Federal Communications Commission (FCC) to extend coverage of the Communications Assistance for Law Enforcement Act (CALEA), passed by Congress in 1994. CALEA initially targeted telephone companies and required network upgrades to make it easier for law enforcement to place wiretaps.[15] In early 2004 the FBI and several other federal law enforcement agencies petitioned the FCC to extend CALEA to the Internet. Many educational organizations, including ALA, sent the FCC formal comments objecting to such an extension.[16] However, in an order released in August 2005, the FCC did extend CALEA to "facilities-based Internet service providers."[17] This action recognized that considerable personal communications are now taking place over the Internet and outside of the more traditional public switched (voice) telecommunications network. Private networks and libraries are exempt from the order extending CALEA. But, the FCC's Order further explains that the private network exemption only applies if such networks are not connected to the public Internet.[18] Thus, the issue of *where* CALEA compliance falls for private networks connected to the Internet is still open to debate. The library exemption means libraries will not be direct parties to possibly compromising patron privacy. However, libraries' Internet Service Providers (ISP) are still covered by the law. Therefore, even if patron privacy is not compromised in the library, it may still be compromised at the ISP level.

In late 2005 the ALA joined a coalition of groups in initiating legal action in federal circuit court against the FCC's extension of CALEA.[19] In a decision announced June 9, 2006, the court upheld the FCC's authority to apply CALEA to the Internet.[20] In response to this decision, ALA President-Elect Leslie Burger stated, "Libraries remain concerned that the court deferred to the FCC's reasoning extending

CALEA to entities providing the facilities that connect private networks to the Internet."[21]

In other activity, the federal Department of Justice has met with large ISPs to discuss issues of tracking Web site use.[22] While the exact parameters of the Justice Department's proposal are not known, the department stated an interest in having ISPs retain data for up to two years, allowing law enforcement to identify individuals who visited specific Web sites. There are concerns that Internet monitoring could go well beyond ISPs to include other entities that provide Internet access, including universities and libraries.[23] In addition, there have been Congressional attempts to mandate that the FCC develop regulations requiring all providers of "Internet access services to retain records to permit the identification of subscribers to such services for appropriate law enforcement purposes."[24] It must be noted that the Electronic Communications Privacy Act (ECPA) already allows law enforcement agencies to request that any provider of electronic communication services, including ISPs and libraries, retain records of specific accounts (i.e., users) for up to 90 days.[25] (A warrant is required for law enforcement to actually obtain the data.) But recent Justice Department and Congressional attempts to require that *all records* from *all accounts* be retained for lengthy periods go far beyond current statutory requirements. The issue of how much tracking or monitoring should be done of a person's Internet use, who can do it, how it should be done, and what safeguards should be in place to prevent abuse, are extremely important issues that directly impact everyone's personal privacy. These questions deserve a larger debate beyond just the library community.

Another expansion of Executive authority to address national security issues has been the disclosure of wiretapping, without warrants, by the National Security Administration (NSA). This program, first revealed by the *New York Times* in December 2005,[26] was authorized by President Bush in 2002. While much of this program is shrouded in secrecy, the White House has said that it only tracks phone calls when at least one party is located beyond the borders of the country. In January, the American Civil Liberties Union (ACLU) filed suit against the NSA claiming that its wiretapping program violated citizen privacy rights under the Fourth Amendment and free speech as defined in the First Amendment.[27] In other NSA-related activity, it was reported in May 2006 that several large telecommunications carriers were cooperating with the NSA in amassing a database of millions of phone call records made by residents within the U.S.[28] The NSA is also reported to be funding research into data mining the wealth of personal information available from the millions of people who have created profiles on social networking sites like MySpace.[29] (Admittedly, no one posting information on such sites should assume it is private, regardless of what safeguards or restrictions the site claims are available to protect subscriber's privacy.)

Data mining by either government or the private sector is made easier by the millions of people who are all too willing—consciously or unconsciously—to compromise their privacy by revealing personal information as they surf the Web. Young people are particularly vulnerable, because they lack the real-world experiences of adults and tend to transfer the interpersonal activity of the social networks they form in school to their online activities via sites like MySpace and Facebook. We are also now seeing the first generation of high school graduates who cannot remember a time before the Internet, Web, e-mail, and interactive chat. In a 2005 Harris poll of school-aged children, just 55 percent said their teachers had discussed the issue of giving out personal information online, although 75 percent said their parents had discussed this issue.[30] The same poll showed that 7 percent of high school students claim they know more about how to use the Internet than their parents. Young people can find it easy to conceal their online activities from their parents, even when parents take an interest in what their child is doing; we need to think about libraries' and librarians' roles here.

The proliferation of social network sites and their ubiquitous use by young people has, unfortunately, resulted in these sites also being frequented by unsavory and criminal elements, including financial scam artists and pedophiles. A 2006 study showed that 61 percent of 13 to 17 year olds have a profile on a social network and 14 percent have actually met in-person with someone they knew only online.[31] In July 2006, the Deleting Online Predators Act (DOPA) passed the House by a wide margin. The bill would prohibit access to social network sites in K–12 schools and public libraries that receive E-rate funds for Internet access.[32] The bill did not pass the Senate before Congress adjourned, but similar legislation was expected to be introduced in 2007. Tracking and apprehending online predators is another reason why the U.S. Justice Department wants to extend CALEA to the Internet.

Privacy in the Library

The PATRIOT Act, CALEA, and NSA intercepts of electronic communications do have very real potential to compromise the privacy of citizens, including patrons in our libraries. Regardless of how you feel about these laws or programs, though, library staff and advocates are limited to expressing their feelings via normal democratic processes. However, within the context of our own libraries, we do have much more control of, influence on, and responsibility for ensuring patron privacy. For example, we cannot lose sight of the fact that everyday library staff are directly responsible for protecting the circulation records and other library use information of millions of patrons. The protection of a patron's personally identifiable information (PII)[33] rests on three important and interrelated elements: (1) state library privacy statutes; (2) privacy principles articulated by ALA; and (3) local library privacy polices (Figure 9.1).

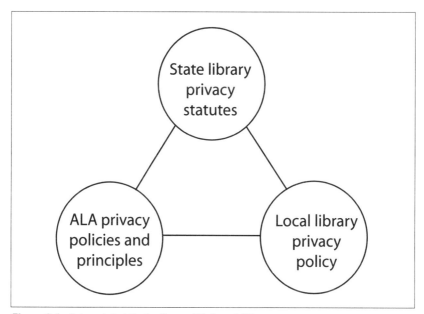

Figure 9.1   Interrelated Protections of Patrons' PII

State Library Privacy Statutes

Legal protections of patron privacy are based on state statutes. According to the ALA, 48 states have laws addressing library privacy.[34] What libraries are covered, the types of PII covered, and the extent of coverage varies from state to state. While the specific language differs, most states' library privacy laws address three basic areas:

- What is protected? Most state laws protect patron PII in the use or checkout of a library's print material. Many statutes have not been updated to cover patron use of electronic databases or the Internet.

- Who is protected? In some states, minors are not afforded the same protections as adults.

- When can protected information be released? Statutes often have language related to use of a patron's PII by library staff in the normal course of carrying out their responsibilities. In addition, statutes usually cite the circumstances by which law enforcement authorities can request access to patron information.

Who is protected and when protected information can be released are usually well defined in the law and require little interpretation. But the first area—what is protected—is where technology has outpaced explicit statutory language. Protection is often referenced in statutes to include titles a patron has checked out from library collections. For example, the Illinois statute reads, "The registration and circulation records of a library are confidential information. Except pursuant to a court order, no person shall publish or make any information contained in such records available to the public."[35] Most library privacy statutes were enacted before libraries offered Internet access and thus lack language specifically protecting Internet use. When such explicit language is lacking, protecting the privacy of Internet use in the library becomes a legal exercise in statutory interpretation. An example of this is the Wisconsin library statute that refers to the protection of patrons' information related to their use of the "library's documents or other materials, resources, or services."[36] The Wisconsin state library interprets the phrase "resources, or services" to cover Internet access.[37] (Issues of privacy and Internet use, beyond statutory issues, are addressed later in this chapter.)

Privacy and the American Library Association

The American Library Association has a strong and longstanding commitment to patron privacy and confidentiality. The ALA's Code of Ethics, adopted in 1939, states: "It is the librarian's obligation to treat as confidential any private information obtained through contact with library patrons."[38] Several other ALA documents more specifically target privacy issues. For example, the *ALA Policy on*

Confidentiality of Library Records advises libraries to "Formally adopt a policy which specifically recognizes its circulation records and other records identifying the name of library users to be confidential in nature."[39] The association's 1991 *Policy Concerning Confidentiality of Personally Identifiable Information About Library Users* has inclusive language stating that: "Confidentiality extends to 'information sought or received, and materials consulted, borrowed or acquired, and includes database search records, reference interviews, circulation records, interlibrary loan records, and other personally identifiable uses of library materials, facilities, or services."[40]

The ALA has taken a strong position on privacy and Congressional actions, including passage of the USA PATRIOT Act. Some of these efforts have been widely publicized, like the group of Connecticut librarians who successfully challenged the PATRIOT Act's gag order.

Library Privacy Policy

The library's privacy policy should be built on the foundation of state statutory protections and the privacy principles and statements from the American Library Association. Any privacy policy should be reviewed by legal counsel with some familiarity in this area.

The implementation and ongoing observance of any library policy obviously rests on an informed staff and a supportive governing body. Educating staff at all levels on the legal and policy protections afforded to patrons' privacy must be an integral part of any staff training and in-service regimen. It is essential that all staff be knowledgeable about their state's library law and that they know exactly what procedures to follow if law enforcement authorities seek information protected by law. This is particularly important, because often a library clerk or part-time student may be at the circulation desk, and it is this person that law enforcement officials are likely to approach first.

It is management's responsibility to make certain that the library's governing body understands both the library's privacy policy and the library's legal obligations. This understanding is critical to help ensure that the governing body speaks with one voice when challenged by those who may not understand the value that the library profession places on privacy or the legal protections that underlie this value. Another management responsibility is to inform local law enforcement about the library's privacy policy and the legal circumstances by which law enforcement can request protected data. Such outreach efforts to law enforcement can help prevent misunder standings and the potential fallout of negative publicity.

Libraries should be proactive and inform their patrons of the obligations the library has to protect its patrons' privacy and how such obligations are incorporated into library policy. Equally important is to make certain patrons know the limitations of such obligations, for example, the need to release PII as a result of a court order, or that patrons' external e-mail accounts (e.g., Gmail or Hotmail) are not protected by library privacy statutes. From a public relations perspective, the library should have a flyer or brochure that succinctly states the library's privacy obligations and key points from the policy itself. The flyer should be routinely provided to new patrons when they register and copies should be as readily available, just like other popular information the library provides (such as lists of new acquisitions).

Much of the specific information in any library's privacy policy should be based on the results of a privacy audit. This is a several step procedure that includes:

1. A discovery process: What types of PII does the library collect? What programs or services use the patron's PII?

2. An evaluation/assessment process: Why is the patron PII being collected? How long is it retained? Can deleted PII be reconstructed from archived files? How do the programs or services that use patron PII interact with each other?

3. An implementation process: What are the factors associated with protecting patron PII? What specific steps must the library take to protect patron PII and to delete it?

Several organizations, including ALA and the University of California, have developed good resources on conducting a privacy audit. These are listed in the Recommended Reading section at the end of this chapter.

Privacy and Key Library Services

There are many services for which libraries collect patron PII, and a thorough privacy audit should be able to properly identify them. The two core services most often associated with privacy issues are the integrated library system (ILS) and Internet access.

Integrated Library Systems (ILS)

With the adoption of integrated library systems (ILS) over the past 20 years, the library community has witnessed a dramatic change in the circulation process and a parallel change in collection access via the online patron access catalog. The library's privacy policy may not have changed with the implementation of the ILS, but upholding the policy has certainly resulted in considerable changes. For example, the substantial security and backup requirements of an ILS simply did not exist in manual (paper-based) systems. Data security is critical in any network environment, and libraries are no exception. Security assumes even greater importance because so many ILSs are accessible over the Internet. An added security factor is that many libraries are in large, regional, shared integrated systems. It is not unusual for shared systems to include more than 50 libraries and a million or more registered patrons. Like local area networks (LANs) in the library, wide area networks (WANs) connecting all the libraries in the ILS require stringent security measures. Regardless of the network topology (e.g., LAN, WAN), network security and privacy protection are closely related. While an in-depth review of security measures is beyond the scope of this chapter, to state it in simple terms: The more secure the network, the greater the degree of privacy protection.

A small but increasing number of libraries are using Radio Frequency Identification (RFID) tags to replace more traditional barcodes for tracking item-level circulation. RFID technology has been used by industry for decades, but is new to the library environment. Like any new technology, RFID must be closely scrutinized to ensure that privacy is not compromised and that procedures are implemented to address any privacy threat. While RFID has many advantages over barcodes, it has generated its own debate related to privacy concerns. Most of the debate that has reached the public's attention has centered on libraries in the San Francisco Bay area.[41] In the current library environment, some of these concerns are overstated. For example, a scenario where anyone with a cheap transponder can walk by your house and determine what titles you have checked out from the library is possible—in theory. In practice, however, it is unrealistic because of the ways in which libraries have implemented the technology. Library RFID tags are passive devices,[42] and a tagged item generally has to be within two to three feet of a transponder to be read. To further enhance privacy, there should be no bibliographic data stored on the tag itself. It should have all the intelligence of a standard barcode, which is to say, none.

Internet Access in the Library

Internet access for both staff and patrons closely followed implementation of integrated systems in libraries. The degree of patron privacy when using the Internet generally depends on the type of library, and is reflected in the library's Internet acceptable-use policy. Academic libraries are usually at one end of the spectrum, with little oversight of Internet use. On the other end are K–12 schools, which usually have the most restrictions. Privacy issues are closely related to how open or how restrictive the library is regarding Internet access and use. As mentioned earlier, state library privacy statutes should be closely examined to establish whether their language expressly includes patron use of the Internet and ancillary issues such as sign-up sheets, temporary Internet files, and cookies. The library's Internet use policy must not only cover appropriate use, but specifically inform the patron about what PII is kept and what the library's policy and legal responsibility is regarding the confidentiality or protection of the patron's PII.

Whenever you surf the Web, in the library, at home, or at work, you leave a clear trail of where you are coming from and where you have been. Web servers track the incoming request based on the Internet protocol (IP) address of the workstation that originates the request. It is not unusual for servers to log several weeks' worth—or even months' worth—of such data. As we have seen, these data have become of interest to federal law enforcement and some in Congress as a way to track the Web surfing habits of millions. The IP number itself is of limited value, but can be tied back to a particular user via authentication software. Such software is being used by an increasing number of libraries.

The workstation's Web browser also tracks where patrons have been via temporary files, cookies, and a listing (history) of visited sites. The two most popular browsers (Internet Explorer and Firefox) have options to limit these Web tracks, but staff have to be proactive and set the options for minimal intrusions. For example, Firefox has the option to delete any browsing history, cookies, and other temporary files upon exiting the browser. Third-party software programs also offer many options for tracking and deleting Web tracking files.

Because libraries often do not have enough Internet workstations to meet patron demand, many keep paper sign-up sheets or have installed time management software to allocate limited Internet access resources. It is easy enough at the end of each day to shred paper sign-up sheets, but the library's privacy policy must address the retention or deletion of patron logins when using software to manage Internet face time.

Over just the past year or two it has become popular for many academic institutions and public libraries to offer wireless Internet access to their students, staff, and/or patrons. In a recent survey of Internet use in public libraries, 36.7 percent offer patron wireless Internet access.[43] For convenience, many wireless connections of this type are open networks and anyone within range can attach to them. The networks seldom use any encryption, such as wired equivalent privacy (WEP). Any institution's Internet Acceptable Use Policy (AUP) should clearly alert users to the open nature of their wireless connection and that the transmission of data is not secure.

The library profession will continue to confront a host of technical and administrative challenges as we continue to implement services that rely on technology. Making a commitment to maintain privacy, and keeping our patrons informed of library policies and privacy protections, must be an inherent component of any technology we implement. We also have a professional responsibility to offer patrons privacy resources and information so that they can become better informed about privacy issues, both within the library and those that extend well beyond the boundaries of the library.

Recommended Reading

American Civil Liberties Union, www.aclu.org
   Among its many interests, the ACLU is one of the leading organizations promoting privacy, and has questioned federal law enforcement efforts on the issue of national security vs. privacy.

American Library Association. The following ALA sites will be of interest:

1. Office of Intellectual Freedom (OIF), www.ala.org/oif

2. Privacy Tool Kit, www.ala.org/oif/iftoolkits/privacy – The Tool Kit is an excellent resource. It is designed to help

librarians understand privacy and its relationship to information access in libraries. It includes links to various ALA privacy statements, policies and other documents and guidelines for developing a privacy policy.

3. Conducting a Privacy Audit, www.ala.org/ala/washoff/contactwo/oitp/emailtutorials/privacya/27.cfm

4. RFID in Libraries: Privacy and Confidentiality Guidelines, www.ala.org/ala/oif/statementspols/otherpolicies/rfidgu idelines.htm

Center for Democracy and Technology, www.cdt.org

The center works to promote democratic values and constitutional liberties in the digital age. With an expertise in law, technology, and policy, the CDT Web site has many resources related to privacy and how it is impacted by technology. It is an especially good resource on government attempts to track Internet usage.

Computer Professionals for Social Responsibility (CPSR), www.cpsr.org

One of the best-known computing organizations, the CPSR's Privacy and Civil Liberties page (www.cpsr.org/program/privacy/privacy.html) is always a good resource.

Electronic Frontier Foundation, www.eff.org

The Electronic Frontier Foundation is one of the best organizations on privacy and First Amendment issues related to Internet use. The EFF covers a variety of issues including biometrics, surveillance, and financial privacy.

Electronic Privacy Information Center, EPIC, www.epic.org

EPIC is one of the best sites on the interaction of privacy and technology. It is an especially good source for the latest news on privacy issues. Highly recommended.

LibraryPrivacy.org, www.libraryprivacy.org

LibraryPrivacy.org is sponsored by the California Library Association and the ACLU of southern California. It provides links to many sites related to reading and privacy, the PATRIOT Act, and more.

University of California Privacy Audit, libraries.universityofcalifornia.
edu/sopag/privacytf/privacy_audit.html

University of California Privacy Audit is a good resource for obtaining more information on conducting a privacy audit.

Privacy and Security in Library RFID: Issues, Practices, and Architectures, by David Molnar and David Wagner, www.cs.berkeley.edu/~dmolnar/library.pdf

This is a detailed, technical paper on RFID use and privacy issues in libraries.

Endnotes

1. *Griswold v. Connecticut*, 381 U.S. 479, 1965, laws.findlaw.com/us/381/479.html (accessed June 15, 2006).
2. *Griswold v. Connecticut*
3. *Roe v. Wade*, 410 U.S. 113, 1973, laws.findlaw.com/us/410/113.html (accessed June 15, 2006).
4. U.S. Federal Trade Commission, Privacy Act of 1974, www.ftc.gov/foia/privacy_act.htm (accessed May 23, 2006).
5. U.S. Department of Education, "Family Educational Rights and Privacy Act (FERPA)," www.ed.gov/policy/gen/guid/fpco/ferpa/index.html (accessed May 26, 2006).
6. The White House, Office of the Press Secretary, "Executive Order: Strengthening Federal Efforts to Protect Against Identity Theft," May 10, 2006, www.whitehouse.gov/news/releases/2006/05/20060510-3.html (accessed May 15, 2006).
7. Joan Starr, "Libraries and National Security: An Historical Review," First Monday 9:12 (December 6, 2004), firstmonday.org/issues/issue9_12/starr (accessed May 14, 2006).
8. "Remarks by Herbert Foerstel, former Head of Branch Libraries at University of Maryland and board member of the National Security Archive," March 29, 1999, www.aaas.org/spp/secrecy/Presents/foerstel.htm (accessed June 30, 2006). A detailed account of the Library Awareness Program can be found in Foerstel's book *Surveillance in the Stacks*, published in 1991 by Greenwood Publishing Group.
9. "Remarks by Herbert Foerstel"
10. "The USA Patriot Act in the Library," American Library Association, www.ala.org/ala/oif/ifissues/usapatriotactlibrary.htm (accessed June 21, 2006).

11. "Analysis of the USA Patriot Act related to Libraries," American Library Association, www.ala.org/ala/oif/ifissues/issuesrelatedlinks/usapatriot actanalysis.htm (accessed June 30, 2006).

12. "Four Connecticut Librarians Shed John Doe Gag," American Library Association, June 2. 2006, www.ala.org/ala/alonline/currentnews/ newsarchive/2006abc/june2006ab/Default7266.htm (accessed June 10, 2006).

13. Letter from the U.S. Department of Justice, Federal Bureau of Investigation to Kenneth Sutton, Library Connection, Inc., Windsor, CT, May 19, 2005, www.aclu.org/images/nationalsecurityletters/asset_ upload_file924_25995.pdf (accessed July 1, 2006).

14. "USA PATRIOT Act Reauthorization Analysis," American Library Association, www.ala.org/ala/washoff/WOissues/civilliberties/theusa patriotact/usapatriotact.htm#reauth (accessed May 11, 2006).

15. CALEA General Frequently Asked Questions," EDUCAUSE, www.edu cause.edu/CALEAFrequentlyAskedQuestions/9355#faq1103 (accessed May 22, 2006).

16. Joint Comments of the American Library Association et al., in the Matter of Various outstanding Issues Concerning the Implementation of the Communication Assistance for Law Enforcement Act, RM10865, April 12, 2004, www.internet2.edu/pubs/20040413-Comments-CALEA.pdf (accessed June 2, 2006). For more comments filed with the FCC, see the ALA CALEA Web site at www.ala.org/ala/washoff/WOissues/techinttele/ calea/calea.htm (accessed June 2, 2006).

17. U.S. Federal Communications Commission, "In the Matter of Communications Assistance for Law Enforcement Act and Broadband Access and Services; First Report and Order." p. 1, August 5, 2005, www.askcalea.net/docs/20050923-fcc-05-153.pdf (accessed May 18, 2006).

18. U.S. Federal Communications Commission, 19.

19. "OITP Technology Policy Brief: The Communications Assistance for Law Enforcement Act (CALEA) and Libraries," American Library Association, www.ala.org/ala/washoff/WOissues/techinttele/calea/CALEA_Tech_Brief. pdf (accessed June 29, 2006).

20. "OITP Technology Policy Brief," 3.

21. "ALA expresses Disappointment in CALEA ruling," American Library Association, June 9, 2006, www.ala.org/ala/pressreleases2006/june2006/ CALEAruling.htm (accessed June 15, 2006).

22. Saul Hansell and Eric Lichtblau, "U.S. Wants Internet Companies to Keep Web-Surfing Records," *New York Times*, June 2, 2006, p. A15,

proquest.umi.com/pqdweb?did=1046390411&sid=1&Fmt=3&clientId=1 7733&RQT=309&VName=PQD (accessed June 15, 2006).

23. Nancy Libin and Jim Dempsey, "Mandatory Data Retention—Invasive, Risky, Unnecessary, Ineffective," Center for Democracy and Technology, June 2, 2006, www.cdt.org/privacy/20060602retention.pdf (accessed June 28, 2006).

24. Record Retention by Providers of Internet Access Service, Title VII of the Communications Act of 1934, section 718, Amendment to the Committee Print Offered by Ms. DeGette of Colorado, energy commerce.house.gov/108/Markups/04262006/degette_001_XML.PDF (accessed June 20, 2006).

25. U.S. Code, Title 18, Crimes and Criminal Procedure Part I, Chapter 121, Stored Wire and Electronic Communications and Transactional Records Access, frwebgate.access.gpo.gov/cgi-bin/getdoc.cgi?dbname=browse_ usc&docid=Cite:+18USC2703 (accessed June 29, 2006).

26. James Risen and Eric Lichtblau, "Bush Lets U.S. Spy on Callers Without Courts," *New York Times*, December 16, 2005, www.nytimes.com/2005/ 12/16/politics/16program.html?ex=1292389200&en=e32072d786623ac1 &ei=5090&partner=rssuserland&emc=rss (accessed May 3, 2006).

27. "NSA Lawsuit—Stop Illegal Surveillance," American Civil Liberties Union, www.aclu.org/safefree/nsaspying (accessed July 1, 2006).

28. Leslie Cauley, "NSA has massive database of Americans' phone calls," *USA Today*, May 11, 2006, www.usatoday.com/news/washington/2006- 05-10-nsa_x.htm (accessed May 16, 2006).

29. Paul Marks, "Pentagon Sets Its Sights on Social Networking Websites," *New Scientist*, June 9, 1996, www.newscientist.com/article/mg 19025556.200?DCMP=NLC-nletter&nsref=mg19025556.200 (accessed July 5, 2006).

30. "Kids More Likely to Take Online Risks at Home than School, New Study Shows," Business Software Alliance, www.bsa.org/usa/press/news releases/kids-online-risks.cfm (accessed November 4, 2006).

31. "Teen Internet Safety Survey," Cox Communications and the National Center for Missing & Exploited Children, March 2006, www.cox.com/ takecharge/ survey_results.asp (accessed November 10, 2006).

32. "What is DOPA?" American Library Association, www.ala.org/ala/ washoff/WOissues/techinttele/dopa/DOPA.htm (accessed November 10, 2006).

33. Personally Identifiable Information (PII) is information that can directly identify an individual or lead to such an identification. Typical PII includes your name, home address, and unique ID numbers like your

Social Security number. PII usually does not include more general group identifiers like gender or income level.

34. "State Privacy Laws Regarding Library Records," American Library Association, www.ala.org/alaorg/oif/stateprivacylaws.html (accessed May 14, 2006).

35. *Illinois Compiled Statutes*, Chapter 75, Illinois Local Library Act, Article 1, www.ala.org/ala/oif/ifgroups/stateifcchairs/stateifcinaction/illinois privacy.rtf (accessed May 13, 2006).

36. *Wisconsin State Statutes*, Chapter 43.30 (1m), www.legis.state.wi.us/statutes/Stat0043.pdf, (accessed May 3, 2006).

37. Michael Cross, Interview by Robert Bocher, Madison, WI, May 23, 2006.

38. History of the Code of Ethics: 1939 Code of Ethics for Librarians, American Library Association, www.ala.org/ala/oif/statementspols/codeofethics/coehistory/1939code.pdf (accessed May 24, 2006).

39. Policy on Confidentiality of Library Records, American Library Association, www.ala.org/ala/oif/statementspols/otherpolicies/confidentialitylibrary records.pdf, (accessed May 24, 2006).

40. Policy concerning Confidentiality of Personally Identifiable Information about Library Users, American Library Association, www.ala.org/ala/oif/statementspols/otherpolicies/confidentialitypersonally identifiable.pdf (accessed May 24, 2006).

41. See "Radio Frequency Identification and the San Francisco Public Library: Summary Report," Prepared by the San Francisco Public Library Technology and Privacy Advisory Committee, October 2005, www.sfpl.org/librarylocations/libtechcomm/RFID-and-SFPL-summary-report-oct2005.pdf (accessed June 3, 2006) and Matthew Artz, "Library's New Technology Sparks Controversy," *The Berkeley Daily Planet*, www.berkeley dailyplanet.com/text/article.cfm?issue=02-15-05&storyID=20728 (accessed June 12, 2006).

42. Richard W. Boss, "RFID Technology for Libraries," *PLA TechNote*, www.ala.org/ala/pla/plapubs/technotes/rfidtechnology.htm (accessed May 14, 2006).

43. "Public Libraries and the Internet 2006: Study Results and Findings," Information Use Management and Policy Institute, Florida State University, www.ii.fsu.edu/projectFiles/plinternet/2006/2006_plinternet.pdf (accessed Nov. 10, 2006).

CHAPTER 10

An Experience to Remember: Building Positive Experiences on Library Web Sites

David Lee King
Digital Branch & Services Manager
Topeka & Shawnee County Public Library

Online experience design is still an emerging concept. In fact, depending on who you ask, the concept could be referred to as: experience planning, experience design, user experience design (UX), experience architecture, interaction design, or experience staging. A search in your favorite search engine will find all these terms (and possibly some others)—as well as a whole lot of junk. A search for "experience planning," for example, will find relevant information, but will also find the resume of someone with "experience planning the layout of a garden." With that in mind, here are some helpful definitions of experience design and planning:

1. "The sensation of interaction with a product, service, or event, through all of our senses, over time, and on both physical and cognitive levels. The boundaries of an experience can be expansive and include the sensorial, the symbolic, the temporal, and the meaningful."[1]

2. Here's another one that's close: "The term used to describe the complete interaction a visitor has with all aspects of an attraction."[2]

3. Nathan.com has a few definitions, and here's an even better one: "Experience Design is an approach to creating successful experiences for people in any medium. This approach includes consideration and design in all 3

> spatial dimensions, over time, all 5 common senses, and interactivity, as well as customer value, personal meaning, and emotional context. Experience Design is not merely the design of Web pages or other interactive media or on-screen digital content. Designed experiences can be in any medium, including spatial/environmental installations, print products, hard products, services, broadcast images and sounds, live performances and events, digital and online media, etc."[3]

Nathan goes on to explain that creating a solid definition is difficult, since experience design is a relatively new field. Some see experience design as a concept applying primarily to digital media, while others see it as encompassing "traditional, established, and other such diverse disciplines as theater, graphic design, storytelling, exhibit design, theme-park design, online design, game design, interior design, architecture, and so forth."[4]

So, how does this relate to Web sites? Think back to the experiences you've had at retail stores. Some have been negative: You've experienced poor customer service, rude cashiers, and uninformed staff. Others have been great: Employees were knowledgeable, helpful, and friendly, and the products were logically shelved. You left thinking: "Wow—I'll be shopping there again!"

Now, translate that experience of shopping at a physical store to the Web. A Web site might include some of the information about and branding of the product you purchase—but will lack employees, whether helpful or unhelpful. All you have is your interaction with the digital interface. According to Kevin Mullet, an experience designer at Macromedia (now Adobe), "the online experience must compensate for the absence of a sales professional who stands ready to greet customers as they arrive and to cheerfully help them accomplish their goal."[5]

Three Paths to Experience

Various viewpoints about experience design and planning are beginning to emerge. This is such a new concept that there aren't many articles or books written about experience; those that are out there, though, serve as excellent beginning points. Let's take a look at three and the concepts they include, each of which will be discussed more in-depth later in this chapter.

Experience Economy

The first and probably most important work to examine in any discussion of experience planning is Joseph Pine and James Gilmore's *The Experience Economy: Work Is Theatre & Every Business a Stage*, which has been the catalyst for many others' ideas. Their work involves "staging" experiences, and the book primarily contains general concepts about the experience economy. Pine and Gilmore discuss how we've moved from the industrial economy, to the service economy, and now to the experience economy. They give tips on operating in an experience economy, and employ a theater metaphor to teach us how to stage experiences.

Interaction Design

In November 2003, Macromedia (now Adobe) published Kevin Mullet's white paper on *The Essence of Effective Rich Internet Applications*. Mullet discusses the concept of user experience design as well, but frames it squarely within the realm of interaction design and interactive experiences. Mullet starts where Pine and Gilmore left off, taking their concept of experience staging and applying it to Internet-based application design. Mullet writes that "a great interactive experience must be seamless, focused, connected, and aware."[6] He then applies each of those concepts to interactive application design.

Experience Architect

Tom Kelley's *The Ten Faces of Innovation: IDEO's Strategies for Beating the Devil's Advocate & Driving Creativity Throughout the Organization* has a chapter devoted to the "Experience Architect." Kelley defines what an experience architect does and how an experience architect is useful to a team, and then provides ideas about architecting experiences.

Using These Ideas on Your Library's Web Site

Each of these works contains great ideas that can be easily applied to a library's Web site. In all three, the focus is on various aspects of the user experience—whether that experience addresses the nuts and bolts of creating a usable Web site, or eliciting an emotional response from the customer. This next section provides examples from these three works and applies them to library Web sites. Experience design encompasses seven main concepts:

1. Focus on Users

2. Focus on Your Staff

3. Save the Customer an Extra Step

4. Find Trigger Points

5. Map a Journey

6. Be Seamless and Focused

7. Theme an Experience

Focus on Users

The first—and most important—way to provide positive, useful experiences on your library's Web site is simple: Focus on your users when creating anything. This can be accomplished in a number of ways.

First, think about doing a usability study on the library's current Web site. A usability test will help quickly discover what is and isn't working for visitors. These tests can also pull out those things that do work, but could use improvement. You can use the information gathered through this test throughout a Web site redesign.

Before creating a new Web site, you can also hold focus groups and take a few user surveys. Focus groups and surveys don't test usability; they provide opinions. At this stage, however, opinions can be useful. Ask your users these types of questions:

- What do you like on our Web site?

- What do you not like?

- What services would you like to see?

- What other sites do you regularly visit?

- What two things would you like to see on our site?

Through questions like these, you can discover what your patrons are looking for—mainly in the design and functionality of your Web site, but also in terms of the types of information and services they expect. Use this information to build improved services and Web sites for your customers, which in turn will provide a better, more positive user experience.

Another way to focus on your users is to examine your Web site for negative or neutral experiences, then work on improving these.[7] For example, many library Web sites have an online library card application form. Usually, when encountering this type of form, here's what your users will experience: They'll discover the form, fill it out, and press the submit button. That's when the negative/neutral experience starts. At that point in the transaction, customers are left staring at a big "thank you for filling out the form" message—and nothing else.

The unstated goal for any Web site is to make the site "sticky," so that customers stay after their initial transaction is completed. Instead of giving patrons the usual "thanks for your time" message, how about providing "next step" pointers for them? Here are a couple of ideas:

1. Give them their new library card number (if possible), so that they can immediately start checking out or reserving library materials.

2. Provide pointers to the catalog, subject guides, or even to a new books or new videos list.

Providing this type of solid information after a transaction is completed will keep Web site visitors browsing your library Web site, and will help to quickly integrate Web site visitors into the library system as patrons.

Focus on Your Staff

Your library staff is another type of Web site customer. They interact with the site, sometimes daily, and work to provide the information presented. So, make sure to address their needs as well. Here are three important questions to ask staff:

1. Ask staff what they'd like to see changed.

2. Ask them what they want to see on the site that's not there. This could be either information or services they'd like to provide.

3. Ask about their experiences with patrons: Have they observed patrons having problems with the site, not understanding its organization or information, or not finding information? This staff feedback can provide

extremely valuable information that you can turn into a better user experience.

Remember that library employees tend to use the library Web site in different ways than do library patrons. They might want you to create something that would work great for staff, but leave a patron hopelessly in the dust. In that case—still do it. Treat your staff like a special type of library Web site customer, but build them a different product that they can access from a link on your staff intranet. This will provide better user experiences for your library staff, while still keeping the public Web site focused on library patrons.

Save the Customer an Extra Step

Always save the customer an extra step when possible,[8] which will improve their experience. To discover these extra steps, explore your Web site, and look for places with "extra clicks." Think about important library services; are they accessible within one click of the main Web site? If not, change the link, and advertise the change to your users. Do your online forms ask for information you don't really need? If so, stop asking for that information—this will cut down on the time patrons need to fill out the form, thus improving their experience.

Find Trigger Points

Often, improving the customer's experience boils down to improving one or two major shortcomings of your current Web site, rather than having to do a complete overhaul of the site. Kelley calls these "trigger points."[9] For example, when Kansas City Public Library redesigned their Web site a few years ago, they focused on pushing Web site visitors to their newly created Subject Guides. All the library's subscription databases can be found using the Subject Guides—there's even a subject guide devoted to library databases.

Unfortunately, focusing on Subject Guides also made the library's databases harder to find. To access the databases, site visitors had to browse to the Subject Guides, find an appropriate subject, and then hope the needed database was listed on that Subject Guide. Alternatively, customers could click a drop-down horizontal menu bar item labeled Subject Guides; library databases appeared on that list. Although there were several access points for the databases—and the list of databases was technically accessible within one click from any page of the Web site—it was hidden underneath the broad term

"Subject Guides." This wasn't what our customers or our staff expected; it was a trigger point for both.

The Web team decided to improve this trigger point. Instead of forcing Web customers to use the menu bar and guess what the terms "subject guide" and "library database" meant, the team added a large link on the main page of the Web site labeled "Magazines, Articles, and Databases."

Has this fixed the problem? Web statistics for the library databases subject guide have shot up, and many staff members have commented that adding that link on the main page has really helped improve customer access to our databases.

Map a Journey

Let's say that your library's site has a page devoted to taxes, including forms, books about how to do taxes, and so on, which you put up around tax season every year. That's great! It's good customer service, and helps your patrons find things they'll need. But, you can take this one step further by mapping their journey.[10]

The concept of mapping a journey is similar to the concept of "personas." A persona is "a user archetype you can use to help guide decisions about product features, navigation, interactions, and even visual design."[11] Personas are great, and can be very helpful tools when designing a Web site. The basic idea here is, rather than designing a Web site for everyone (which makes user satisfaction nearly impossible), you design for three to seven "personas," which are developed through analyzing usage patterns in your library. It's much easier to meet the needs of these personas, and to therefore meet the needs of your largest user groups.

Mapping a journey takes the concept of personas and places it in the context of a probable situation and the information on your Web site. Looking at our tax page example in the context of mapping a journey, instead of thinking about the *library's* outcome for the tax page (that of placing useful information online), imagine yourself as *the patron* who needs to access your library's tax page. Ask yourself questions like: Why am I (the patron) coming to the tax page? How am I feeling? What day is it? (April 14 or April 16? That will make a difference.) Then, create a story based around the answers to your questions. For instance:

Jim is extremely anxious this year, because he's put off doing his taxes until a week before they need to be mailed. He's a creative person who is also a small business owner, so he'll have a mound of paperwork to process. He's stressed, and needs some quick pointers to the proper forms and instructions … and, if there's a step-by-step video or a *Dummies Guide to Business Tax Season*, he'll check it out.

So for our tax page example, instead of creating a persona of "a person needing to access our tax page," we can take the persona idea a little further by also mapping journeys, which that persona would take to an individual item on our Web site. To change our presentation of information on the tax page for this persona's journey, we can do a number of things:

- Instead of arranging the taxes booklist in alphabetical order, list the how-to books first.

- Create a separate page or section about how to do business-related taxes.

- Create larger font sizes to emphasize certain forms or instructional guides, especially as "Tax Day" gets closer.

That's how mapping a journey works. Think about the experience from start to finish. But, do so by thinking about the *patron's* version from start to finish—not just at the point when they click through to your Web site.

Be Seamless and Focused

Make sure your site provides a seamless and focused experience for visitors. For Mullet, a seamless experience "provides immediate responses and smooth transitions … within the application."[12] By this, he means that when using an application or a page of a Web site, nothing stops you. There are no interruptions, no hiccups, no having to do things twice.

The goal of most Web sites today is to keep users on the site. If your site pauses for a long time or if the natural flow of finding something is interrupted, that gives your user time to reflect. He will think about other things, and wander off somewhere else. Remember, many browsers now have a Google search engine box built right into the menu bar, so it's extremely easy for customers to drift away from your site.

What can you change to provide a seamless user experience? Basically, you need to remove distractions when possible. One easy way to do this is to make sure your Web site has a consistent look and feel. Make sure all of the little things—the titles, headers, menus, colors—are in the same place, and that they are consistent across the whole site. This will make your site much less distracting, providing a more seamless experience for the user.

Also, be on the lookout for newer scripting languages, like AJAX and Ruby on Rails. AJAX (Asynchronous JavaScript And XML) is emerging as a tool to create interactive Web applications; many Web 2.0 sites currently use AJAX. Google's Gmail (Google's e-mail product) is one good example of AJAX in action. The Gmail interface includes a left-hand side menu bar. When you click to read an e-mail message, instead of the whole page disappearing for a second to reload (like most current Web sites function), the menu stays right where it is; only the right-hand side content changes. That's AJAX in action. It provides a much smoother user interface.

Ruby on Rails also helps provide a more seamless interface, but works more on the backend. Ruby is a programming language, much like Perl, PHP, or JavaScript. Rails is a *Web application framework*. From the Ruby on Rails Web site: "A framework is like the 'support structure' of a program. Believe it or not, the majority of the time that programmers spend writing big Web applications isn't actually spent on the specifics of the program's functionality, but instead it's spent doing much more general programming—writing reusable pieces of code that can be called throughout the main application."[13] This framework is called Rails.

Ruby on Rails, then, makes the creation of database-driven Web sites easier. It includes handy tools like a database access library "that simplifies the process of using SQL databases from within an application."[14] Once understood, Ruby on Rails makes the life of a programmer much easier. These newer languages, when used correctly, can save the time of the user, make the user's experience much more seamless, and provide a better experience.

"A focused experience has a purpose that is clearly defined at the outset and continuously reinforced."[15] A focused experience translates well to Pine and Gilmore's concept of staging a themed experience. There are two primary areas on which to focus:

1. Focus on clearly defined information.

2. Focus on one theme (discussed in the next section).

When your customers click a page for specific information, they should get that information, and nothing else. You want the user's destination to concentrate on a few things in-depth, rather than providing a broad survey. Simply put, make sure you have everything you need on one page. If a user has to log in to part of the site, provide all the boxes needed to complete that function. For example, you would not want to require someone to type her name, click to the next page, and add a PIN number. Extra clicks create a less-focused experience for the user.

Theme an Experience

Pine says "retailers ... talk of 'the shopping experience' but fail to create a theme that ties disparate merchandising presentations together into a staged experience."[16] For an example of a retailer who does this very well, think for a moment about Home Depot. (For those not familiar with Home Depot, it's a home improvement store in the U.S. and Canada.) Visitors to Home Depot are greeted with an in-store atmosphere of large aisles, helpful signage, friendly staff, and do-it-yourself help booklets. Its Web site mimics the in-store atmosphere, with lots of white space (large aisles), good labels on menu bars and page titles (helpful signage), images of staff members on many pages, an easy-to-reach 1-800 number (friendly staff), and a useful Know-How section (mimicking the do-it-yourself help booklets). Home Depot's themes of customer service, an open, friendly environment, and a DIY spirit come through both in their stores and on their Web site.

What can we learn from this? Library Web sites can mimic their physical space (the library building) on their digital space (their Web site and other digital services). Use colors, labels, and signage from the physical space to continue the library experience online. Put pictures of real staff members up on the Web site. Have library staff write articles for the Web site about their favorite books. Having these types of themes and continuing them online will help create a solid themed experience, which is much stronger than having separate online and offline experiences.

Experience and the Future

There are a great variety of experiences to be had on the Web—some great, some not so great, and many forgettable. In the near future, however—maybe even as soon as five years from now—I believe that many types of transactions will be taking place in the digital realm. People will start to expect many normal, everyday services to at least have a digital component, if not to be completely digital. What's going to set one digital service apart from the others, when they all reside in digital space?

Simply this: a positive experience. People will choose an experience that doesn't get in the way, that isn't a roadblock. That memorable experience will bring customers back for more, and those customers will tell their friends, who will also be looking for positive digital experiences. If your library is able to provide memorable digital experiences, then you will be well on the way to not only surviving, but also succeeding in the emerging digital space.

Get Ready, Get Set …

This chapter has presented a number of ways to stage experiences using your library Web site as the stage, your staff members as the actors, and the information presented as the props and costumes. Your job now is to figure out a starting point—all these ideas don't have to be acted on at once—and start to improve your Web site visitors' experience.

To get started, do two things. First, create a simple online survey, and place it on the main page of your Web site. Ask your users questions like the ones mentioned in the section about focusing on your users. Find out what your customers like and don't like; find out what they'd like to see changed. Then, change those things. That will go a long way toward improving your customers' online experience.

Secondly, create a persona and map a journey. See if what you are providing really meets the needs of that persona in the given situation. Again, meet the needs of that persona, and you will go a long way toward meeting the needs of your users. Those users will, in turn, be greeted with a better experience … and will come back for more.

Endnotes

1. Nathan Shedroff, "An Evolving Glossary of Experience Design," www.nathan.com/ed/glossary (accessed May 16, 2006).
2. Iwerks Entertainment, "Glossary: technology terms," www.iwerks.com/notshocked/iwerks/i-glossary.html (accessed May 16, 2006).
3. Nathan Shedroff, "An Evolving Glossary of Experience Design."
4. Nathan Shedroff, "An Evolving Glossary of Experience Design."
5. Kevin Mullet, "The Essence of Effective Rich Internet Applications," Nov. 2003: 5, download.macromedia.com/pub/solutions/downloads/business/essence_of_ria.pdf (accessed May 16, 2006).
6. Mullet, 14.
7. Tom Kelley, *The Ten Faces of Innovation: IDEO's Strategies for Beating the Devil's Advocate & Driving Creativity Throughout the Organization* (New York: Currency Doubleday, 2005): 168.
8. Kelley, 170.
9. Kelley, 171.
10. Kelley, 180.
11. Kim Goodwin, "Perfecting Your Personas," www.cooper.com/newsletters/2001_07/perfecting_your_personas.htm (accessed May 16, 2006).
12. Mullet, 14.
13. Ruby on Rails, "StartAtTheBeginning," wiki.rubyonrails.org/rails/pages/StartAtTheBeginning (accessed May 16, 2006).
14. Ruby on Rails, "StartAtTheBeginning"
15 Mullet, 17.
16. Joseph B. Pine and James H. Gilmore, *The Experience Economy: Work Is Theatre & Every Business a Stage* (Boston Harvard Business School Press, 1999): 46.

Part 3

2.0—and Beyond

CHAPTER 11

Library 2.0

Jenny Levine
Internet Development Specialist and Strategy Guide
American Library Association

During the summer of 2006, I found myself at a Little League baseball game on a Saturday morning, listening to some of the moms talk about the normal things moms talk about when they get together. I let my mind wander elsewhere until I heard one mother say, "I like to get up early before my kids so I can use my computer." Of course, what she really meant was that she likes to get up early before her kids so that she can use *the Internet*.

More and more of us use our computers primarily for connectivity, and connectivity is increasingly taken for granted. In 2002, 12.2 million Americans used online bill payment services. By 2008, 60 million Americans are expected to be using this service.[1] Ask anyone who takes advantage of online bill paying and banking if they would ever go back to the way they used to pay bills; inevitably they laugh and heartily declare, "No way!" Why? Because it's more convenient than licking envelopes and purchasing stamps. Because it's faster and more efficient. Because tracking bill payment history is simpler. Because every point in the process is about helping the user complete tasks. Because it's just easier! More and more, we're living in our Web browsers, and *doing* things there, rather than simply reading things there.

Part of "Library 2.0" (or "L2") involves taking these concepts—easier, faster, more convenient, more efficient—and applying them to libraries. Libraries do a pretty good job of understanding the needs of users who walk through the doors of their physical buildings and have spent decades refining ways to serve them. In general, however, libraries still need to improve how they help users online, in their Web browsers. How can online library services be made easier, faster, more convenient, and more efficient—and even, more fun? In other words, how can they be made as wonderful to use as online bill payment services? How do we get our users to say they would never go back to the way they used to do things, because using the library is so easy?

This is a natural next step in the evolution of our online services. It neither denigrates what has come before nor ignores the wonderful efforts made by our colleagues during the last century. Instead, it extends those services, with a renewed focus on our users and a realignment of our services with where users have moved to. Additionally, it aligns our services with what we have to offer users in the age of ubiquitous, always-on, high-speed Internet access and connectivity. This is an evolutionary step, not a revolutionary one. In this world, how do we renew our commitment to the baseball mom who is up early in the morning—before the library is open—and who has information needs that have to be met in the hour before her kids wake up? Where do our services fit into her life? How do we meet her at the point of her information needs in the most convenient way possible, rather than forcing her into using our rigid box of services? How do we shift our services to where she is, when she needs us?

Many libraries have started to think about their online services in this way, asking how they can wrap themselves around the user, rather than the other way around. Some librarians have responded to this challenge by re-examining their long-held assumptions about library service and what our users want, especially our long-held beliefs about what constitutes "real" library services.

What Is Library 2.0?

When some librarians first read about Library 2.0, they initially associate the term strictly with technology or Web-based services. This renewed emphasis on the user, though, does not apply only to the online world. Just as families, businesses, and the world in general have failed to stand still during the last decade, neither should libraries. Libraries need to constantly look at the outside world and make sure they are offering services in ways that meet the changing needs of users. Sometimes it's easier to see how these needs have changed in the realm of technology (ebooks, audio ebooks, Internet access, remote access to databases, virtual reference, instant messaging …). This should not, however, preclude us from performing similar assessments of the already-familiar services offered within the four walls of the library.

How, then, do we define "Library 2.0?" It is almost impossible to provide a single definition, because L2 encompasses a set of concepts in continuous evolution, which are being created and distilled through an iterative conversation among interested librarians. Unlike AACR2 and MARC—accepted standards of practice that have been approved and which librarians have a context for understanding — Library 2.0 is not a standard, but is a new, or renewed, philosophical and practical commitment to users. Library 2.0 is an emerging movement whose proponents generally agree on the following tenets:

- The library is everywhere. (Chad & Miller)

- The library has no barriers. (Chad & Miller)

- The library invites participation. (Chad & Miller)

- The library uses flexible, best-of-breed systems. (Chad & Miller)

- The library encourages the heart. (Michael Stephens)

- The library is human. (Michael Stephens)

- The library recognizes that its users are human too. (Michael Stephens)

- The library puts users in touch with information and entertainment wherever they may be. (Michael Stephens)

- The library breaks down the barriers of space, time, and outdated policy. (Michael Stephens)

- The library is comfortable in the new reality of constant change. (Michael Casey)

- The library reaches out to new users. (Michael Casey)

- The services change, the mission does not. (Michael Casey)

This is by no means a comprehensive list, and these concepts are constantly being added to, updated, and discussed. What seems clear, however, is a consensus that we already know how to offer adult programming, youth programming, instructional classes, readers' advisory, reference service, and other traditional library services to the users who enter our doors. But in a world where the norm is now constant change and increasing online activity, how can all types of libraries help users? What of the larger population that does not use libraries—what can we offer them in this new landscape? We need to re-examine our profession's sacred cows and long-held beliefs about what constitutes a "library" or "library service." All types of libraries need to re-examine how best to serve users, given the changes of the last decade.

Michael Casey, author of the blog LibraryCrunch, was the first person to use the term "Library 2.0." In December 2005, he provided a concise overview of his thinking:

> Every library has a different starting point. Every library has a different set of constraints it must operate within—most often financial and political. And every library has a slightly different mission. Crafting better and better services, giving customers more and more control over library offerings, and reaching a greater and greater proportion of the population—all while seeking to fulfill that mission—is the goal of Library 2.0.[2]

To sum it all up in one tidy generalization, Library 2.0 is about constant change, making the library user-centered (in all areas), encouraging user participation, reaching out to new users in new ways, creating community (in both our physical and online spaces), and shifting services to where our users are (instead of forcing them to come to us). It can also be neatly summed up in a catchy mnemonic: "the five C's," which stand for community, conversation, collaboration, connections, and commons. Neither of these definitions is static, however, and the debate about the meaning of L2 is sure to continue and to evolve—especially since we cannot implement "Library 2.0" without "Librarian 2.0." Michael Stephens, author of the blog Tame the Web, expands on this need to revise our own professional tenets by noting:

> As we reach out to users, we must remember all of the folks we serve. To me, Library 2.0 will be a meeting place, online or in the physical world, where my emotional needs will be fulfilled through entertainment, information, and the ability to create my own stuff to contribute to the ocean of content out there—the Long Tail if you will. Librarian 2.0, then, will be available to guide me and teach me to use the systems provided by the library to do just that. As Abram said, librarians will provide clarification: 'Librarians need

to position themselves and the library to help with finding the answers to: how? and why?'[3]

In the end, however, it's all about renewing and extending our focus on the user, meeting her information or recreational needs where she is, and creating communities both online and in our physical buildings that allow our users to interact in new and collaborative ways. As Stephen Abram says, "Libraries are no longer able to drive the good bus 'library' alone."[4] The key, however, is to realize that L2 goes beyond just jumping on a bandwagon, or, as Michael Stephens cautions, succumbing to technolust simply for the sake of having a "cool" new technology. Instead, it is important to recognize that L2 offers very real services and products for those libraries that are willing to re-examine themselves in the context of these new Web 2.0 tools and the "five C's." It does so using a broad array of technological and professional applications. In some ways L2 is bounded only by the imaginations of libraries and librarians, and by the adoption of L2-inspired services by actual users.

Re-examining Services

In March 2006, John Blyberg proposed four realms in which libraries could apply L2 thinking when re-examining services:[5]

1. Physical Spaces

2. Programming

3. Policy

4. Technology

Let's look at an example from each of these areas to see how L2 ideas could be used to improve patron services. Using this model helps illustrate how Library 2.0 is about much more than just technology, Web sites, or online services. In fact, Michael Casey drives this point home when he states:

> I think it's fundamentally flawed to say that technology is to libraries as oxygen is to our lives. Were technology to disappear (or stop advancing) today, libraries would be able to continue providing critical services and would be able to expand and change to meet the needs of our users

(and those we want to be our users), all within the framework of what is available. This fluidity, this ability to use
whatever resources are available, be they high tech or not,
in an efficient and effective manner, is what Library 2.0
symbolizes.[6]

Physical Spaces

How can we apply L2 thinking in our physical spaces? As Beth Gallaway
notes in Chapter 6, one way is to reach out to nontraditional patrons,
using new ideas that come from their world, not ours. Gallaway illus-
trates that we can offer almost any user a neutral, commercial-free,
inviting space to come together and play video games as a social and
recreational activity (similar to the ways in which we offer space for
movies, book discussion groups, knitting groups, and others). We can
renew our mission of community, of the library as "third place"—that
is, a place that is neither home nor work nor school—to groups that
traditionally have not seen us this way before. They have never
thought of going to libraries to just "be" (as they go to the mall), or for
recreational use, but we can change that.

Programming

Libraries can use gaming to create connections, connotations, community, and even commons, especially for teens. Service to this
group has suffered over the years as we focused more heavily on children, adults, and seniors. In the past, we've viewed this demographic
almost purely as "students," rather than as recreational users, especially in the academic world. Should we not be trying to serve their
recreational needs in ways that give them the same sense of community and connection as adults and faculty? When viewed as content,
are video games really all that different from romance novels, story-
times, fiction in academic libraries, and other recreational uses?
When viewed in this way, gaming also becomes an excellent illustra-
tion of applying L2 principles to library programming.

Policy

The one piece of Library 2.0 that truly does seem to be a departure
for our profession is the movement to include users in the decision-
making processes, and even in the day-to-day activities, of the

library. Again, traditionally we have been better at doing this in the physical world (with user surveys, focus groups, usability studies, suggestion boxes), but there appears to be a new emphasis on doing more than just asking users what they want. We are now seeing the implementation of new services that have seemed inappropriate (or have even scared us) in the past, simply because we adhered to what librarians think the library should be, rather than taking into account what *our users* think it should be.

Ask any teenage boy if he'd like to play video games with his friends at the library, and he is likely to respond with an enthusiastic, "Yes!" Ask a librarian if that same boy should be able to do this, and the response is often, "No." Should libraries offer every possible service? Of course not. However, for all of the reasons Gallaway mentions, gaming is a wonderful example of libraries offering community and a place for (what kids today view as) content. This is a way of meeting this group of users' needs, and is a valid service. Librarians need to think differently and to take a long, hard look at what we can offer our users, especially in the realm of policy—which basically looks at what we allow, what we restrict, and who decides these things.

Technology

Online, this can seem more difficult, especially for libraries with limited budgets and declining resources. However, the emerging world of Web 2.0 (the Read/Write Web) that Michael Stephens discusses in Chapter 8 actually means that libraries can offer a new and powerful collaborative environment to our users. Taking advantage of free technology such as blogs, RSS, wikis, instant messaging, and other social software tools, we can now easily add an online component to the central theme of Library 2.0—*user participation*. In the past, this seemingly innocuous phrase meant, at best, providing an online feedback form that patrons could use to contact the library. While the transfer of the traditional suggestion box to the online world is a no-brainer, we haven't taken advantage of the Web 2.0 world to improve it for the benefit of our users. Currently, when a user fills out one of these forms, she has no idea who will see the message or if there will be a response. Often, she doesn't even receive a copy of the message or a confirmation e-mail that it was received by library staff. She is left to await some response, someday. How can we transform this simple feedback experience in the 2.0 world? How can we allow greater user participation and encourage community and connections online, to improve just this one service?

One relatively easy and increasingly efficient way to do this is to start a blog, regardless of your type of library. Using blogging software for "what's new" and announcements pages not only makes staff more efficient (making it easier to add content to the library Web site), but turning on comments for posts allows users to provide feedback in a much more immediate and communal way. This one easy— and free—act creates community, as users post their comments in a very open and transparent online environment. Conversations start online and staff can respond in the same way, creating an immediacy that simulates an in-person conversation and that satisfies the need for response and involvement. Instead of that e-mail from the user disappearing into the ether, she enters her comment in a box, clicks on the "submit" button, and immediately sees it posted on the library's Web site. Talk about participation! Now staff (and even other users) can respond and engage in conversation, providing richer, fuller answers in a collaborative environment.

Interestingly, some of the most vivid examples of L2 practices, especially regarding user participation, were initiated before the L2 concept had been expressed. This shows that librarians alert to changes in how people are interacting with their worlds were able to begin creatively adapting library practices to those changes. The most fascinating example of this to date has been Michigan's Ann Arbor District Library's (AADL) Web site. In July 2005, AADL migrated to a blog-based site and opened up comments on almost every item posted. The thought of users adding opinion and potentially non-authoritative content to library Web sites scares us, flying in the face of our expert-based profession. But what better way is there to engage a community online and to dialogue with them in a way that says, "We have nothing to hide, and we welcome your input?"

One can see the potential of this approach in so many posts on the AADL site (Figure 11.1). On almost any day, their home page shows comments from users who are engaging the staff and each other in discussions about the library. The conversation draws us in because it displays a new possibility for human interaction on a library's Web site—it surprises us. These conversations occur within library buildings every day, but for the first time, libraries are opening up their online presences to create this same type of community and participation via their Web sites.

Submitted by markjwilson on Wed, 08/24/2005 - 6:31am.

How do you account for an 8% increase in visits generating a 33% increase in circulation? Is everyone checking out 3 books instead of 2?

This is also interesting in its contrast with this article

http://www.cbsnews.com/stories/2005/08/23/tech/main791462.shtml

which describes how the UT undergrad library removed all of its books.

Submitted by steve on Wed, 08/24/2005 - 11:27am.

I would guess that renewing materials from home via computer probably accounts for a significant amount of the increase in circulation over the last few years.

Submitted by markjwilson on Wed, 08/24/2005 - 5:15pm.

Do we count a renewal the same way we count the original checkout? That doesn't seem right.

Submitted by technocrat on Wed, 08/24/2005 - 8:33pm.

What's wrong with it? How is a renewal different than returning a book and checking it out again the next day? Both involve a transaction and the book being unavailable to anyone else.

Submitted by markjwilson on Thu, 08/25/2005 - 8:40am.

I read a lot and have 16 items checked out right now in a Darwinian rotation. I renew everything online about once a week. When an item comes up as not renewable, I decide whether to move it to the top of the stack, or to return it unread. When I return an item unread, I usually put in a new request for it.

Figure 11.1   Patron Comments on the AADL Web Site

For example, on some posts on the AADL site, patrons have left comments raising concerns about environmental degradation due to the construction of a new library branch, the migration to a new OPAC that didn't send out e-mail notices *before* items were due, and even a debate (between the patrons, mind you, not the staff!) about whether a renewal should count the same as a new circulation! To our well-established professional minds, the thought of allowing patrons to post their thoughts about these issues on library-owned Web pages is very scary, but not so for the Ann Arbor Library staff. Instead, they relied on the notion of "radical trust" and provided a platform for dialogue. At the time they did this, Darlene Fichter had not yet defined the term "radical trust" in the context of libraries and explained its importance to "Library 2.0." In fact, at the time the AADL staff broke with tradition and decided to let patrons collaborate with them on the library's Web site, the term "Library 2.0" itself had not yet been coined by Michael Casey.

Radical Trust

As Fichter defines "Library 2.0" in an April 2, 2006, blog post on the subject, L2 equals "(books 'n stuff + people + radical trust) x participation"[7] (Figure 11.2). She goes on to say:

> Libraries have always been about books 'n stuff and people. The notion of **radical trust** and applying this to online library activities introduces a new dimension to the work that we've been doing in libraries. You'll also notice that the scaling up factor in this simple formula is based on participation. Without the first three ingredients you can't start to scale rapidly and create new wealth (richness) and value for participants. …
>
> We can only build emergent systems if we have radical trust. With an emergent system, we build something without setting in stone what it will be or trying to control all that it will be. We allow and encourage participants to shape and sculpt and be co-creators of the system. We don't have a million customers/users/patrons … we have a million participants and co-creators.
>
> Radical trust is about trusting the community. We know that abuse can happen, but we trust (radically) that the community and participation will work. In the real world, we know that vandalism happens but we still put art and sculpture up in our parks. As an online community we come up with safeguards or mechanisms that help keep open contribution and participation working.

Radical trust, therefore, is a new element for libraries and librarians, exemplified by the openness and collaborative transparency of the AADL Web site. This holds true for the user participation realm, especially if we again think about new and useful ways to create community with our patrons using L2-ish tools such as blogs. For an equally participatory and radical idea, we turn to the Western Springs History site (IL), created in April 2005 by library staff member Aaron Schmidt and consultant Jessamyn West. Many libraries have digitized local history projects they then offer via the Web. Typically, content is

Figure 11.2   Theory of Radical Trust by Darlene Fichter

created by librarians and posted to the Web for users to read (one-way, not interactive), and usually the user has to search to find something (as opposed to being able to browse).

In the Western Springs History project, Schmidt and West used L2 principles (again before the concept had even been named) to transform the traditional local history project into a community conversation, simply by using a blog with images as the infrastructure for the site. Instead of creating a purely searchable database, they used the blog format to create categories that consisted of street names, making the site searchable as well as browsable. Each image and its metadata became a separate blog post—but more importantly, they opened comments on every post/image. For the first time, the community could contribute directly to the community history project! And while some of us might have worried that vandals or spammers would have posted inappropriate—or at best, inaccurate—comments, the community stepped up and contributed real value to the project, value the library staff could never have provided on their own. This has developed a community understanding of local history based on memories and on the experiences of the people of that community.

For example, look at the record for 4620 Grand.[8] Not only are there comments from someone who lived in the house during the years 1938–1945, as well as comments from the current owners (Figure 11.3), but someone has left a comment about the house next door—because there is no separate record for it yet! This is the true power of Fichter's definition of L2, in particular the radical trust and participation tenets. It's amazing what can be built when we allow ourselves to trust and collaborate with our users. This is a different way of thinking for our profession, but one that increasingly proves to hold great promise for transforming our services, and therefore our relationships with users.

❀ 4 Comments »

Comment by Leta Merle Behling

My grandparents Rose and Fred Merle owned that house. I lived there from 1938 to 1945. It had a wrap around porch, 2 pantries and a formal Sunday parlor. They also owned the lot next door. My grandfather was a very talented gardner, wood carver, and artist. It was a wonderful house to grow up in and the gardens were magical.

Leta Merle Behling

Posted on July 30, 2005 at 5:42 pm

Comment by Administrator

Thanks for the wonderful comments. The information you give us really adds to the website. Glad you saw it.

Aaron @ the TFML

Posted on August 1, 2005 at 12:25 pm

Comment by Diana Whelton

I currently live in this sky-blue house with my husband Jim, and two boys, Jack (3) and Ryan (1). A two-story addition (plus basement) was added by previous owners. When we bought the home in 2002 there was a very old-fashioned photograph of a family hanging on the wall (the back is unmarked). I believe much of the front half of the home is original (front door, staircase, fireplace,

---

Figure 11.3 Patron Contributions to Western Springs Local History Blog

The User Is Not Broken

Although some have taken issue with the label "Library 2.0," it is important to differentiate between the name and the concepts. Every month, we are seeing new examples of libraries of every size and type implementing L2-based services using L2-ish tools that promote collaboration, conversation, and community. The common theme? A focus on the user. As Karen Schneider so eloquently stated in her post The User Is Not Broken: A Meme Masquerading as a Manifesto[9]:

> The OPAC is not the sun. The OPAC is at best a distant planet, every year moving farther from the orbit of its solar system.
> The user is the sun.
> The user is the magic element that transforms librarianship from a gatekeeping trade to a services profession.
> The user is not broken.

For the first time, we have new tools that allow us to more easily put *users* at the *center* of our services online and actually let them *contribute* to the *conversation*!

We can use instant messaging to provide reference services where our users already are, instead of forcing them to come to our Web sites. We can use blogs to generate RSS feeds of our most current information and then display those feeds on other sites where our users might already be going (local government, newspapers, college portals, parent organizations). We can let the users contribute their knowledge of the community to the community wiki or to the local history project.

For the users we do see every day, we need to reassess all of our services and policies to re-create the library as the persistent heart of the community and to make users the center of our services. It is imperative that we refocus on why we do what we do (asking ourselves along the way if we need to continue doing what we're doing and the way we are doing it) and begin shifting our services to where our patrons are, making services as easy to use as possible for people like busy moms—at home, on Saturday mornings, or at any other time. L2 philosophies, tools, and practices allow us to increasingly span time and space to truly put the user at the heart of library services, in all types of libraries, and in both physical and virtual spaces.

Endnotes

1. Robyn Greenspan, "E-Banking, Online Bill Paying Growth Ahead," ClickZ, www.clickz.com/stats/sectors/finance/article.php/3112511 (accessed July 12, 2006).
2. Michael Casey, "Whatever Tools Take Us There Are the Ones We Will Use," Library Crunch, www.librarycrunch.com/2005/12/whatever_tools_take_us_there_a.html (accessed July 14, 2006).
3. Michael Stephens, "Do Libraries Matter: On Library & Librarian 2.0," ALA TechSource Blog, www.techsource.ala.org/blog/2005/11/do-libraries-matter-on-library-librarian-20.html (accessed July 12, 2006).
4. Stephen Abram, "The Library 2.0 'Bandwagon,'" Stephen's Lighthouse, stephenslighthouse.sirsi.com/archives/2006/02/the_library_20_1.html (accessed July 13, 2006).
5. John Blyberg, "Find the Edge, Push It," Blyberg.net, blyberg.net/2006/03/22/find-the-edge-push-it (accessed July 14, 2006).
6. Michael Casey, "Whatever Tools …"
7. Darlene Fichter, "Web 2.0, Library 2.0 and Radical Trust: A First Take," Blog on the Side, library.usask.ca/~fichter/blog_on_the_side/2006/04/web-2.html (accessed July 11, 2006).
8. Thomas Ford Memorial Library, "4620 Grand," Western Springs History, westernspringshistory.org/4620-grand (accessed July 12, 2006).
9. Karen Schneider, "The User Is Not Broken: A Meme Masquerading as a Manifesto," Free Range Librarian, freerangelibrarian.com/2006/06/the_user_is_not_broken_a_meme (accessed July 12, 2006).

CHAPTER 12

Get a Second Life!
Libraries in Virtual Worlds

Rhonda B. Trueman
Reference Librarian, Johnson & Wales University

Tom Peters
Founder, TAP Information Services

Lori Bell
Director of Innovation, Alliance Library System

In April 2006, the Alliance Library System (ALS) launched Alliance Second Life Library 2.0 (SLL; www.infoisland.org). ALS, which serves central Illinois and is headquartered in East Peoria, is one of nine multitype regional library systems in the state. At the time, our public libraries were worried about their lack of young adult users, and wondered how we could provide services to them, get them interested in books, and encourage them to come to the library. One of our members, Bloomington Public Library (BPL), had been offering gaming nights and attracting large crowds of teens who then checked out books on a variety of topics. Working with BPL, we wrote grants to try to introduce gaming in some of our smaller rural libraries in order to attract young adults.

Unfortunately, our grant applications were not funded, so we continued thinking of ways we could help our libraries attract young adults. We learned of Second Life (SL) and began investigating it after reading about the Gaming and Libraries Symposium held by Metropolitan Library System in December 2005, hosted by Jenny Levine. We also tried other virtual realities, such as Active Worlds (www.activeworlds.com) and There (www.there.com), but Second Life seemed the best of all possible virtual worlds to begin an initial exploration of providing in-world library services.

We included "2.0" in the SLL project name because we wanted to implement and build upon some of the excellent ideas and principles emanating from the Library 2.0 movement. Once the SLL was officially under development, volunteer librarians from all types of libraries, all around the world, began contributing their time and expertise to the project. The Alliance Second Life Library 2.0 has evolved into Library 3D, as it has moved quickly beyond text and graphics; SLL has all the qualities and interaction of any Library 2.0 initiative, but adds a third dimension.

Virtual Worlds vs. Gaming

What is the difference between virtual worlds and gaming? A gaming environment is one in which the characters, the goal of the game, the rules, and other rudiments are already established. A quest or purpose to the game often is explicitly understood by all the participants in the game, who may gain powers or move to higher levels based on their earlier accomplishments. Second Life, Active Worlds, There, and other virtual environments, on the other hand, are places where people go to create "avatars"—virtual representations or surrogates for themselves—who can look however they want and can interact with other avatars. Virtual worlds don't necessarily present a goal to be achieved. In virtual worlds, the avatars themselves play a major role in building the virtual world and deciding on the rules and mores of the "residents" or "citizens" of each region or world.

What Is Second Life?

Second Life is a virtual world entirely built and owned by its residents, or avatars. Participants build their avatar or alternate persona to actively participate in the creation of media, instead of participating in more passive modes such as watching television or viewing a static Web page. The Wikipedia article about "Avatar (icon)" provides some historical context about the use of the Hindu concept of avatars to name the residents of virtual environments:

> The use of *Avatar* to mean online virtual bodies was popularised by Neal Stephenson in his cyberpunk novel *Snow Crash* (1992). In *Snow Crash,* the term *Avatar* was used to describe the virtual simulation of the human form in the

Metaverse, a virtual-reality version of the Internet. Social status within the Metaverse was often based on the quality of a user's avatar, as a highly detailed avatar showed that the user was a skilled hacker and programmer while the less talented would buy off-the-shelf models in the same manner as a forumer today. (en.wikipedia.org/wiki/Avatar)

Since opening to the public in 2003, Second Life has grown explosively. As of June 2007, Second Life was inhabited by close to 7.5 million people from around the globe, compared with about 180,000 in mid-April 2006. New residents discover a vast digital continent teeming with people, entertainment, and opportunities. After exploring this virtual world, individuals might decide to buy land, purchase a home, or start a business. They will also be surrounded by the creations of fellow residents. Because residents retain the rights to their digital creations, they can buy, sell, and trade with other residents. Everything you can imagine (and some things you cannot!) can be found in Second Life. There are museums, 19th-century worlds where residents dress in period clothing and live in Victorian homes, immersive learning environments such as an Egyptian tomb, simulations of weather and seismic phenomena, Star Trek futuristic realms, re-creations of real-world areas (such as the French Quarter in New Orleans), and much more. Residents can also go to the virtual library and use a number of resources.

Starting the Second Life Library

We started the SLL because we wanted to see if and how avatars needed libraries and library services in a virtual world. With the 'net generation now starting college—those who have grown up using video games for learning and entertainment—many educational institutions, corporations, and nonprofit organizations are moving into virtual worlds. We think libraries should be there, too. We started the library with seed money from a revenue-generating project ALS had undertaken, a small plot of land in Second Life (Info Island), and a traditional-looking library building. We invited any interested librarians to join us, and soon had over two dozen volunteers, with a variety of skill sets, joining us in Second Life.

Starting a library in Second Life was much like starting a library in a new culture or country where you do not know the language, the tools, or how to get around. One advantage you have in Second Life is that you can fly—but this doesn't prevent you from flying into buildings! Our group of volunteers had library skills, but the question was how best to put them to good use to meet the actual information needs of avatars in this particular virtual world. We conducted training and orientation programs on Second Life for our librarians, answered reference questions, learned how to make books, and had several authors give live, in-world programs. Traffic on Info Island was good, and more and more librarians—and others—became interested.

In May 2006 we received an anonymous donation of an island, much larger than the previous SLL location. We were able to have a large library built, where we put public domain books in different formats, audio books, exhibits, and special collections built by librarians interested in genealogy, anime/manga, and other subjects. We had a Goth castle built called Mystery Manor, where avatars can visit, view posters of mystery authors, and participate in mystery book discussions. We had a spaceship built, which holds the science fiction and fantasy gallery. (Unsurprisingly, there are many science fiction fans in Second Life.) This building will be used to host science fiction and fantasy authors and promote their works. Each of these areas has a dedicated group of volunteers who work as a group to provide services.

Now we have a Google group with more than 500 members (groups.google.com/group/alliancesecondlife), a Second Life group with more than 500 members, and a friends group in Second Life with more than 1,000 members. The numbers for all these groups are growing. At our grand opening in October 2006, we had flags in our outdoor auditorium for all the countries represented by volunteers working on the library; nearly every continent was represented (except for Africa and Antarctica).

We have a second main library, Parvenu Tower, where each floor emphasizes a different subject area developed by a collection team under the leadership of Abbey Zenith (SL name). For instance, there are floors focused on government documents, humanities and social sciences, higher education, and science and technology. On the top floor of Parvenu Tower there is an auditorium that seats 40. From the very beginning, Namro Orman from the Netherlands built a medical library and led the way in the use of Second Life tools and technology to offer library services.

We also have nonlibrary organizational partners we work with and provide space for on both Info Island and the adjacent islands. For example, Tech Soup, which provides technology services to many nonprofits, has a space and has offered a "mixed reality" event where the participants in Second Life could see what was happening at an event in real life and the participants in real life could see the Second Life activities. We also provide a spot for World Bridges, which assists us with Web and audio casting. We have a booth where you can search Amazon.com and buy books in several different languages, and a search central area where avatars can search Google, Wikipedia, and WorldCat. We also have an art gallery run by Abbey Zenith, where we—as real-life libraries do—try to promote the artists, creators, and authors in Second Life. In October 2006 we held our first art show of photography from Bucky Barkley, which was attended by more than 80 people; his exhibit was featured in the *New York Times*. Each month or two we plan to sponsor a new exhibit by a Second Life artist, holding an event and providing publicity so that artists may share their work.

Just as many real-life libraries offer live, in-person programs, SLL also has one or more live, in-world events each week. We have had great attendance for our author events, some of whom write both in real and Second Life, and some of whom write only in Second Life. The real-life husband-and-wife team of Pamela Woodward and Wilbur Witt, who wrote *Dobbit Do*, a science fiction thriller published in real life and in Second Life, packed the outdoor auditorium for their talk. Another real-life wife-and-husband author team, Sharon Lee and Steve Miller, talked to a packed island about how they used the Internet to begin publishing and gain readers. They are now well-known and highly regarded authors in real life, and have a presence in Second Life to provide snippets of their books. We have had another author who writes on a Web site and built a virtual reality of her book within Second Life where her fans could role-play and be a part of the book. JC Hutchins (in real life, JC Ripley in Second Life) writes the *7th Son*, which was podcast to more than 50 people who then visited scenes from his book he had re-created in Second Life.

We have also had programs on technologies used in Second Life. Jeff Barr from Amazon.com talked about the technologies they are employing, and more than 60 avatars attended. We have held historical reenactments to bring figures like Henry VIII and Anne Boleyn to life with avatars. The audience is able to interact with them—and even to enjoy heckling Henry VIII about his six wives! With immersive environments and technology we are working with technologists in Second Life to make exhibits more interactive, immersive, exciting, and lifelike, and to make learning more fun.

In September 2006, OCLC generously donated trial access to its Question Point virtual reference service to help us learn if virtual users want virtual reference. Yes, they do! We started staffing the reference desk a few hours per week, and we have been fairly busy. We put ourselves at the point where people come into our island in order to greet them. We get a lot of people new to Second Life, so we actually do get both reference questions and a lot of questions on where to go and what to do in Second Life. We plan to continue offering reference services and are also looking into adding instant messaging reference via meebo.

Why Libraries Should Be Involved in Virtual Worlds

Just as it was important for libraries to experiment with earlier technologies, such as telephones, photocopiers, and the Web, libraries should also be involved in virtual worlds. Libraries need to have a presence wherever their users are, and, as the use of virtual worlds is increasing, libraries need to extend their presence into these worlds. As of 2007, we are at a stage with virtual worlds similar to where we were in 1995 with the graphical Web. Libraries were there to help their communities and patrons get online with the Web, teach them how to find and evaluate information, and provide access to those who could not access the Web for lack of a computer or ISP. Libraries need to be early adopters of technology.

Many naysayers wonder why librarians should explore technologies and applications that affect only about 5 percent of the general population. As can be seen from numerous examples—consider the migration of audio books from cassette, to CD, to downloadable audio—all technology applications begin with a small group of early adopters, with costs of entry that initially can be quite high. At the rate things are changing and growing, it will not be long before virtual worlds impact a significant percentage of people worldwide.

How We Expect to Expand Our Role

Within two months of obtaining Info Island I, in August 2006, a private donor donated Info Island II for museums and special collections.

In October 2006, we received a grant from the National Library of Medicine Greater Midwest Region to create a Healthinfo Island to provide training and resources on consumer health. Also in October 2006, with the sponsorship of the library automation vendor Talis, we were able to create Cybrary City. This island allows libraries and librarians to have a local spot for virtual office hours, for a collection they wish to show off, or just a place to meet with avatars from their core service populations. Cybrary City also has a large training conference classroom center that members may use to train librarians or have conferences. In exchange for giving two hours a week to the collaborative library through reference work, programs, cataloging, or collection creation, libraries may have their own spot on Cybrary City.

On the other side of Info Island is the Commonwealth Island for nonprofits, created and built by Hayduke Ebisu (SL name). Next to that is a Web development firm. We now have EduIslands I, II, III, and IV for both colleges and universities and individual educators.

We are currently working with a number of technology developers in Second Life to learn the tools, the scripting, and how best to deliver information in Second Life. We will continue to work there to create immersive environments promoting literature and reading and to deliver information in new formats. We are definitely now part of the community of Second Life, just as real-life librarians are of their communities, creating partnerships and working on projects that benefit everyone. We also continue to promote reading through author visits and places dedicated to promoting or serving information on a particular genre.

Collections in Second Life

If collections are defined as a library's accumulation of books and materials, organized and cataloged for easy access and use by library patrons, then the potential for collections in Second Life surpasses all expectations of real-life collections. At this time print, video, and audio materials are limited to public domain materials and materials freely given by Second Life creators, writers, and librarians. Despite this limitation, Second Life Library 2.0 is not limited by the physical restraints of storage for materials that a real-world library faces. Although SLL is confined to a virtual space that corresponds to a physical space—a parcel of land on which to place structures that hold collections—our collections are not limited to materials that can be seen or touched. A virtual book on a virtual shelf can provide as many copies as there are people who want them. Each user "touches" the object by right-clicking on it. The object can be transferred to that user's inventory to be read or used as many times as desired—nothing to wear out, nothing to return. There is no "borrowing" from SLL; collections are freely shared.

While most libraries have collections of ephemera, on SLL it is possible to collect any items that are free to share. This would include not only books, audio books, digital collections, and other types of literary materials, but also teaching aids like whiteboards, scripts that enable others to create objects that perform special functions, and even clothing, buildings, vehicles, and plants. In Second Life, an object can hold detailed information in the form of a notecard that the library patron is able to keep; it can hold links to related Second Life places; it may even contain other related objects that the patron may keep. In addition, a patron may also be able to obtain a copy of the original object. For example, a brightly colored toadstool could contain information on Lewis C. Carroll, a link to an area of Second Life based on *Alice in Wonderland*, a dress with a pinafore or a Mad Hatter's hat, a digital copy of the book—and, to top it off, the patron can keep the toadstool to decorate his or her own Second Life garden.

Despite the magical qualities that the Second Life environment allows, our aim on SLL is to be first and foremost a library that is responsive to our patrons' needs. Some may question the need for books at all; Second Life is not an environment where people go to read. So far the technology does not allow us to share objects that are stored on the patron's computer for later use; it does not allow us to bring the Internet in-world. Books that are found in-world are expensive to make and awkward to read. So, why books? Because, even today, books are the icons of librarianship. Our visitors to SLL expect to see books. The most frequent question I am asked when working reference is "Where are the books?" One patron was even highly irate that our copy of *War of the Worlds* was not allowing him to "take" it.

In addition to several forms of Second Life books, SLL has an extensive collection of Internet URLs organized into subject areas. As in real life, we group collections together by subject and we try to make the "physical" space accommodating for our users. Each area is arranged to be aesthetically pleasing. The academic resources are in an area with comfy looking chairs and a huge fish tank; the business area has desks and chairs, a soothing fountain, and racks for newspapers; the humanities floor has leather wingback chairs, paintings, collections of coins, a teakettle, and a map chest; and the science area has specially made desks for research, lab tables, Bunsen burners, and a free floating euglena. Again, the reason for familiar spaces is iconic. We tend to expect certain things, and we seem to seek familiar surroundings, even in a virtual world we create from scratch.

The collections available through the Medical Library and the Consumer Health Library are without doubt some of the most useful and most used collections. They include database resources and RSS feeds in addition to the standard methods of delivering information on Second Life. This area has been pioneering the use of a Jnana search, which is a decision-tree-based engine, preprogrammed to function through questions asked. It is able to provide objects, documents, Web sites, Flash technology, notecards, and even contact information for further inquiry through e-mail. The collections in this area make it possible for users to seek healthcare information anonymously. Carolina Keats (Second Life name) reports that most inquiries start as casual conversation and then move into more direct questions about one health issue or another.

In a virtual world, collections can be augmented by audio and visual effects that add layers to the experience of the user. A special collection on government documents could conceivably have speeches playing in the background. An area dedicated to mystery fiction can play an audio book throughout the building, or could have sound effects like screams and creaking doors. QuickTime allows movies in Second Life, and where available these can be used to add depth to the resources found in the collection.

Collections can be quickly changed, updated, or moved. Special collections can be created to enhance exhibits like our first one on Vachel Lindsay or the 9/11 memorial that was created in September 2006. Once the exhibit is complete, collections can be moved to a different area or kept in inventory until needed again.

New and innovative ways of presenting information and new items for collections become available quickly on Second Life. In a world where creations are the sole property of the creator, the impetus to develop products for recognition or for profit encourages creativity. We have volunteers on Info Island who have developed new ways to link to the Internet, to provide training, to give orientations, to develop exhibits, and more.

The Library of Congress' American Memory division has a changing exhibit developed by Shadow Fugazi (SL name). An exhibit on the United States Declaration of Independence provided text and audio information along with bigger-than-life copies of the Declaration of Independence, the Preamble and Articles, and other important historical documents. There is a book rack containing "America During the Age of Revolution, 1764–1789" in sections that provide notecard text. Visual elements also contain information, and a computer monitor is set up to lead visitors to the Library of Congress' American Memory Web site.

Another special collection of SLL is the Caledon Branch Library's collection. Caledon is a 19th-century Sim where residents dress in the clothing styles, speak the vernacular, and live in homes of the period. Caledon's collections consist of materials published before 1900, which also include fiction and nonfiction for research on the period; a group within this library's patronage has a high interest in the Steampunk genre of fiction. The library also provides a collection of items that residents in this area use, such as textures, gestures, and animations. All this is packaged into a branch library of the period, managed by a librarian perfectly suited in style and wit to the position, JJ Drinkwater (SL name).

Librarianship in Second Life may bear little resemblance to real-world librarianship. Patrons are not borrowers; events and programs may be more important than collections; collections can be as vast or as specific as needed; change can be managed with a minimal amount of time invested; communication is instantaneous and direct. Yet still, the mission of libraries in Second Life is to serve the information needs of our users—and in Second Life we are able to do this just as we do in real-world libraries.

Educators in Second Life

Educators have been quick to assess the potential for education in Second Life. The experiential nature of Second Life provides an arena in which theories can be tested, methodology can be explored, and results can be measured. Education in Second Life is creative, collaborative, and immersive. It allows faculty to reach out to students on a level that most students, children of the technological age, may already consider a comfort zone—virtual worlds and online gaming. Gamers learn by exploring, by doing, by making errors and correcting them. Second Life, which seems like a game yet is not a game, allows students to work in an environment that is simultaneously fun and educational.

In many cases educators have pioneered their institution's involvement in Second Life, but in the case of Alliance's SLL it is the librarians who have blazed trails, set up camp and invited educators to sit by the fire. Our EduIslands were developed specifically for educators who want to begin using this platform for teaching. Space is provided at cost for educators to use in class instruction. Linden Lab, the creator of Second Life, currently offers a small parcel to educators free for one semester, and there are other facilities that rent out space on Second Life for profit. SLL allows educators not only to have a space of their own, but to use our facilities for larger meetings or events. We are happy to work with faculty to provide the resources needed for a successful virtual classroom experience. EduIslands I, II, III, and IV are located directly next door to the island for individual libraries. It is now possible for a university or college to have space for classes with their own library support in the same area! We even have library schools that are creating a presence on the library island in order to train students or provide meetings and distance education. These are wonderful examples of how educators and librarians can collaborate in Second Life.

Educators and librarians share common goals and common challenges with Second Life. Challenges include: navigation, obtaining Second Life skills, finding funding, developing in-world instructional skills, and providing access to space and resources for students or patrons. There is much to consider when venturing into Second Life to hold classes or provide educational resources, and it can often be overwhelming to someone with only a cursory knowledge of virtual worlds and games. SLL has made significant progress in paving the way for interested educators and librarians. We offer assistance in the form of tours and classes, which are organized by librarians and designed to help orient new Second Life residents. One of our partners on Info Island, the Information and Communication Technology (ICT) Library, offers free or inexpensive teaching aids and a library of scripts that enable instructors and students to manipulate their virtual environment.

Perhaps more important than the skill sets, resources, and materials we help to provide is the personal interaction and community SLL nurtures. We are a volunteer community—librarians, library staff, library students, library supporters, and library friends—working on this project on our own time. Educators can come to Second Life and find not only a place, but a growing thriving community that exists, not for our own aggrandizement, but for the service we can provide to others. The culture of collaboration and sharing already is firmly rooted in Second Life. There may not always be someone officially on duty at the reference desk, but more often than not educators will find someone who can give assistance, directions, instruction, information, or just a human connection. And, if the first person you meet on Info Island doesn't have all the answers, they will most likely introduce you to someone else who can offer further assistance, or to another educator working in Second Life, or help find places in Second Life that are relevant to your subject.

As stated on the Second Life Web site (secondlife.com), this virtual world is "imagined, created & owned by its residents." Across the Info Archipelago, librarians and other volunteers have imagined, created, and taken pride in their "ownership" of the community they have worked so hard to build. On SLL, educators will find a place to begin, a place of support, and a place to communicate with others who share similar goals.

Shifty Thoughts About the Future of Libraries in Virtual Worlds

Most major technological developments eventually require some sort of shift in thinking. The development of word processing software, for example, led to a rethinking of the processes of writing (and rewriting) and sharing documents. The Alliance Second Life Library Project is motivating many people involved in the project (and many people not directly involved) to rethink key components of librarianship. As the presence of librarianship in Second Life and other virtual worlds continues to rapidly develop and evolve, we may see a general departure in the development of in-world architecture from real-world architecture. In virtual environments, inclement weather happens only if some avatar wills it. As a result, "outdoor" meetings, exhibits, and presentations are very accessible and welcomed by many avatars. For in-world buildings, there is no need to worry about load and stress, HVAC, restrooms, pests, and vermin. Other building factors, such as signage, lighting, location of service points, and the arrangement of collections and resources, are as important in virtual worlds as they are in the real world. There are several ways to move from one floor to another, including stairs, teleportation, and flying; some buildings in SL hover in the air.

Interactive, immersive exhibits and a wide variety of live, in-world events may quickly become as central to the mission of libraries in virtual worlds as are collections to most real-world libraries. Our experiences during the first few months of SLL indicated that more formal presentations with podiums and presentation slides are less well-received by attending avatars than are more relaxed and interactive presentations and events. The presenter often assumes less of the role of a professor and more of the role of a facilitator of some sort of group-learning experience. The possibilities for exhibits in Second Life are almost limitless.

As librarians continue to explore these virtual worlds and conceptualize and implement library systems and services that best meet the needs of their residents, we may see in-world libraries morph to include elements and styles that in the real world are more often associated with museums, theme parks, and other cultural and social institutions. When it comes to in-world formal education, academic and school libraries may be perceived and used by student-avatars and instructor-avatars as spaces that are much more integrated with other in-world formal learning spaces, such as classrooms, research labs, and field stations.

The future of library services to residents of virtual worlds seems bright. The growth of Second Life overall since 2006 has been phenomenal, and the rapid growth and evolution of the Alliance Second Life Library 2.0 project and the Info Archipelago has been astounding. Over time, we may learn that some avenues we have pursued turned out to be dead ends or false starts, but even this knowledge will be useful as the overall exploration of librarianship in virtual worlds continues apace.

CHAPTER 13

Librarianship + Technology + Instructional Design = Blended Librarian

John D. Shank
Instructional Design Librarian and Director of the Center for
Learning Technologies
Pennsylvania State University (Berks Campus)

Steven J. Bell
Associate University Librarian for
Research and Instructional Services
Temple University Libraries

> *The future of the library is that there is no library; the functions that the library performs have been blown up and are scattered throughout the universe.*
>
> —Leigh Watson Healy, Outsell Inc.

Although librarianship is often perceived by outsiders as a dull, static profession, those of us working in the field—at least anytime over the last 20 years—know the truth. Our constantly changing profession battles to keep pace, both with endlessly shifting external forces such as technology and demographics, and with high-pressure internal forces demanding our unfailing ability to connect our user communities with the information they need (wherever they are, in whatever format it's needed, and doing it all yesterday!). To maintain the library's position as a valued source of information, all librarians must evolve to meet rapidly changing user expectations and to prevent the marginalization that comes from failing to stay in touch. This chapter discusses one way in which academic librarians can meet these expectations, by blending traditional skill sets with new and different ones.

Several years ago, we began feeling that academic librarians were being marginalized by new forms of information competition. We decided that we needed to undergo a transformation in order to maintain our relevance to the user communities we served. Rather than sitting in the library waiting for faculty or students to come calling on us, the path to staying valued was to be where the users were. That meant becoming better integrated into teaching and learning spaces, both physical and virtual. Accomplishing this, we realized, would require skills we didn't learn in library school and developing a collaborative relationship with faculty—a goal that many academic librarians find elusive.

Toward this end, we identified a new skill set that, when added to existing library and information science skills, would enable academic librarians to succeed in avoiding marginalization through integrating themselves into the teaching and learning process. That new skill set combined instructional design and technology.

"Blended librarianship" is the term we use to describe the combination of librarianship, information technology, and instructional design and technology skills. Over the last few years, a growing number of librarians have been obtaining formal training in instructional design and technology, working more closely with instructional designers and technologists, or discovering how becoming more adept with the design of instructional products can lead to a greater level of involvement in teaching and learning. In particular, we advocate using these skills to create better connections, and hence better collaborative relationships, with faculty. In this chapter, we will provide an overview of blended librarianship and then explore the ways in which blended librarians use these skills to integrate themselves into learning spaces on their campuses.

A Brief History

The roots of Blended Librarianship date back to a paragraph in a 2003 article Bell published in *portal: The Library and the Academy:*

> Librarians will need more than technology savvy to achieve true integration into the teaching and learning process. Our colleagues in information technology and

instructional technology are endowed with technology skills as well. How do we differentiate ourselves in this arena? We can pursue a new role, one I refer to as the 'Blended Librarian.' The Blended Librarian first combines the traditional aspects of librarianship with the technology skills of an information technologist, someone skilled with software and hardware. Many librarians already demonstrate sound technology skills of this type. To this mix the Blended Librarian adds the instructional or educational technologist's skills for curriculum design, and the application of technology for student-centered learning. Few librarians have instructional technology skills. Library science curricula need re-structuring that adds some pedagogical foundation to the academic librarian's professional education. The Blended Librarian is the academic professional who offers the best combination of skills and services to help faculty apply technology for enhanced teaching and learning.[1]

A chance meeting took an idea from an article and turned it into something concrete. In the fall of 2003, we met at a regional teaching and learning conference when we sat next to each other during a presentation. The conversation soon turned to the Blended Librarian concept, and it occurred to us both that Bell's position was a potential model. We decided to commit the idea to further study, and to take that single paragraph and develop it into a more detailed description of what exactly Blended Librarianship would entail.

In November of 2003, after we had developed a skeletal framework for our ideas, we shared the idea with Steve Gilbert, President of the TLT Group. While Gilbert was initially curious (and possibly even skeptical) about the idea, he did provide some valuable insights into how Blended Librarianship could provide support for librarians in the area of information literacy. He also thought that an online workshop on Blended Librarianship could be of interest to academic librarians, faculty, and other academic support professionals, and asked us to develop a workshop for the TLT Group's collaborative workshop series with ACRL. The first Blended Librarians workshop was offered in April 2004. We decided to develop an articulation of our ideas about Blended Librarianship in conjunction with the workshop, which became the Blended Librarians Manifesto (later rewritten for publication in *College & Research Library News*). This document identified the rationale for Blended Librarianship, the principles upon which it was based, and the ways in which it might be practically integrated by academic librarians.

Conducting the TLT Group/ACRL online workshop also led to another significant development in Blended Librarianship. We knew from the start of our discussions about the concept that we wanted it to be more than just an article published in a journal or a one-time workshop. We sought a way to give library practitioners an opportunity to learn about Blended Librarianship, develop instructional design and technology skills, and contribute to the growth of Blended Librarianship within the profession. That opportunity presented itself when we met Hope Kandel, a production specialist at the Learning Times Network. We thought that the Network, which hosted the TLT Group online workshop, would be an ideal virtual space for a learning community for Blended Librarians.

With support from the Learning Times Network, we were able to create the Blended Librarians Online Learning Community in 2004. After two years and several more TLT Group/ACRL workshops, face-to-face workshops around the country, multiple Webcasts, and discussion board postings, the Blended Librarians Online Learning Community is a thriving enterprise with well over a thousand members. Along with the Blended Librarians Web site (blendedlibrarians. org), academic librarians now have excellent opportunities to learn about Blended Librarianship and to integrate instructional design and technology skills into their traditional skill set. In the future, Blended Librarians will be able to further explore academic librarianship by design as these principles become further integrated into Blended Librarianship.

Blended Librarian's Manifesto

This chapter began with a quote from Leigh Watson Healy of Outsell, Inc. This notion that the "future of the library is that there is no library" resonated strongly with us, because an initial impetus for our thinking about Blended Librarianship was the observation that academic librarianship was at a critical professional juncture. Our initial treatise, "The Blended Librarian's Manifesto," emerged in response to what we viewed as forces converging to marginalize the academic librarian. We called it a "manifesto" because it put forth the issues confronting academic librarianship and ways in which members of the profession could respond. First, the manifesto identified a set of observations about the current information landscape. These observations reflected on a number of trends that were contributing (or had the potential to contribute) to the marginalization of academic librarianship:

- Ubiquitous courseware systems allow faculty to create information silos that serve as gateways to all course-related information, including research sources that may or may not include the campus library.

- Textbook publishers are moving to incorporate traditional library database content into Web sites that are companion tools for students as they use the text.

- Google and other search engines! Need more be said?

- Radical transformation in scholarly publishing is creating new avenues by which scholars make their research available, potentially heralding the demise of traditional journals upon which our collections are based, and throwing into question whether libraries will continue to serve as the primary conduit for scholarly literature.

- Personalized subscription databases are marketed to individuals as an alternative to existing libraries. Questia has struggled to make this concept viable, but it's only a matter of time until a better model evolves.

- Amazon and Google "book searching," despite their inadequacies, become immensely popular almost immediately, receive tremendous media adulation, and make libraries, despite our technology, seem old and shopworn.

- The "Googlelization" phenomenon, in which librarians and database producers are driving a movement to make our systems emulate Google, makes us look desperate and fearful that our days of teaching end-users to develop efficient research skills are over.

To us, these trends suggested that if the future is one in which there is no library—or at least the library that exists as our traditional communal paradigm of what an academic library is supposed to be— then our profession was at the perfect time to take the opportunity to transform the academic library and the role of the academic librarian. In the Manifesto, we wrote:

> It is imperative and no exaggeration to claim that the future of academic librarianship depends on our collective ability to integrate services and practices into the teaching and learning process. While the evolution of information literacy is a positive sign, the academic librarian is still largely tangential to what happens in or beyond the classroom. Strategies, techniques and skills are needed that can allow all academic librarians, from every sector of the library organization, to proactively advance their integration into the teaching and learning process. The framework envisioned depends largely upon the ability to collaborate with faculty, but also other campus information and instructional technologists. This framework is best expressed as the 'Blended Librarian.'[2]

Although the premise of the Blended Librarian was more theory than practice at this early stage, a simple definition evolved: "A Blended Librarian is an academic librarian who combines the traditional skill set of librarianship with the information technologist's hardware/software skills, and the instructional or educational designer's ability to apply technology appropriately in the teaching–learning process."[3] To expand further on the definition, we identified six principles for Blended Librarianship. They are:

- Taking a leadership position as campus innovators and change agents is critical to the success of delivering library services in today's "information society."

- Committing to developing campus-wide information literacy initiatives on our campuses in order to facilitate our ongoing involvement in the teaching and learning process.

- Designing instructional and educational programs and classes to assist patrons in using library services and learning information literacy that is absolutely essential to gaining the necessary skills (trade) and knowledge (profession) for lifelong success.

- Collaborating and engaging in dialogue with instructional technologists and designers, which is vital to the development of programs, services and resources needed to facilitate the instructional mission of academic libraries.

- Implementing adaptive, creative, proactive, and innovative change in library instruction can be enhanced by communicating and collaborating with newly created Instructional Technology/Design librarians and existing instructional designers and technologists.

- Transforming our relationship with faculty to emphasize our ability to assist them with integrating information technology and library resources into courses, but adding to that traditional role a new capacity to collaborate on enhancing student learning and outcome assessment in the area of information access, retrieval, and integration.

As originally perceived, Blended Librarianship would reverse the marginalization of academic librarianship by making it more central to what happens in learning spaces, both physical and virtual. The goal was never to eliminate other information competitors from those same learning spaces or to brainwash students to use only the academic library's information resources. Even in the unlikely event this could be accomplished, the actual intention was simply to integrate the academic library into the teaching and learning process in a way that would enable faculty and students to achieve better balance in their research, as well as to use the tools most appropriate for their research, from the library or otherwise. Through faculty collaboration, by providing faculty and students with digital learning materials to support their understanding and use of the library's resources, and by applying design thinking to achieve important goals, we believed Blended Librarianship could help academic librarians connect more effectively with faculty and students seeking information.

Applying Blended Librarianship in Teaching and Learning

Now that you are more familiar with Blended Librarianship, we would like to introduce some ways in which we have been putting our ideas into practice by combining design and instructional technology skills in our work. Most of these practices are geared toward creating connections with faculty. In our workshops, one of the most frequent sources of frustration for academic librarians is their inability to engage faculty in collaborative projects. For example, although Blended Librarianship can apply in many areas of librarianship, it is often regarded as a technique for enhancing an information literacy initiative—because that service is often closely connected to teaching and learning. Successful information literacy programs depend heavily on faculty collaboration; without it, they fail. So, many of the ways in which we put our Blended Librarianship philosophy to work are directed to creating the connections with faculty that will lead to more collaboration.

We often promote the idea of WIIFM, or "What's In It For Me." We have found that faculty are most engaged with library resources when they believe this will further support or promote good principles of teaching. A good example of what we mean by "good principles" can be found in Chickering and Ehrman's "Implementing The Seven Principles: Technology As Lever" (www.tltgroup.org/programs/seven.html). Their framework demonstrates how various technologies can enhance instruction and assist in selecting the most appropriate educational technologies for instructional needs. They state that, in order for technology to be truly effective, it should be consistent with these Seven Principles:

1. Good practice encourages contacts between students and faculty.

2. Good practice develops reciprocity and cooperation among students.

3. Good practice uses active learning techniques.

4. Good practice gives prompt feedback.

5. Good practice emphasizes time on task.

6. Good practice communicates high expectations.

7. Good practice respects diverse talents and ways of learning.

When faculty are introduced to a new resource, service, or teaching technique that helps them to achieve one of these principles, their "What's In It For Me" drive is satisfied. Here, we present some of our techniques that meet the WIIFM test.

Courseware: Facilitating Collaboration in the Virtual Classroom

Collaboration with faculty is one of the greatest challenges for all academic librarians, regardless of the size of their college or university. However, collaboration becomes absolutely vital if the library and its services are going to be further integrated into the curriculum, and this is an area where Blended Librarians can make a difference. An extensive body of literature discusses the various ways and means by which librarians can seek to more effectively connect with and collaborate with faculty. However, much of that literature ignores how technology tools can be used to facilitate partnerships with faculty. One such tool is courseware, or course/learning management systems like Blackboard, WebCT, and ANGEL. These courseware systems can assist librarians in sharing resources and communicating with faculty and students.

There are some barriers to overcome before librarians can use courseware to collaborate with faculty to reach their students. Many institutions have yet to involve their librarians with the campus courseware. Consequently, librarians become marginalized in the courseware environment, tangential to courseware use, and badly integrated into instructors' courses. Librarians may not even be able to establish a library presence in the courseware (other than a token link that connects students and faculty to the library's Web site). Librarians must seek to establish connections with the department that runs and maintains the courseware so that they can get access to the system and explore ways to integrate the library into the virtual course environment. Forming administrative, faculty, librarian instructional partnerships (A_FLIP)[4] lets us utilize courseware to create a greater connection with library resources and services, as well as a direct link to students who get their information from courseware.

There are two primary ways that librarians can go about integrating the library into courseware. The first is the systems-level approach, which requires librarians to collaborate at the highest level (with the administrators, developers, and programmers of courseware) to integrate a standard, global presence for the library into the system. This method allows faculty and students access to a broad range of preexisting, familiar library services and resources from within courseware. This also takes advantage of the high degree of scalability in integrating preexisting digital library services and resources, allowing large university or small college libraries to achieve this integration equally easily.

The second, course-level approach requires faculty to partner with librarians to develop customized library resources for specific courseware-enhanced courses. This differs from the systems-level method in that it is geared to customizing the content of an individual instructor's course (or possibly multiple sections of a single course). While this approach is more time-consuming and labor-intensive, it can be advantageous in that an instructor can have a librarian tailor resources specifically for his or her assignments.

As mentioned previously, courseware can be a useful tool in creating and maintaining relationships with faculty and students. Especially at the course level, courseware's resource-sharing and communication tools are two primary features that can enhance collaboration between librarians, libraries, and faculty.

Resource-sharing components of courseware can facilitate collaboration between faculty and librarians in various ways. For example, Penn State University libraries have successfully partnered with the university's ANGEL (A New Global Environment for Learning) courseware administrator to create "librarian" status user accounts, letting instructors add a librarian to their course. This feature allows a librarian to be a member of the course, with direct access to syllabi and assignments. Librarians' ability to contact a faculty member and ask to be added as a librarian to a course benefits both librarians and faculty members. The librarian sees firsthand what the instructor is assigning, which in turn saves the instructor from having to forward the information. Additionally, this feature lets librarians post information without faculty members needing to take the time to receive and load it in the course. Direct access from their course encourages students to view these materials, lowering barriers to access and providing ease and convenience.

Another benefit to both the librarian and instructor is that the resource-sharing feature can enhance librarian instruction sessions. Since librarians are now free to post materials prior to the instruction session, students get exposed to information literacy skills that better prepare them for instruction. This allows librarians to create a level playing field for all the students, and lets them move away from lecture-style instruction in favor of a more active learning approach, and faculty members benefit when students learn more of their information literacy skills outside of the classroom. Additionally, faculty members can benefit from the courseware tool that enables students to submit assignments, because this enables librarian partnerships with instructors to evaluate works related to a research assignment.

The communication elements of courseware (e-mail, chat rooms, and message boards) allow faculty to save time and increase communication with their students—as well as with librarians. A faculty member, for example, could include a librarian in a message board about a research assignment, allowing him or her to answer when students have research-specific questions. The entire class could then see the response, saving both the instructor and librarian time.

Librarians could also benefit from these communication features. By becoming a member of an entire course, the librarian has an unprecedented ability to develop and strengthen contacts with students and faculty. Not only does this lend credibility to the librarian, it also facilitates his or her ability to identify and inform faculty about students who lack basic information literacy skills.

Courseware is only a tool, and cannot in and of itself increase the collaboration between librarians and faculty. However, if used properly, courseware can be an effective tool for saving an instructor valuable class time, while also letting him or her communicate with librarians more easily. This also allows students to achieve new ease and convenience in using library resources, as well as to have increased access to and assistance from the librarian.

LTAs: Helping Faculty Save Time on Task

The phrase "low threshold application" (LTA) was coined several years ago by Steve Gilbert, President of the TLT Group. When Gilbert visited Philadelphia University in 2002, he spoke to the faculty about integrating technology into their teaching. During the talk, Gilbert explained that in his discussions about technology with faculty across the country, the top reason faculty give for avoiding the integration of technology is lack of time. Faculty claim they lack the necessary time to learn and internalize existing and new technology applications. At the time, Philadelphia University had just introduced course management software, and the adoption rate was certainly slow. During the course of Gilbert's presentation, Philadelphia University faculty identified several issues that made them resistant to learning new technologies.

In recognizing the time and learning curve barriers to faculty adoption of new technology, Gilbert described a relatively new initiative that would offer simple step-by-step instructions to give faculty a hands-on method of learning a new technology. He described this new initiative as the low threshold application, which:

- Is a new technology easily learned by faculty
- Is any technology that enhances productivity or adds a new application of technology for teaching or learning
- Takes no more than 30 to 60 minutes to learn
- Requires minimal documentation
- Is available to faculty at no cost

To promote the development and sharing of LTAs, the TLT Group sponsors an LTA section on its Web site (www.tltgroup.org/ltas.htm; you'll find an inventory of existing LTAs at zircon.mcli.dist.maricopa. edu/lta). An LTA is really a simply designed and formatted tutorial; most contain a set of step-by-step instructions supplemented with screenshots or links. Creating an LTA requires little more than a word processor and screen capture software; all LTAs are edited to ensure consistency and ease of use. Examples of the technology applications described in LTAs include "Integrating RSS Feeds Into Courseware Sites," "Using Digitized Recordings to Respond to Student Writing," and "Partnering With Students to Avoid Cut and Paste Plagiarism." Each of these LTAs is designed to introduce faculty to a new technology application that can help save time on task, enhance communication with students, or promote any of the other seven principles for good implementation of technology—and to do so in a minimal amount of time, with a short learning curve.

Although Gilbert provided multiple examples of LTAs during his Philadelphia University visit, none included library technologies. Many library resources (such as aggregator databases), however, are the exact types of technologies faculty have little time to master. Our library technologies are often thought of as simply gateways to information, but, when integrated into the learning process, they can easily be included along with other teaching technologies. A visit to the LTA site after Gilbert's presentation showed one existing library-related LTA, which described the library electronic reserve and provided some basic information and steps faculty could use to discover and make better use of the library's e-reserve service. Clearly, more LTAs about library technologies could be developed.

Bell decided to develop his own LTA that he hoped could be added to the collection. This was inspired by an actual incident in which he realized that, with some proper instruction, a faculty member could save significant time in getting course-related reading material to students. One afternoon Bell received a call from a frenzied faculty member who wanted to add a document to her e-reserve but had discovered that the library's e-reserve fax option was offline. Over the course of the conversation, Bell found that she would find an article in a newspaper or magazine that she wanted her students to read for the next class, photocopy it, fax it to the e-reserve module, and then create an entry for that document on her e-reserve page. Since most of the readings were from popular newspapers and magazines, Bell realized that the faculty member could instead simply add a persistent link to the document in one of the library's aggregator databases. That would save a great deal of time, help integrate library resources into the course, and eliminate copyright issues.

To facilitate the faculty's ability to add persistent links to their e-reserve or courseware sites, he created what is now LTA #26, "Durable Links and Downloads: Create E-Reserves with Library Content" (zircon.mcli.dist.maricopa.edu/lta/archives/lta26.php). This was the first of several library technology-based LTAs that Bell created to both promote library technologies as learning resources and make them easier for faculty to integrate into their courses. What are some other existing and potential LTAs for library technologies?

- Using table of contents alert services in e-journal collections (e.g., ScienceDirect, Kluwer Online, Emerald, ACS)

- Capturing database articles as text files and uploading captured files into courseware or e-reserves

- Locating articles in databases using exact citations supplementing the addition of articles to course sites or e-reserves

- Using direct borrow ILL options in systems such as First Search

- Using citation-formatting features found in library databases

- Using RSS technology to create "alerts" in library aggregator databases

When you think about it, many library resources make good LTAs. Our user community sees no added cost for these resources; the library has already paid for them, and, if LTAs can encourage greater use, this benefits the entire community. While library resources have sometimes come under fire for being too complex, they are hardly beyond the learning capacity of any community member. Despite a modest learning curve, when aided by an LTA, faculty members can learn how to use these resources for specific teaching and learning applications in less than an hour. They certainly meet the WIFFM test; in the long run, the learning time invested will reap many hours of saved instructional and research time. Finally, library technologies increase faculty productivity by creating easier-to-navigate paths to needed content for teaching and research.

A Blended Librarian can create an LTA. No specialized technology or programming skills are needed, but it is helpful to approach the development of an LTA with some instructional design thinking:

- Consider what information or instructional gap the LTA is intended to fill.

- Identify outcomes that the LTA should achieve when completed.

- Develop some quick prototypes to test on faculty before deciding on a final format.

- Conduct some formative evaluation during the LTA development process to identify weaknesses that require improvement.

All of these steps derive from the blending of instructional design and technology skills into our existing knowledge of library technology. Rather than simply creating tutorials, handouts, or pathfinders that we then mount on a Web site, we should allow our instructional design and technology influences to give us a different and more thoughtful approach to the development of resources like LTAs.

Digital Learning Materials: Enhancing Student Learning

Digital learning materials (DLMs), or Web-based digital resources that can be utilized for instructional purposes, are part of the next generation of digital informational formats that can be used to augment the instructional process and improve student learning. Blended Librarians can use DLMs to improve their instruction sessions, as well as assist faculty in locating and utilizing these digital resources.

Because DLMs are new, it will be helpful to further outline what they are—and what they are not. DLMs can include "learning objects," "instructional objects," "education objects," and "knowledge objects." However, some specific components help clarify DLMs. The informational elements that make up digital learning materials can include text, graphics, animations, audio, and video. DLMs can come in numerous format flavors, such as HTML, Flash, JavaScript, AVI, WMV, MP3, WAV, JPEG, and TIFF—to name just a few. Additionally, digital learning materials can take various forms, including: tutorials, simulations, demonstrations, exercises, online modules, games, experiments, and case studies. What sets them apart from more traditional formats such as monographs, periodicals, and conventional media (TV, film, photos, and overhead projectors) is that DLMs include both active-learning and assessment components that promote student learning.

DLMs offer several advantages. First, these digital resources allow students to more effectively match their ideal learning style through interaction with the content in various modes. For example, DLMs often incorporate audio and visual content, which in some cases might be the primary way students can succeed at learning. Secondly, students can practice with DLMs both inside and outside the classroom, multiple times, and at their own pace. Students also receive immediate feedback from the DLMs. This testing of their knowledge helps provide them with guidance and direction in learning new concepts and skills.

Below are a few examples of DLMs that demonstrate the new approaches to presenting, interacting, and assessing library concepts and skills:

- Texas Information Literacy Tutorial, or TILT, tilt.lib. utsystem.edu

- Plagiarism and Academic Integrity Simulation, www.scc. rutgers.edu/douglass/sal/plagiarism/intro.html

- Boolean Operators Tutorial, library.nyu.edu/research/ tutorials/boolean/tutorial.html

Librarians who utilize DLMs enhance face-to-face instruction, rather than replacing it. These digital materials promote active learning, are geared for multiple learning styles, and provide feedback and assessment. Librarians who employ DLMs in their instruction sessions will be better able to assist students in experiencing, and ultimately learning, library skills and concepts.

Faculty similarly benefit from making use of DLMs in their instruction. However, in the current environment, it is difficult for faculty to locate existing DLMs. Librarians could play a vital role in helping faculty find course-appropriate DLMs. This creates yet another tie with faculty and demonstrates the relevance of the library, as well as helps to improve student learning.

A number of institutions now create DLMs and make them available. These include nonprofit educational and professional organizations, governmental organizations, entertainment providers, and for-profit publishers. Librarians could guide faculty to these, as well as assist them in searching the various repositories, referatories, and digital libraries that house these materials. Below are a few examples of well known digital referatories and libraries that can be searched to locate DLMs:

- MERLOT, www.merlot.org/Home.po
- PRIMO, www.ala.org/CFApps/Primo/public/search.cfm
- Wisconsin Online Resource Center, www.wisc-online.com

Besides improving librarian instruction sessions, libraries can benefit when librarians collaborate with faculty to identify course appropriate DLMs, further demonstrating their relevance in the "Information Age."

Creating Community: Learning Opportunities for Blended Librarians

When thinking about Blended Librarianship, we realized that the next step should be a working organism through which library practitioners would help each other to improve their knowledge of and ability to apply the theory and practice of instructional design and technology. We wanted to provide those interested in Blended Librarianship with a mechanism to improve their ability to connect with faculty for the purpose of achieving student learning outcomes. Among the possibilities we considered were an online journal and an electronic discussion list. However, neither of those options offered the opportunities for community-type interaction we sought with others who shared our interests.

One option that did appeal to us was an online learning community. From our previous experience with the communities developed by the Learning Times Network (when Shank participated in the 2004 Online Library Conference and then again when we both delivered online Blended Librarian workshops), it seemed that LTN's online learning environment could provide an outstanding platform for a librarians' online learning community. Elluminate, the software used by Learning Times, provides a number of useful features. It allows for online conferencing; presenters can narrate their slides and respond to questions, and attendees can speak (with a microphone) as well. It contains a discussion board, which helps engage members in community conversations, and a variety of resources can be posted to the community. Members can be notified of new events and resources through regular e-mail, and those who want to join can register with ease. To facilitate our vision, we worked with Hope Kandel of the Learning Times Network, and they agreed to allow us space within their Library Community area to develop the Blended Librarian online learning community (blendedlibrarian.org).

What do members get from joining the Blended Librarian Online Learning Community? For one thing, those who attend the formal workshops we conduct can extend their learning; the community enables them to continue participating in discussions, ask questions of others with similar interests, and get access to a series of six to eight Webcasts each academic year. Our Webcast presenters have included faculty who teach instructional design, instructional designers who've provided advice on using technology for learning, and librarians using instructional design and technology to better serve their users, as well as designers and librarians who are conducting unique and cutting-edge research projects related to the integration of the library into the teaching and learning process.

The community discussion board is used to disseminate information, opinions, and reactions. Community volunteers share with members the latest articles, Web-based videos or other sources of information that communicate new methods or models in fields related to pedagogy; most focus on some application of technology for learning. Members may choose to add their own resources or comment on those identified by others. As in any community, one benefit is discovering individuals with shared interests or experiences; librarians can make contact with others working on similar projects. The community also supports learning by providing archives of all Webcasts and associated resources (reading lists, links) so that members can use them at their convenience. Members receive regular e-mail alerts from the community when new resources, archived material, or discussion board posts are added. It is clear that, in the future, online communities are going to be a powerful resource for continuous learning for librarians. The Blended Librarian Online Learning Community is a part of the exciting future of lifelong learning.

Beyond Multitasking

We hope this chapter provided greater insight into Blended Librarianship. As we have explored this concept and continue to ground it in practice, we realize that it can sometimes be misunderstood. Most frequently we find that librarians equate multitasking with being blended. That is, for the uninitiated, being blended means wearing many hats in the workplace. There are few librarians who don't juggle many jobs, each of which can include some mix of traditional library skills, such as reference, and information technology, such as using specialized computer software.

Multitasking, though, is far from synonymous with Blended Librarianship, which involves more than just being a jack-of-all-trades. Blended Librarianship focuses on the combination of specific skills, in particular instructional design and technology, to enable a library professional to better assess learning gaps and then develop and evaluate the instructional products that will resolve those gaps. The Blended Librarian is also comfortable with different instructional technologies, from document cameras to smart boards, knows how to assess which technology is most appropriate to achieve a specific learning outcome, and is aware enough to know when a technology solution may be the inappropriate choice. Though a Blended Librarian is tech savvy, he or she never forces technology on a situation; technology is sometimes the wrong solution to the problem.

What's next? Blended Librarianship is still a relatively new and forming set of concepts and practices. Its future shape will be influenced by both the needs of our user communities and those who participate in our online community. We hope you become involved in the process.

Endnotes

1. Steven J. Bell, "A Passion for Academic Librarianship: Find It, Keep It, Sustain It—A Reflective Inquiry," *portal: Libraries and the Academy* 3:4 (2003): 637.
2. Steven J. Bell and John Shank, "The Blended Librarian: A Blueprint For Redefining the Teaching And Learning Role Of Academic Librarians," *College & Research Libraries News* 65:7 (2004): 373.
3. Bell and Shank, 374.
4. John Shank and Steven Bell, "A_FLIP to Courseware: A Strategic Alliance for Improving Student Learning Outcomes," *Innovate: Journal of Online Education* 2 (2006), www.innovateonline.info/index.php?view=article&ID=46 (accessed July 3, 2006).

References

Bell, Steven J. "A Passion for Academic Librarianship: Find It, Keep It, Sustain It—A Reflective Inquiry." *portal: Libraries and the Academy* 3:4 (2003): 633–642.

Bell, Steven J. and John Shank. "The Blended Librarian: A Blueprint For Redefining The Teaching And Learning Role Of Academic Librarians." *College & Research Libraries News* 65:7 (2004): 372–375.

Brown, Tim. "Strategy by Design." *Fast Company* 95 (June 2005): 52–54.

Chickering, Arthur and Stephen C. Ehrmann. "Implementing the Seven Principles: Technology as Lever." *AAHE Bulletin*, October 1996: 3–6. Available www.tltgroup.org/programs/seven.html (accessed May 23, 2006).

DeBlois, Peter B. "Leadership in Instructional Technology and Design: An Interview." *EDUCAUSE Quarterly* 28:4 (2005): 12–17.

CHAPTER 14

Training Librarians for the Future: Integrating Technology into LIS Education

Meredith G. Farkas
Distance Learning Librarian
Norwich University

Schools of Library and Information Science (LIS) struggle with the ongoing tension between teaching theory and practice. LIS faculty tend to argue that librarians need a firm grounding in the foundational theories of the profession, while employers of information professionals often argue that library schools should be teaching students the practical skills they need to succeed in the workplace. Most library schools usually try to provide some combination of the theoretical and the practical in their curricula, but neither group seems really to feel that sufficient attention is being paid to what they believe should be the focus of LIS education.

Obviously, it is important to provide students with an understanding of the ideas that underlie what we do as librarians, especially with regard to how information is organized. Regardless of where you stand on the issue of theory versus practice, however, library school graduates have to face an increasingly competitive job market, many armed only with the knowledge and skills they develop in graduate school. If they lack the skills employers are looking for, they will find it very difficult to get a job. Library schools can offer whatever courses they feel to be important, but if they stray further from teaching students what they need to know to be successful librarians in the real world, they will be doing a grave disservice both to their students and to the profession.

Technology in Today's Libraries

Technology is now interwoven throughout every aspect of the library profession. Whether you are in public services, technical services, systems, or administration, chances are that some knowledge of computer technologies is integral to your work. This can range from understanding the ILS to designing Web content to searching databases to evaluating new library technologies to troubleshooting printer problems. Most libraries lease access to at least a few electronic databases, which has led to increased interest in the quality of the library's Web presence, since many patrons may be accessing the library from a distance. In academia, the enormous growth in distance learning over the past decade has forced public service librarians to learn how to translate their traditional services into the online medium. The growth of content in digital form has led to concerns about how to preserve and provide access to that content. Libraries have long had a key role in providing access to and preserving knowledge, and we will be an important part of ensuring continued access to knowledge in digital form. Librarians in all settings will need to become more comfortable with and knowledgeable about technology, in order to do their jobs and to meet the needs of an increasingly tech-savvy population.

While looking for my first job out of library school, I found that many employers were seeking applicants with technology skills and experience. Considering the lack of technology education in the core requirements in my program, it was rather surprising to see the skills and knowledge that employers expected of a new librarian. Obviously, for positions like Web Services Librarian or Systems Librarian, employers assume that the ideal candidate will have a strong knowledge of computer technologies. However, the jobs I was looking at were more general public service positions, such as reference, instruction, and liaison. In both public and academic libraries, I saw a large number of entry-level openings that required technology skills. Looking at job advertisements for public service librarians between February and June 2006, I found similar requirements for more than 20 positions. The ads, all requiring between zero and two years of experience, included a number of technological requirements, including the following:

- "Basic familiarity with computer programming, strong Web development skills."

- "Familiarity with course management software such as WebCT."

- "Ability to adapt to rapidly changing technologies."

- "Experience with Web page creation and editing, including familiarity with various tagging and scripting languages such as XML, HTML, PHP, etc."

- "Experience in integrating new technologies into the delivery of information services."

- "Experience instructing adult learners, particularly in the area of computer literacy."

- "Participates in the creation, enhancement, and implementation of technological tools, products, and interfaces that facilitate 24/7 study and research and promote student engagement."

- "Experience with innovative uses of technology in support of reference and instruction."

- "Experience providing virtual reference services."

- "Plays an active role in the development of institutional repository programs and digital collections."

- "Experience working with an integrated library system."

- "Knowledge of instructional design principles and techniques for both in-person and distance learners in a higher education setting."[1]

Public service librarians these days are expected to be able to translate traditional reference and instructional services to the online medium. Many create their own online pathfinders and subject guides. They develop online tutorials using HTML and screencasting software (which generates a Flash movie of one's desktop for demonstration purposes). They use social software tools to communicate with their patrons and deliver better online library services. They provide reference services via online chat and instruction via co-browsing. While at the reference desk, they may be asked to do everything from online research, to troubleshooting a remote student's database access problem, to dealing with a printer jam. Public service librarians who don't have these skills will find themselves unable to provide the services needed by their patrons, and may end up frequently taping out-of-order signs on computers and printers they don't know how to troubleshoot.

As library budgets shrink, fewer administrators have the luxury of hiring both a Web developer and a reference librarian, or a systems librarian and a liaison to the sciences. Instead, administrators are forced to ask much more of their job candidates. Over the past few years, we've seen more and more positions with titles like Web/Reference Librarian and Research Librarian/Information Technology Specialist. Especially in libraries where much of the staff has been employed for a decade or more, administrators expect new librarians to come in with the technology skills the rest of the staff may lack. A recent study of entry-level job advertisements between 1982 and 2002 found that employers over the years have been asking more and more of their applicants, and that now "employers require experience and knowledge that cannot always be gained from library school."[2] The study found that for reference librarian positions, computer experience was required in more cases—26 percent vs. 17 percent—than was reference experience. Of entry-level reference positions, 39 percent required computer knowledge and skills. With employers asking so much more of new librarians, it's important that what is taught in library school reflects these changing expectations.

At the same time that public service jobs are calling for stronger technology skills, we are also seeing an explosion of new positions that simply didn't exist a decade ago. In academic libraries, in particular, but also in some larger public libraries, we are seeing a growing number of Digital Services Librarians, Distance Learning Librarians, Electronic Resources Librarians, Metadata Librarians, Web Services Librarians, eBranch Librarians, and Digital Repository Services Librarians. Libraries that create positions like this recognize the need to keep up with the latest technologies and with their patrons who may be accessing resources remotely. New library and information professionals also have opportunities to work outside of libraries as consultants, technology evangelists, and knowledge managers. All of these positions tend to require a high comfort level with bleeding-edge technologies—something rarely taught in library schools. Where are LIS students supposed to obtain the skills they need for positions like these? Often, those who land these positions have prior experience in the technology sector or have learned markup and programming languages as a hobby. People who enter library school with no technology experience and expect to land one of these jobs may find it difficult to get the skills they need through their LIS program.

Whether or not specific jobs explicitly require these technological competencies, it is still important for librarians to have tech skills. We must begin to play a leading role in shaping new technologies, rather than simply being swept along with the tide. The lack of usability in most OPACs is due, in part, to librarians asking for the wrong things and not thinking enough about usability on the patron's side. We need to understand usability principles and how our library systems work so that we can advocate for things that would benefit our patrons. We need to be able to evaluate different products, such as link resolvers, citation managers, and chat reference software. We need to be able to create a Web presence that engages visitors and effectively communicates information to our patrons. We need to be able to talk to our IT department about the things the library needs. How will we be able to speak the language of our IT staff if we know nothing about technology? If they say something can't be done because of security concerns, for example, how will we know if that is even true? Ignorance of technology puts us in a position where we can easily be taken advantage of and where we may not be able to provide adequate services to our patrons.

The argument could be made that librarians can simply hire technologists without a library degree to run the ILS, design and maintain the Web site, create online tutorials, and do any other computer-related tasks. While most libraries run on the work of many non-degreed library workers, it is wrong to assume that the development of library technology fails to require an understanding of library science. Often, online library services are simply virtual translations of library services in the physical world. Librarians with Web design skills can better translate information literacy objectives into the online medium than someone with no background in library science. They can better design online library services based on traditional library principles. Librarians should treat the development of online tools the same way they treat those in the physical world. It isn't just about being able to create a Web site, or being able to use a piece of software. Technology shouldn't be thought of as completely divorced from traditional library services; it is complementary, and its implementation requires a thorough grounding in the foundations of library science. While technologists can certainly help develop online tools, librarians need to be able to act as a bridge between the tech world and the library world.

LIS Education in a Changing Tech Landscape

LIS schools have recognized this changing landscape to varying degrees. Some library schools offer degrees in Library Science (MLS) and Information Studies (MSIS), one focusing more on *people* and the other focusing more on *computers*. Some only offer a few technology-related classes as electives, while sticking to a very traditional library school curriculum. Other schools design specializations in areas such as digital librarianship, information architecture, human–computer interaction, or information technology. Very few schools, though, make technology education a part of the core required courses for the degree; technology is seen as somehow separate from librarians' core competencies. Making technology a separate (and often elective) part of the curriculum, though, ignores the importance of computer knowledge for new librarians. In order that library schools truly prepare students to be 21st-century library and information professionals, technology needs to be a central part of the curriculum, and needs to be integrated into every course.

I went into my Master of Library and Information Science (MLIS) program wanting to become a traditional public service librarian—but also wanting to be prepared for the future of the profession. To me, being a 21st-century librarian meant being tech-savvy and understanding how to apply technology to traditional library services. In spite of the fact that many of my classmates were not getting their degree in order to work in a library, most of the core-required classes were designed to prepare individuals to work in libraries as traditionally conceived. While they introduced us to information policy, how to do scholarly research, how to provide reference assistance, how to manage people, and how information is organized, none of the core courses really taught us anything about technology. According to the requirements, a student could actually go through the entire program without ever having to take a technology-related course. This sends a message to students that technology is only a part of some library positions. It tells them that if they want to be a reference librarian or a youth services librarian, they really won't need to know how to design a Web site, fix a printer, or evaluate technologies. When providing library services to an increasingly mobile and tech-savvy patron population, though, librarians of all kinds will need not only some basic computer skills but the ability to keep up with the rapid changes in the way in which we provide library services.

Another problem with technology instruction in the LIS curriculum is the extent to which technology classes are disconnected from traditional library school classes. I took 18 of my 42 credits in technology related courses (literally, all of the technology classes offered for distance learners), and learned about database design, information retrieval, Web design, usability, and network administration. Libraries were mentioned rarely in these courses. When discussing usability, we didn't evaluate *library* Web pages. In my Web design classes, we didn't discuss how to design and manage *library* Web sites. Network administration didn't cover proxy servers, managing an ILS, or even maintaining a network in a library. The classes were not at all geared toward being practical *for librarians,* and could just as well have been taught through a completely different department.

Libraries were integrated into the technology courses as little as technology was integrated into the library courses. While I learned how to design a Web page in library school, I really didn't learn the first thing about how library Web pages are designed and organized, much less how to create an online tutorial. This further promotes the idea that "library work" and "information science work" are two very different things. No classes taught us ways to cope with technological change, how to manage technology projects, or how to evaluate technologies. These "big picture" topics are among the most important technological competencies librarians can have in the coming years, as technologies continue to change at a rapid pace.

Ideas and Examples

Not all library schools are doing a poor job of teaching technology. Some programs have managed to integrate technology into their core curriculum, to develop courses that offer skills for integrating technologies into libraries, or to ensure that their students have enough practical knowledge about information technologies to succeed in the profession. At the University of Maryland College of Information Studies (www.clis.umd.edu), for example, information technology is one of the five core courses required for the MLS. The program also offers a course on the principles of software evaluation to help librarians learn to evaluate applications for use in libraries—a skill that will prove useful, even as specific technologies change. The University of North Texas (www.unt.edu/slis) and Syracuse University (www.ist.syr.edu) both

offer courses related to technology project management and managing technological change in libraries. Other schools offer courses in
Web design and other technologies and how they can specifically be
applied in libraries and related environments.

Some schools have technology requirements outside of their
course offerings. One way to ensure that students attain a minimum
acceptable level of practical computer knowledge during their LIS
education is to require that they pass an exam covering the computer
knowledge necessary to at least meet the requirements of most entry-
level librarian positions. For instance, whether they took HTML
classes in library school, learned their Web design skills previously, or
simply studied a book, all grads would leave with enough Web design
skills to provide basic services to patrons online. Simmons Graduate
School of Library and Information Science (www.simmons.edu/gslis)
developed a Technology Orientation Requirement (TOR) that every
student must complete before registering for their second semester of
classes. This requirement includes a series of tasks—including designing a Web page in HTML—to demonstrate the minimal level of technological proficiency that a GSLIS student should have. While the
requirements of the TOR are not as rigorous as the skills library
employers seek, the idea of ensuring that all students meet a minimum level of technological competence is a step in the right direction.

The Information School at the University of Washington
(www.ischool.washington.edu) requires MLIS students to complete a
portfolio demonstrating that they have developed the skills and
attributes needed by a successful information professional. This list
of attributes includes technology skills and experience. Most students in the program develop their portfolios online, which serves
the dual purpose of sharpening their Web design skills and of creating a portfolio to show to potential employers post-graduation.

Integration, Translation, and Change

It is impossible to identify one specific core list of technological
knowledge that every librarian needs to be successful; this will differ
with each job. Web design and the ability to translate reference and
instructional services into the online medium seem to be the skills
currently most in-demand for public service librarians, but different
position types will require different skills. No 36-to-42 credit LIS program can offer students enough courses to give them both a thorough

grounding in the topics central to librarianship and enough technology competence to become an expert systems administrator or Web designer. Librarians, of course, will also acquire a great deal of practical knowledge during their practicum (if offered) and in their first professional library job. However, LIS schools should at least teach the basic foundations of information technology.

A successful LIS program will not only offer courses in information technologies such as Web design, database administration, and network administration, but will also offer courses that teach students how to manage and evaluate technologies. The one constant in the technological landscape is change, and the best skills LIS schools can teach graduates include how to see the big picture, manage change, critique and troubleshoot technologies, and plan for the technological future of their institution. Technology should be integrated throughout the LIS curriculum and should be a part of nearly all courses, just as technology is a part of nearly all library functions. Programs should give students the opportunity to practice their technological skills in the same ways that they will likely be using the technologies in their professional lives; technology should never be divorced from the environment in which it will be practiced. Requiring a practicum can help library school students to see the realities of the profession they're about to enter and the ways in which technology permeates everything librarians do.

The ideal librarian of the future will be comfortable with technology, able to view it as the tool that it is, and have the vision to see how technologies can be applied in their environment to provide better services to patrons. It is up to our LIS schools to nurture these skills in the library leaders of tomorrow.

Endnotes

1. These job advertisements appeared in American Libraries' Hot Jobs Online (www.ala.org/ala/education/empopps/careerleadsb/hotjobs online/hotjobsonline.htm) and Combined Job Postings from Library Job Postings on the Internet and LISjobs.com (www.lisjobs.com/jobs) between February and June 2006.
2. Claudene Sproles and David Ratledge, "An Analysis of Entry-Level Librarian Ads Published in American Libraries, 1982–2002," *Electronic Journal of Academic and Special Librarianship* 5:2–3 (2004): 19, southern librarianship.icaap.org/content/v05n02/sproles_c01.htm (accessed June 18, 2006).

CHAPTER 15

Technophobia, Technostress, and Technorealism

Jessamyn West
Community Technologist

It's easier to obtain technology for a library than to obtain technology know-how and enthusiasm, both among library staff and library patrons. As more of the information we provide is digital, more different kinds of library workers have to add "working with technology" to their job descriptions and their skill sets. However, while collection development, for example, is a skill many of us learned in school, creating and working in a library technology environment is not. While we grapple with the changing face of our profession, we need also to look at the large and important social and emotional component involved in dealing with change in general, and technological changes in particular. Stress is a part of most working environments, so what makes working with computers and technology different?

In part, this difference is due to the technology environment and the ways in which it is unlike any other environment that has come before. With most mechanical labor-saving or entertainment devices, we have both an expectation of certain levels of knowledge and competence among users (think driving a car), as well as clear lines of responsibility when something goes wrong (call the electrician, the TV repair man, or the cable company). The quirky technological combination of hardware, software, and Web-based tools, though, defies easy compartmentalization and analysis; the interconnectedness of all things technological makes fixing nebulous "computer problems" more like going in for a physical and less like grabbing an aspirin from the medicine cabinet. Add to this the rapid pace of change, the widely varying levels of competence and experience among both staff and patrons, and the murky meld of free, cheap, and expensive hardware and software bundled with dense and intractable licenses and terms of service and it's no wonder that many people find this environment stressful.

Technostress, however, is truly a human problem, brought about by human attitudes toward machines and toward other people dealing with machines. While this stress manifests itself around computers, it's simply a repackaging of existing communication breakdowns and missteps. The fact that computers persist, and that their role in our profession is uncertain, yet growing, exacerbates a problem that might otherwise be better attended to. This chapter focuses on anecdotes, suggestions, and a look at the human and mechanical systems that affect libraries' ability to deal effectively with technology—with an emphasis on realistic approaches to some fairly typical scenarios. I'll be mostly talking about computer- and Internet-based technologies, though many of the issues described could just as easily apply to any new workplace system.

Where I'm Typing From

As a librarian, as well as a technology user and educator, I have spent the last decade observing how technology has moved into libraries, how it has been received by staff and patrons, and how it has been presented to the public. As a librarian blogger, I've watched library workers and patrons use the Internet to spread their ideas about how technology in libraries works, how it doesn't work, and how it should work.

I move between worlds. I spend much of my time helping rural libraries and their patrons learn to use technology. I also travel widely and talk to people in nonrural areas about the digital divide, what they can do about it, and why it matters. I'm a second generation technology power user and advocate—my father built mainframe computers in the 1970s and 1980s—and I've always thought that mucking about with computers was more like playing video games than actual work. I'm definitely older than the "born with the chip" generation, and yet I approach technological challenges as someone who looks at new opportunities with technology and says "Why not?"

It took me a while to realize that this approach is atypical in our profession. While there are many technology advocates among our ranks, they are the exception rather than the rule. There is a bit of a conflict between the roles of organizing and archiving the collected knowledge of a culture, and advocating new ways of connecting and accessing new (and old) information.

Or is there?

What Is It?

Technostress is a made-up word that describes a particular sort of reaction to technological change and expectations. Many librarians have attempted to hammer out definitions, a few of which I'll list here:

- "A condition resulting from having to adapt to the intro-duction and operation of new technology, particularly when equipment, support, or the technology itself is inad-equate." —Nina Davis-Millis[1]

- "A modern disease of adaptation caused by an inability to cope with the new computer technologies in a healthy manner. It manifests itself in two distinct ways: in the struggle to accept computer technology, and in the more specialized form of over identification with computer technology." —Craig Brod[2]

- "'Technostress' (computer-related stress), a common problem for reference librarians in the 1990s, is a combi-nation of performance anxiety, information overload, role conflicts, and organizational factors." —John Kupersmith[3]

As you can see even by reading these brief definitions, technos-tress is a loaded term that is very tightly wrapped up in people's atti-tudes and concepts about what a normative approach to technology might look like. People who love and enjoy technology think that the root of technostress lies with those reluctant to "embrace change." People who dislike or distrust technology often blame the people who approach technology decision points with "technolust" in their hearts. While our profession usually likes to hammer out best practices for everything, the customizable nature of technology, as well as the way its usage has grown in libraries, makes a one-size-fits-all approach to technostress impractical, if not impossible.

I should also note the related term "technophobia," in which attitudes about technology actually impede people's ability to use technology in their daily lives. We must be mindful that, while stresses are not necessarily negative—they can encourage us to seek changes or improve systems—a phobic reaction to something that is necessary in the workplace is a problematic situation.

The Information "Don't Care" and Others

In presentations about the digital divide, I often talk about the information poor, but I also discuss a group that I call the "information don't care." These are people who don't use computer technology, aren't tech-curious, and, when given technological approaches to problem solving, will often opt for a nontechnological solution if one is available. Many of us know people who are like this in some facet of their lives. I don't have a cell phone, for example, even though there are times when one would be convenient. I have a neighbor who doesn't drive, relying on neighbors to take him to and from the supermarket and doctor's appointments. I know people without computers, credit cards, cable television, and other conveniences that others consider indispensable.

The question becomes: "At what point is your lack of ability to use a technology to do basic tasks inhibiting your ability to interact with society?" Generally, I try to respect people's choices about how they want to live their lives, and I rarely proselytize about computers to people who have no interest in learning about them. However, more and more often, we are seeing people for whom the lack of computer ability becomes a sudden troubling impediment. Here are a few examples:

- A person newly on the job market wants to apply for jobs at a local employer and finds that the only way to fill out a job application is through a somewhat complicated multi-page form, which is only available online.

- A person who is elected to a governance position within an organization realizes that communication with other members of the organization is entirely via e-mail. (I have seen this happen with organizations as large as the American Library Association and as small as the local garden club.)

- A person in an area that is hit by a natural disaster must apply for emergency relief and has two options: trying to make a phone call to a number that seems constantly busy, or filling out a series of forms online.

In a library situation, educating and assisting computer novices in doing these things is challenging, but doable. The job becomes significantly more difficult if patrons—or especially staff—are laboring under the weight of added technostress.

Technostress Is Other People

The previous examples could be made even more problematic by misunderstandings, miscommunications, or, more frequently, policies that come between the technology users, the technology providers, and the technology itself. A few more technostressful examples follow, modified from the first set.

- A person who is not very computer savvy has to fill out a job application online and needs staff assistance, as well as more time than the 45 minutes allowed by the computer scheduling software. Staff are anxious about giving the patron too much assistance, and do not know how to override the computer timer software.

- A person in a new governance position within her organization gets a new e-mail account and suddenly has to deal with 10 to 20 messages per day, many of which are difficult to read on the library's computers. Staff cannot change the settings on the monitors on a per-patron basis, so suggest she just print out the messages she wants to read at a larger font size.

- A person using a library computer to apply for disaster relief discovers that the library's computer will not reproduce the forms that he needs to fill out online. Staff are unclear if the problem is with their browser, their PDF reader, the Web site the patron is trying to access, or their security settings.

When I tell people I am writing about technostress, the first thing they tell me about, without exception, is some crazy new computer policy that they have to deal with at work. Usually this policy is in response to some other Bad Computer Event that happened at work. The second round of stories usually involves patrons at the public library and the chaos that they cause, or public library computers and the way they are unlike any other computers on earth. If there's still time, the third round of computer stories usually concerns the person's own computer and something that's hinky with it. However, the factor that always makes a normal "I had a bad day with my computer" story into a tale of technostress is the addition of *other people*. There's a tech guy in Bangalore, or a nephew who tried to help, or the mandates of the Gates Foundation, or the busy librarian, or the confused patron, that took a normal human–computer interaction and made it stressful—technostressful.

So Much Technostress, So Close to Home

Technostress is both a relative and an absolute condition. Most frequently there is a statement of self-evaluation that people use when describing their relationships to technology either at work or at home. Often, this is not described as "technostress" per se, but as basic problems with computers that are difficult to deal with and hard to adequately resolve. Usually the technostress moniker is applied to *other people* who have this problem, either by people who are managing them, or being managed by them. Not understanding a specific technology is an individual problem, exacerbated by real or imagined feelings of "having" to be able to use it. Technostress is a reflection of a systemic problem—an outgrowth of expectations and abilities that don't match, along with no clear end to this mismatch in sight.

Put another way, when I can't use something technologically in my personal life, I have a clear set of choices:

- Learn to use it.

- Find someone else who can use it and get them do whatever I need to do with it.

- Decide I can live without whatever benefits that particular technology offers me.

When I can't use technology at my job, I have a much more muddled set of choices, including some of the ones listed earlier but also options such as:

- Assigning someone else to handle the technology that I can't use.

- Getting my manager to make someone else responsible for the technology I can't use.

- Modifying or fixing the technology so I can use it.

- Getting someone else to repair the technology so that I can use it.

- Switching technologies to one that I can use (especially software).

- Obtaining on-the-job training to learn the technology.

- Determining that what I am being asked to do technologically isn't part of my specific job, or even part of the library's job in general.

- Quitting, crying, having a tantrum, becoming sullen and surly—and other unrealistic options for librarians, but perhaps sometimes seen in our patrons.

Most of the time, even for library professionals, it can be tough even to determine where the problem lies. My gut feeling is that there are many people, in libraries and elsewhere, who would happily live their lives without computers if their jobs didn't require a certain level of technological interaction. Similarly there are other people, myself among them, who would have a difficult time conceiving of a job—or even a living situation—without computers or the ubiquitous Internet. When these two types of people work together, depending on who is in charge, conflicts arise. This often results in technostress.

One of the largest contributors to technostress is the difficulty in determining a "normal" amount of computer know-how or ability, especially in a professional setting. At the same time as we try to develop lists of core competencies, we are still having the debate about whether technological skills generally are important, or even essential, skills for all new librarians. I went to library school in the mid-1990s—does this mean that I don't need to learn to use Google? Of course not. And yet many members of the profession, both old and new, make the argument that they should be held to a low standard of technical know-how where computers are concerned. There are many oft-cited reasons for this, a few of which I outline here:

1. They didn't learn how to do it in school, and therefore it's not one of their competency areas.

2. The library has other people who "know computers." Therefore, it's not their job, just like everyone doesn't need to know how to be a children's librarian.

3. Technology is changing so quickly that attaining competency is impossible.

4. It's not the library's job to teach people how to use computers. We don't teach them how to read; we just provide books.

5. The job didn't require technology skills when the librarian applied for it.

You can see the lines being drawn in the sand. Unlike an *obvious* requirement for a library job, like literacy, for example, it's harder to explain exactly why tech-savviness is required and in what instances. This explanation becomes harder still for managers who may not possess these skills themselves.

Technostress in Libraries, a Management Issue

John Kupersmith is a reference librarian at the University of California, Berkeley, who has written about technostress in libraries. He breaks down the problems involved in technostress and reference librarians into a few discrete categories:

- *Performance anxiety* – Being concerned that you are being judged by your ability to use technology, especially when trying to demonstrate it to someone else. As Kupersmith says: "It is hard—and stressful—to suppress one's anger at clumsy design when teaching a user how to get around in a frustrating system, yet we know that we must do this and project a positive attitude for the user's sake."[4]

- *Information overload* – This involves not just learning about an ever-expanding set of new resources and tools, but also quickly achieving a level of competency so that you can explain it to new (or experienced) users.

- *Role conflicts* – Librarians feel that they are shifting from highly skilled reference work to doing more general tech support for everyone, which seems like a "deprofessionalization" of their position as well as a demotion of sorts.

- *Organizational factors* – The larger organization makes choices about how many people are needed to address a certain task, or how much technology is needed to assist a certain number of patrons. When these numbers are off, or the perception is that they are off, people feel overworked, or that they are not being supplied with technology they feel that they need.

- *Burnout* – When day-to-day stresses build up, staff and sometimes patrons can become exhausted.

Kupersmith's list was originally published in 1992. I would add a couple of my own points:

- *Money* – In today's lean budgetary times, technology is still expensive. Trying to determine how to budget for technology in the present and future when there are already budget shortages is a real challenge, and the proper balance of tech to nontech expenditures is often contested by patrons and staff.

- *Middleman syndrome and powerlessness* – Vendors and their products make up a larger part of the library budget than they did 10 years ago. Many technology products come in barely customizable forms with uncertain pricing structures and pricey support agreements. More libraries are members of consortia that make technology decisions in a one-size-fits-all fashion. The librarians work with technology that is not of their choosing and not customizable by them.

Kupersmith has suggestions for what people can do on a personal level: relaxation, time management, being healthy, setting sensible goals, and thinking positively. He also has a longer list of what organizations can do for their stressed-out employees, and, to a lesser degree, their patrons. These include such solutions as being supportive in word and deed, training staff, distributing expertise among many staff members, lowering everyone's anxiety level by not being a taskmaster, and not setting the stakes so high.

If the problems and their solutions are so straightforward, why are these issues—which were raised 15 years ago—still plaguing us today?

In short, problems arise when there is more than one stakeholder in a library interaction involving technology—often the patrons vs. the institution, or staff vs. management. The lack of clear technology directions and priorities causes anxiety, which, when left unmanaged, leads to ongoing stress. Technological problems often involve the classic "too many cooks" scenario, where everyone has *some* responsibility, but it's difficult to determine who has final responsibility.

What We Talk About When We Talk About Technostress

When technostress is seen as a communication problem rather than simply a problem of bad technology or stubborn people, we can work toward solutions. When you discuss technology in your organization, or with your patrons, here are some strategies for making sure your discussions address some of the fuzzy edges of computer problems.

Jessamyn's Technostress Talking Points

Clear Outlines

"What we are trying to do for you."

Make sure it's clear what problem you are trying to solve, how you are handling it, and how long you think it will be until there is some resolution.

Examples:

- Don't just say: "We're waiting for the computer guy to come in." Instead, explain that the computers need more memory for the new operating system, he does all your upgrades, and he's here on Wednesdays.

- Don't just say: "We're switching to Firefox." Instead, explain that you are doing this to minimize browser crashes and annoying popups, without creating a steep learning curve.

- When a patron comes in to a library and faces a technological barrier (can't plug in an iPod, can't read files off of a USB drive, can't print from a floppy drive, can't download an attachment), make sure the patron knows when and if that problem will be fixed. If the problem will not be fixed, make sure the patron understands the policy that governs that issue and that they know how to challenge the policy.

Clear guidelines

"What is and is not our problem. What is and is not our responsibility."
We have a Library Bill of Rights to govern our basic policies toward patrons and their rights in our libraries. We should have Internet use policies. What can our patrons expect from our technology? Uptime? Updatedness?

Examples:

- Make sure staff understand the Internet use policy for patrons, including how it is enforced and how it is amended.

- Make sure your organization has an acceptable use policy for staff.

- Make sure your patrons know when computers will be fixed or what is wrong with them.

Clear understanding of the partnership

"We learn as you learn."
Very rarely is any computer issue simple. Staff may be learning on the job as patrons are also trying to understand. Being transparent about this partnership, learning from our patrons as they learn from us, makes us responsive, human, and part of the solution.

Examples:

- When a patron comes in with a new technology that they want to use with library computers—USB drives, iPods, Bluetooth widgets—try to understand what it does and why people use it. Try to make speedy decisions about whether to implement new technologies at the library. If you can't let people use iPods on library computers, at least be able to explain why to patrons.

- Consider some sort of a patron technology board to advise the library on technological directions.

- If your library spends money and time on staff technology training, make sure they come back to the library prepared to share what they have learned.

We are used to always playing the expert, yet the increasing role of technology in our libraries means that, as librarians, we have to be prepared to be part of a larger discussion involving our local communities, our vendors, our staff, and the people who come to our library—both in person and online.

What's Next?

Ours is a polite profession. This can sometimes be our undoing. We want to be able to say yes to every patron, yes to every staff request, yes to every purchasing order. Limited resources, though—time and money in particular—keep us from doing that. Instead of getting good at saying: "No, but here's why ..." we've developed a tendency to say: "Yes, maybe ..." Our inability to deliver becomes more glaring in an age of increasing transparency and accountability.

Technology is part of every librarian's job. Technology will continue to evolve at a rate that will evade our best efforts to stay completely on top of it. Our patrons' range of abilities will widen as the savvy get savvier and the novices remain at square one. This does not threaten us; this keeps us in business.

While we must be mindful of not allowing technostress to turn into technophobia, we should also be listening to what it is telling us. Stress tells us that something isn't working properly. Stress can encourage us to seek changes. Stress can motivate us to improve systems. While working out small solutions to the day-to-day technology interactions that we face, we should also be looking at our systems— computer systems, human systems, procedural systems—seeking out those technostress points, and fixing them.

Technostress is not about hard-to-use computers or cranky librarians or insensate patrons. It is a communication problem and a management problem, and can and should be dealt with accordingly. You can do it. We can do it. This is why we do what we do.

Endnotes

1. Nina Davis-Millis, "Technostress and the Organization. A Manager's Guide to Survival in the Information Age" (presented at the 67th Annual Meeting of the Music Library Association, Boston, Massachusetts, February 14, 1998), web.mit.edu/ninadm/www/mla.htm (accessed September 4, 2006).

2. Craig Brod, *Technostress: The Human Cost of the Computer Revolution*, Reading, MA: Addison-Wesley, 1984: 16; quoted in John Kupersmith, "Technostress and the Reference Librarian," www.jkup.net/tstr_ref.html (accessed September 4, 2006).
3. John Kupersmith, "Technostress and the Reference Librarian," *Reference Services Review* 20:2 (1992): 8–10, www.jkup.net/tstr_ref.html (accessed September 4, 2006).
4. Kupersmith, "Technostress and the Reference Librarian."

Recommended Reading

Assessing and Managing Technostress by Richard A. Hudiburg, www2.una.edu/psychology/alatalk.htm

Library Technostress Survey Results—John Kupersmith, www.jkup.net/tstress-survey-2003.html

A Manager's Guide to Survival in the Information Age by Nina Davis-Millis, web.mit.edu/ninadm/www/mla.htm

Managing Technostress in UK Libraries: A Realistic Guide by Stephen Harper, www.ariadne.ac.uk/issue25/technostress

Technostress and the Reference Librarian—John Kupersmith, www.jkup.net/tstr_ref.html

CHAPTER 16

Reading Tea Leaves:
One Past, Many Futures

Alane Wilson
Former Senior Library Market Consultant, OCLC

The future is here. It's just not evenly distributed yet.

—William Gibson

Libraries of all types in North America exist uneasily in two spaces. One space is physical, a place of history, nostalgia, local presence, and deep roots, a place perhaps now more of the imagination than of reality. The second space is virtual, where geography is as yet not completely discovered, where rules of engagement are not fully formed, and where the titans of physical spaces struggle to define themselves. Libraries, like religious institutions and museums, have been successful in defining their roles in their physical communities—but have discovered that merely translating those roles into the virtual world fails to reproduce that success.

As the data show in OCLC's 2005 report, *Perceptions of Libraries and Information Resources*,[1] awareness of many types of library resources is low, trust in library materials and librarians is about equivalent to that of search engines, and people are not likely ever to start seeking information at a library Web site.

While it is possible that people's information-seeking habits and preferences have not actually changed much since the early part of the 20th century,[2] the abundance of content (and increasingly easy access to that content) brings attention to the continued relevance of and need for libraries. And yet, when asked, the communities served by libraries clearly value the existence of the physical space called "the library." How do we reconcile these two vastly different spaces, one the space of the imagination, and the other the imagination of space? This is the overarching challenge of librarianship in the next few years. The values of one space are sometimes antithetical to those of the second space, but libraries must compete successfully in both arenas.

Predicting the future is a mug's game. Predictions either do or do not come to pass. Unless one is running bets on the predictions, being right or wrong isn't helpful in trying to chart the course of a business or a library. How, then, to read the tea leaves for the future of libraries without falling into the seductive and relatively easy trap of making bombastic predictions about the role and place of technology in this future?

A common technique in library planning is to assume that the future is based on the past and is singular, a straight line extrapolation from the present. But, this type of tea leaf reading usually fails to take into account the environmental factors that may—or may not—change society in general, and which then have an impact on libraries. It is often the case that human nature is underestimated or ignored in straight-line predictions, which go something like this: "Technology has made it possible for all content to be available anywhere, so now there will be no need for libraries." This sort of prediction by technophiliacs ignores the demonstrated human preference to be among other humans in socially neutral and comfortable spaces. The coffee shop, the mall, and the library are not suffering from lack of visitors.

Basing a library's technological future on current tools and services is not really reading any tea leaves; it is indulging in tunnel vision. One example will illustrate. Based on current and past usage of in-house computers, it might seem sensible to plan to add hundreds more computers to a library. However, data[3] suggest that "tethered" computers will likely soon give way to predominantly mobile computers (cell phones and PDAs, for example) in North America—as they already have in countries such as South Korea and Finland. An "inside out" approach to planning would justify the installation of desktop computers, whereas an "outside in" approach would suggest a very different plan.

For reasons too numerous to address here, library planning of the "inside out" sort has focused overly much on technology as the driver of change, rather than on the social trends that drive technology adoption. Indeed, much of the recent discussion about Web 2.0 and Library 2.0 applications and services in libraries has focused on the technology itself, rather than on the trends in human behavior in a Web 2.0 world that suggest the type of services libraries might offer.

Ignoring trends in the use of mobile devices explains in part why so many libraries shortsightedly ban cell "phones"—which are increasingly used to access, create, and house text, video, music, and photos and to share, collaborate within, and inhabit a digital space lying parallel to the physical one. In a world where convenience, accessibility, immediate gratification, and comprehensiveness are valued, library planning in general focuses too much on the mechanics of information delivery, and not enough on the social life of information. The rate of change in the mechanics of information delivery is much, much faster than the rate of change in human behavior. Planning based around the realities of human nature is likely to have a longer shelf life.

In the 2002 preface to their seminal 2000 work (one I strongly recommend readers revisit), *The Social Life of Information,* John Seely Brown and Paul Duguid write:

> Where many old technologies inherently forced people together in factories, office buildings, schools and libraries, new ones tempt them to stay apart, working for organizations without working in one, joining schools or libraries without going to one. … Rather than simply taking place for granted or celebrating placelessness, people must now struggle with these conflicting forces, trying to find the best resolution for particular situations and specific needs. To play a helpful part in this struggle, designers of buildings, organizations, interactions and technologies will find the intricacies of the 'lure of the local' more important than the simplicities of the death of distance.[4]

A better way to read the tea leaves is to recognize that the future is an extrapolation of the present, not a linear path. Librarians can learn about possible futures by looking at trends in many different arenas—technology, demography, politics, social behavior—to develop foresight that helps identify opportunities and challenges, and gain confidence in planning.

Here are a few techniques futurists use in developing foresight[5]:

- *Scanning* – This is an ongoing activity that focuses mainly on identifying and following trends (evolving changes) rather than events. It is a systematic survey of, mostly, media, such as magazines, blogs, videos, and newspapers.

- *Trend Analysis* – Trends are examined to determine their potential impacts on particular arenas. For example, the trend of the rise in reading newspapers on the Web has a different impact for the newspaper industry than it does for libraries.

- *Scenario Development and Analysis* – Scenarios are pictures from the future, seeking to show several plausible ways that current trends might extrapolate into the future. They are helpful in aiding understanding of the impact of particular decisions.

Libraries may exist uneasily in two spaces, the physical and the virtual, but, increasingly, people happily exist in both. In a 2006 article,[6] Scott Bennett distills the factors inherent in the challenge of relevancy for (academic) libraries into three main areas: the substitution of digital culture for the culture of the book; the convenience of digital information and the productivity gains this brings about; and the increasing ability people have to live within virtual environments. And, yet, as he notes, physical libraries continue to be built, celebrated, and used. Planning within this paradox is clearly necessary.

In the *OCLC Environmental Scan*,[7] we wrote of the importance of the physical library as one of the places in the "third space." Ray Oldenburg first wrote about third spaces and their importance to communities in 1989,[8] long before the ubiquity of the Web. But the emergence of digital culture has not dispensed with our need and desire for physical third spaces. Understanding the power of public spaces is central to planning for the physical library where the focus must shift from warehousing content to providing the community with opportunities for coming together in an active social environment. The irony of the preceding sentence is that its imperative has absolutely nothing to do with being written in the early years of the 21st century. In a 1905 speech at the Minnesota Library Association, Gratia Alta Countryman said: "The library has the duty of being all things to all men. It is no longer simply a repository of books. … The sooner we unveil the 'gods of joy and good fellowship' in our library the better; and sooner we make the library a centre for all the activities among us that make for social efficiency the better."[9] Clearly, the library profession has not ever successfully reconciled the idea of the library as an efficient machine, created and supported by technology, and the idea of the library as a social space, whether the paradox is one played out in physical or virtual space.

This has a lot to do with focusing on technology as the end rather than the means to an end. Focusing on the former will build monuments. Focusing on process and social needs will allow for a recombinant physical library, one that adjusts dynamically to its community. Practically, this might suggest such things as movable desks, workstations, and walls, wireless access, adjustable lighting, different acoustical spaces, long opening hours, and flexible policies. Organizationally, this suggests staff with broad and somewhat vague job descriptions and a lot of appetite for trial and error, and the permanent, ongoing participation of both users and nonusers in the evolution of the physical space and its amenities.

It is probably a cliché to suggest that the successful and thriving library is one that is vital to its local community, participates in the life of the community, adds value to the community, and is an "idea amplifier" for community members. This success is very much related to the physical library, to its uniqueness and its sensitivity to its constituents. As long as financial and emotional support comes from the local community, whether this is the university community or the community of local geography, the success of the library will depend on its relationships within that community, not solely on the services and content available to walk-in users.

So, what of the virtual library? Most libraries, whether they are academic, public, or corporate, currently constitute their virtual selves as digital versions of their physical selves. Web sites mimic the physical organizational structure and the separation of content by type. The physical "brand" is extended virtually by offering a lot of widely available content under an institutional brand umbrella to potential users—who do not care if a particular instantiation of a database is offered by University A or Public Library B. The results for people are confusion, bad discovery experiences, and high use of easily accessed content via Google and Amazon. Here, as well, there are too many reasons to go into, but two issues exemplify the challenges.

The first issue is that libraries have constituted themselves around services (and generally still do), and these service groupings are maintained as virtual service points. The virtual seeker must hop from service area to service area to discover resources, request delivery, update personal information, and view content—and that's within a single virtual institution. The process is repeated if another library must be consulted. In the "Amazoogle" world of convenience, accessibility, and immediate gratification, this environment full of seams and walls is unacceptable. The technology is too intrusive.

The second issue is that soon there will likely be very little walk-in demand for library services as they are constituted today. This suggests that the current definitions of success that focus on collection, usage, and transaction statistics—counting widgets—will have to give way to measuring the differences library services make to those served. Jim Collins suggests in his recent monograph *Good to Great and the Social Sectors*[10] that measurement of social institutions should encompass the extent to which they deliver superior performance, make a distinctive impact, and achieve lasting endurance. These measures are ones that rely little on how much or how often or who owns what, and rely not at all on becoming "more like a business."

In a world of ubiquitous content, where there may be thousands of places to access MEDLINE, and Google and others are digitizing books, the challenge for libraries is not in the collecting of common content, whether print or digital. The challenge is in moving from merely being a high-level delivery service, moving content from publisher to library to seeker, to becoming a collaborator and participant in the lives of information seekers.

For libraries, this means dealing with the difficult issues of duplication of content (difficult because copyright and legal issues are beyond our control) and "siloed" information resources. It means removing institutional barriers between and among libraries—not just types of libraries, but all libraries. For librarians, this suggests moving away from being expert gatekeepers to, for want of a better term, content curators, actively selecting and screening information and content based on the needs of the moment. It means moving away from the sequential, "one at a time" artisanal processes of the physical world that make it impossible to teach information literacy to an entire student body, for example (assuming the slightly insulting notion that people are information illiterate survives).

Libraries need to differentiate virtually between a corporate self and a functional self. The corporate entity "the Hometown Library" exists as a part of a larger brand identity, whether that's a university or a town. It is important that this is the case, particularly with regard to funding and political support. Seekers, on the other hand, do not

care about the corporate brand when they are doing research, participating in group work, or looking for information, and should not be
made to navigate the corporate brand in order to find information.
Information and assistance should be where they are, virtually, provided by "the library." Sadly, turf issues between and among libraries,
libraries and IT units, and libraries and boards make this goal difficult, sacrificing seekers to politics.

This matter of needing to differentiate between a virtual corporate
entity and virtual service provision is also the challenge of differenti-
ating between the physical library and the virtual library. Failing to
differentiate clearly leads to confusion: confusion of brand, confusion of purpose, and confusion of service delivery. As I suggested at
the beginning, this is the overarching challenge in librarianship. Lack
of clarity in purpose leads to bad planning and execution. And yet,
the sheer monumentality of the challenge seems to bring about planning fatigue, and the ambitious roadmap for change is diluted and
diminished until the changes implemented in libraries still, often,
look like "inside out" rather than "outside in."

How can libraries be successful in reading their tea leaves and
resist planning for one deterministic future that may or may not
come to pass? I return to Jim Collins' book, *Good to Great and the
Social Sector.* He writes that a great organization must:

> … attain piercing clarity about how to produce the best
> long-term results, and then exercise the relentless disci-
> pline to say, 'No thank you' to opportunities that fail the
> hedgehog test. When we examined the Hedgehog
> Concepts of the good-to-great companies, we found they
> reflected deep understanding of three intersecting circles:
> 1) what you are deeply passionate about, 2) what you can
> be the best in the world at, and 3) what best drives your
> economic engine.[11]

These questions are good ones to use to drive and guide the
process of sustaining and enhancing the physical library, and in
developing useful and usable virtual library services. Question two is
particularly relevant here. What are librarians best in the world at? I
don't have an answer, but I do know that we are collectively not best
at building better search engines, or data storage and inventory control systems, or handling supply chain management, or designing
artificial intelligence systems. And yet, in the 20-year span of my

career, librarians have spent a great deal of time and effort on the development of systems and not a lot of time and effort on the social context in which library systems must exist. (If we had, I dare say we would not find ourselves the owners and architects of local systems that reflect our interests in data management and inventory control, rather than our users' interests in discovery and delivery.)

Collins points out that "[g]reatness is not a function of circumstance. Greatness, it turns out, is largely a matter of conscious choice, and discipline." Planning and implementing change in the physical and the virtual library for the library of the future requires discipline, not just vision.

As a profession, we have become "good" at technology, but we need to (re)discover what makes us great. I am sure that technology alone will not make librarians and libraries great. I have read the tea leaves, and they formed these words: "Many of our libraries are now housed in beautiful buildings, in which case, the building as well as the books become a means of social influence. ... The whole building at all times should be managed in the broadest spirit of hospitality ... do away with all unnecessary restrictions, take down all bars, and try to put face to face our friends the books and our friends the people. Introduce them cordially, then stand aside and let them make each other's acquaintance."[12]

Endnotes

1. *Perceptions of Libraries and Information Resources*, OCLC, 2005, www.oclc.org/reports/2005perceptions.htm (accessed Nov. 21, 2006). OCLC has published *College Students' Perceptions of Libraries and Information Resources* as a companion piece to the earlier full report.

2. See the various volumes of *The Public Library in the United States* (The General Report of the Public Library Inquiry), New York: Columbia University Press, 1949. In particular, data presented in *The Library's Public* supports this.

3. The following sources publish information about Internet usage and cell phone penetration: Internet World Statistics (www.internetworldstats.com/index.html), ClikZ (www.clickz.com/stats), Pew Internet and American Life Project (www.pewinternet.org), and Nielsen/NetRatings (www.nielsen-netratings.com).

4. John Seely Brown and Paul Duguid, *The Social Life of Information*, Boston: Harvard Business School Press, 2002: xix. (Seely Brown and

Duguid note the phrase "lure of the local" in this quote comes from Lucy R. Lippard, *The Lure of the Local: Sense of Place in a Multi-Centered Society*. New York: New Press, 1997.)

5. Edward Cornish, *Futuring: The Exploration of the Future*, Place: World Future Society, 2004.

6. Scott Bennett, "The Choice for Learning," *The Journal of Academic Librarianship* 32(1), January 2006: 3–13.

7. In the Research and Learning chapter: www.oclc.org/reports/escan/research/learning.htm.

8. Ray Oldenburg, *The Great, Good Place: Cafés, Coffee Shops, Community Centers, Beauty Parlors, General Stores, Bars, Hangouts, and How They Get You Through the Day*, New York: Paragon House, 1989.

9. Miss Gratia Alta Countryman, *The Library as Social Centre*. The opening address of the Minnesota Library Association, October 12, 1905, juteux.net/rory/wbm11.html (accessed Nov. 21, 2006).

10. James C. Collins, *Good to Great and the Social Sectors: Why Business Thinking Is Not the Answer*. (A monograph to accompany *Good to Great: Why Some Companies Make the Leap—and Others Don't*.) [Boulder, CO: J. Collins], 2005.

11. He goes on to point out that the third circle is the one that doesn't fit well with social sector organizations, and so he rephrases that to be "How can we develop a sustainable resource engine to deliver superior performance relative to our mission?"

12. Countryman.

Web Sites

Chapter 1

Palm Treos, www.palm.com/us/products/smartphones
Upcoming Nokia Phones, www.nokiausa.com/A4409001
Samsung Flip Phones, www.samsung.com/products/wirelessphones
E Ink, www.eink.com
Sony Reader, products.sel.sony.com/pa/prs/index.html
iRex Illiad, www.irextechnologies.com/shop/products/iliad.htm
dotMobi, mtld.mobi
Skweezer, www.skweezer.com
Iyhy, www.iyhy.com
Harper Teen, www.harperteen.com
Boston—MSN City Guides, cityguides.msn.com/default.aspx?where =bostonma
SplashBlog, www.splashblog.com
Mob5, mob5.com
Blogger Mobile, www.blogger.com/mobile-start.g
WINK, winksite.com
Rabble, www.rabble.com
National Weather Service (mobile), mobile.srh.weather.gov
Hoover's (mobile), mobile.hoovers.com
PubMed for Handhelds, pubmedhh.nlm.nih.gov/nlm
Lincoln Trail Library System (LTLS) PDA Connect, www.ltls.org/ pda.html
LibraryThing (mobile), librarything.com/m
Handango, www.handango.com
Handmark, www.handmark.com
Tucows, www.tucows.com
4INFO, www.4info.net

Medio, www.mediosystems.com

UpSnap, www.upsnap.com

Answers.com, librarians.answers.com/main/answers_librarians_
  presearch.jsp

Teleread, www.teleread.org/blog

OpenReader, www.openreader.org

Project Gutenberg, www.gutenberg.org

Manybooks, manybooks.net

Synfonic, www.synfonic.com

The Library Success Wiki: Libraries Using IM Reference, www.lib
  success.org/index.php?title=Libraries_Using_IM_Reference

Flickr cell phone ban signs,
  www.flickr.com/search/?q=cell+phone+library

Altarama, www.altarama.com.au

The Library of Curtin University of Technology in Bentley, Australia,
  SMS Reference presentation, conferences.alia.org.au/online
  2005/pres/a12.pps

Sims Memorial Library at Southeastern Louisiana University, SMS
  Reference, www2.selu.edu/Library/ServicesDept/referenc/texta
  librarian.html

Dokimas, www.dokimas.co.uk

Talis, www.talis.com

Teleflip, www.teleflip.com

Vazu, www.vazu.com

Wake Forest MobileU, mobileu.wfu.edu

Baruch College of the City University of New York,
  www.baruch.cuny.edu

Southern Illinois University, www.siu.edu

Montclair State University, www.montclair.edu

Audible Air, www.audible.com

Mobitv, www.mobitv.com

LocationFree, www.learningcenter.sony.us/HomeAudioandVideo/
  LocationFree/Research_/LocationFreeFeatures

Mobot, www.mobot.com

Intelligent Spatial Technologies, Inc., www.i-spatialtech.com/
  iPointer.htm

GeoVector, www.geovector.com

Engadget Mobile, www.engadgetmobile.com

Gizmodo: The Gadgets Weblog, www.gizmodo.com

GottaBeMobile, www.gottabemobile.com

Handheld and Mobile Computing Constituent Group, EDUCAUSE,
  www.educause.edu/handheldandmobilecomputingconstituent
  group/7098
The Handheld Librarian, www.handheldlib.blogspot.com
MobileRead, www.mobileread.com
PDAlibraries group at Yahoo!, groups.Yahoo.com/group/pdalibraries
LIBRARY-PDAs Listserv: Library Support for Palmtops,
  www.lsoft.com/scripts/wl.exe?SL1=LIBRARY-PDAS&H=LIST
  SERV.ARIZONA.EDU
PDAs in education, www.jiscmail.ac.uk/pda-edu
PDA-ebook: Users of Electronic Books on PDA devices group, tech.
  groups.yahoo.com/group/pda-book
TeleRead: Bring the E-Books Home, www.teleread.org/blog
Textually, www.textually.org
Wireless Librarian (Bill Drew), wirelesslibraries.blogspot.com

Chapter 2

The GNU Project, gnu.org
Free Software Foundation, fsf.org
GNU GPL, gnu.org/copyleft/gpl.html
Open Source Systems for Libraries, oss4lib.org
Web4Lib, lists.webjunction.org/web4lib
Code4Lib, www.code4lib.org
Opensource.org, opensource.org

Chapter 3

Blyberg.net, www.blyberg.net
ILS Customer Bill of Rights, www.blyberg.net/2005/11/20/ils-
  customer-bill-of-rights
World Wide Web Consortium, www.w3.org/Consortium

Chapter 5

arXiv, arXiv.org
E-LIS, eprints.rclis.org
DList, dlist.sir.arizona.edu
Public Library of Science, plos.org
DSpace, dspace.org

Fedora, fedora.info

EPrints, www.eprints.org/software

CONTENTdm, www.oclc.org/contentdm

Open Repository, openrepository.com

Open Journal Systems, pkp.sfu.ca/ojs

DPubS, dpubs.org

Project Euclid, projecteuclid.org

Protocol for Metadata Harvesting, www.openarchives.org/OAI/
openarchivesprotocol.html

Google Scholar, scholar.google.com

OAIster, oaister.umdl.umich.edu

RLG-Nara Audit Checklist for Certifying Digital Repositories,
www.rlg.org/en/page.php?Page_ID=20769

SPARC, www.arl.org/sparc

Create Change, www.createchange.org

BioMed Central, biomedcentral.com

Newfound Press, www.lib.utk.edu/newfoundpress

Connexions, www.cnx.org

The University of Michigan Library's Scholarly Publishing Office,
spo.umdl.umich.edu

Cornell's Digital Consulting and Production Services,
dcaps.library.cornell.edu

Faculty of 1000, facultyof1000.com

Naboj, www.naboj.com

LOCKSS, www.lockss.org

Portico, www.portico.org

Washington Research Library Consortium's Aladin-RC,
aladinrc.wrlc.org

Greenstone, greenstone.org

Chapter 6

Search Institute, www.search-institute.org

Social Impact Games, www.socialimpactgames.com

Game On! Video Games in Libraries blog, libgaming.blogspot.com

LibGaming Google Group, groups.google.com/group/libgaming

YALSA Gaming Interest group, communities.ala.org

Penguin Baseball, fury.com/mirror/penguin.html

Chicktionary, www.shockwave.com/gamelanding/chicktionary.jsp

Diner Dash, www.shockwave.com/gamelanding/dinerdash.jsp

Online Games, home.comcast.net/~begallaway/gamelist.html
Library Success Best Practices Wiki, www.libsuccess.org
Boing Boing, www.boingboing.net
Electronic Gaming Monthly, egm.1up.com
Entertainment Software Association, www.theesa.com
Game Informer, www.gameinformer.com
Penny Arcade, www.penny-arcade.com
Pop Goes the Library, www.popgoesthelibrary.com
PvP, www.pvponline.com
This Spartan Life, www.thisspartanlife.com
VOYA Teen Pop Culture Quiz, www.voya.com

Chapter 8

Flickr, Librarian Trading Cards, www.flickr.com/groups/
    librariancards/pool
Movable Type, www.sixapart.com
WordPress, www.wordpress.org
Blogger, www.blogger.com
Ann Arbor District Library, www.aadl.org
St. Joseph County Public Library, www.libraryforlife.org/blogs/
    lifeline/index.php
Blog Without a Library, www.blogwithoutalibrary.net
Bloglines, www.bloglines.com
Newsgator, www.newsgator.com
Feedster, feedster.com
Hennepin County Library, www.hclib.org
SeedWiki, SeedWiki.com
MediaWiki, www.mediawiki.org
Wikipedia, www.wikipedia.org
Butler University Library Reference Resources Wiki,
    www.seedwiki.com/wiki/butler_wikiref
Ohio University Libraries Biz Wiki, www.library.ohiou.edu/subjects/
    bizwiki/index.php/Main_Page
St. Joseph County Public Library subject guides,
    www.libraryforlife.org/subjectguides/index.php/Main_Page
Trillian, www.ceruleanstudios.com
Darien Library, Contact Us, www.darienlibrary.org/contact.php
The Library Loft, www.libraryloft.org
PLCMC MySpace, www.myspace.com/libraryloft

Hennepin County Library MySpace, www.myspace.com/hennepin
countylibrary
Flickr, www.flickr.com
Last.FM, www.lastfm.com
YouTube, www.youtube.com
LibraryCrunch, www.librarycrunch.com
LibraryBytes, www.librarybytes.com

Chapter 9

ALA Office of Intellectual Freedom (OIF), www.ala.org/oif
ALA Privacy Tool Kit, www.ala.org/oif/iftoolkits/privacy
ALA, Conducting a Privacy Audit, www.ala.org/ala/washoff/
contactwo/oitp/emailtutorials/privacya/27.cfm
ALA, RFID in Libraries: Privacy and Confidentiality Guidelines,
www.ala.org/ala/oif/statementspols/otherpolicies/rfidguide
lines.htm
Center for Democracy and Technology, www.cdt.org
Computer Professionals for Social Responsibility (CPSR),
www.cpsr.org
CPSR's Privacy and Civil Liberties page, www.cpsr.org/program/
privacy/privacy.html
Electronic Frontier Foundation, www.eff.org
Electronic Privacy Information Center, EPIC, www.epic.org
Libraryprivacy.org, www.libraryprivacy.org
University of California Privacy Audit, libraries.universityof
california.edu/sopag/privacytf/privacy_audit.html
Privacy and Security in Library RFID: Issues, Practices, and
Architectures, www.cs.berkeley.edu/~dmolnar/library.pdf

Chapter 12

Second Life Library 2.0, www.infoisland.org
Active Worlds, www.activeworlds.com
There, www.there.com
Second Life Library Google Group,
groups.google.com/group/alliancesecondlife
Second Life, secondlife.com

Chapter 13

Implementing the Seven Principles: Technology as Lever, www.
   tltgroup.org/programs/seven.html
TLT LTAs, www.tltgroup.org/ltas.htm
LTA Inventory, zircon.mcli.dist.maricopa.edu/lta
LTA # 26, Durable Links and Downloads: Create E-Reserves With
   Library Content, zircon.mcli.dist.maricopa.edu/lta/archives/
   lta26.php
Texas Information Literacy Tutorial, or TILT, tilt.lib.utsystem.edu
Plagiarism and Academic Integrity Simulation,
   www.scc.rutgers.edu/douglass/sal/plagiarism/intro.html
Boolean Operators Tutorial, http://library.nyu.edu/research/
   tutorials/boolean/tutorial.html
MERLOT, www.merlot.org/Home.po
PRIMO, www.ala.org/CFApps/Primo/public/search.cfm
Wisconsin Online Resource Center, www.wisc-online.com
The Blended Librarian, blendedlibrarian.org

Chapter 14

University of Maryland College of Information Studies, www.clis.
   umd.edu
University of North Texas SLIS, www.unt.edu/slis
Syracuse University, www.ist.syr.edu
Simmons Graduate School of Library and Information Science,
   www.simmons.edu/gslis
Information School at the University of Washington,
   www.ischool.washington.edu

Chapter 15

Assessing and Managing Technostress, www2.una.edu/psychology/
   alatalk.htm
A Manager's Guide to Survival in the Information Age, Nina Davis-
   Millis, web.mit.edu/ninadm/www/mla.htm
Managing Technostress in UK Libraries: A Realistic Guide, www.
   ariadne.ac.uk/issue25/technostress
Library Technostress Survey Results, www.jkup.net/tstress-survey-
   2003.html
Technostress and the Reference Librarian, www.jkup.net/tstr_ref.html

About the Contributors

Lori Bell is Director of Innovation for the Alliance Library System, and has been involved in the setup and implementation of the Alliance Second Life Library. She has worked in a variety of library settings, has served as an adjunct instructor at the Dominican University GSLIS and the University of Illinois (GSLIS), and was named a *Library Journal* "Mover & Shaker" in 2004. She received her MS in Library and Information Science from the University of Illinois and certificate of additional study in distance learning from the Instructional Technology and Telecommunications program at Western Illinois University.

Steven J. Bell is Associate University Librarian for Research and Instructional Services at Temple University. Prior to that, he was Director of the Paul J. Gutman Library at Philadelphia University. He obtained his EdD in 1997 from the University of Pennsylvania. He writes and speaks frequently on topics such as information retrieval, library and learning technologies, and academic librarianship. An Adjunct Professor at the Drexel University College of Information Science and Technology, he teaches courses in academic librarianship and information retrieval. He maintains a Web site and blog, "Steven Bell's Keeping Up Web Site" and "The Kept-Up Academic Librarian," that promote current awareness skills and resources. He blogs for ACRLog, ACRL's official blog, and Designing Better Libraries, a blog that promotes design thinking. Steven is a co-founder of the Blended Librarian's Online Learning Community on the Learning Times Network. For additional information about Steven or to find links to the various Web sites he publishes and maintains, point your browser to stevenbell.info.

John Blyberg (BA English, University of Maine, 1998) is currently the Head of Technology and Digital Initiatives at Darien Library in

Connecticut. He was formerly the System Administrator and Lead Developer for the Ann Arbor District Library (AADL) in Michigan. Prior to working in libraries, John was the IT manager for the North American office of the British car company, Lotus Engineering. At AADL, John was responsible for rebuilding the IT infrastructure and numerous software development products such as a custom session management system, RFID circulation client, WiFi registration system, and point-of-sale (POS) software. He is most well-known for his work on AADL's award-winning Web site and social OPAC (SOPAC). In March 2006, John was named a "Mover & Shaker" by *Library Journal*. In September 2006, John took First Prize in the Talis "Mashing-up the Library" competition.

Robert Bocher is the Technology Consultant with the Wisconsin State Library. He keypunched his first programs, which gives you an idea of how long he's been involved in this line of work. Bob works primarily with Wisconsin's public libraries and K–12 schools on various technology issues and projects, including the federal E-rate program. Bob is on the board of WiscNet, Wisconsin's public sector Internet provider. He also serves on the American Library Association's Office for Information Technology Policy Advisory Committee and has assisted the ALA in formulating policies and positions on telecommunication issues and legislation. In 2005, he co-authored the book *Privacy in the 21st Century: Issues for Public, School, and Academic Libraries*, published by Libraries Unlimited. Bob has his MLS from UW-Madison.

Daniel Chudnov is a librarian and programmer currently working as an Information Technology Specialist in the Office of Strategic Initiatives at the Library of Congress. Before taking this position in March 2007, he was lead developer for the Canary Database and unalog at the Yale Center for Medical Informatics, worked as a freelance developer and writer, and contributed to several well-known open source projects, including the initial development and implementation of DSpace at MIT Libraries, the jake project at the Cushing/Whitney Medical Library at the Yale University School of Medicine, and a precursor to the award-winning Prospero project, the first widely used Web-based document delivery toolkit. He is a frequent speaker and author on technology and the importance of free software in libraries, and started the oss4lib Weblog and listserv in 1999 to promote the use of open source in our community. In

January 2007, he started writing the monthly "Libraries in Computers" column for *Computers in Libraries* magazine. Daniel earned an MS at the School of Information in 1997 and studied Economics and Japanese as an undergraduate, both at the University of Michigan. In 2005 he received the LITA/Brett Butler Entrepreneurship Award from the Library & Information Technology Association of the American Library Association.

Jill Emery is currently the Head of Acquisitions at the University of Texas at Austin. Jill has more than 10 years of experience working with serials and electronic resources, and has served as a Member-at-Large on the North American Serials Interest Group (NASIG) Board. She is current incoming Vice-President of NASIG and is the current Past-Chair of the ALA-ALCTS Serials Section. In 2004, Jill was named one of *Library Journal's* "Movers & Shakers," and she is the most recent recipient of the ALCTS Esther J. Piercy Award. Lastly, Jill serves on the International Library Committee for Nature Publishing Group.

Meredith G. Farkas (BA Wesleyan University; MSW Florida State University; MLIS Florida State University) is the Distance Learning Librarian at Norwich University in Northfield, Vermont. She is the author of the book *Social Software in Libraries: Building Collaboration, Communication, and Community Online* (Information Today, Inc., 2007) and writes the monthly column "Technology in Practice" for *American Libraries*. Meredith also is the author of the blog Information Wants to Be Free (meredith.wolfwater.com/word press) and is the creator of Library Success: A Best Practices Wiki (www.libsuccess.org), as well as a number of national conference wikis. Meredith is a passionate advocate for affordable online continuing education for librarians and developed the free online course, Five Weeks to a Social Library (www.sociallibraries.com/course), to teach librarians about social software. In March 2006, she was named a "Mover & Shaker" by *Library Journal* for her innovative use of technology to benefit the profession.

Megan K. Fox is the Web & Electronic Resources Librarian for the Simmons College Library. She manages the library's Web site, negotiates contracts and subscriptions for online research databases, and assists the Public Services department with instruction, faculty outreach, and marketing library services. Megan received her MA in Literature from Boston College in 1994 and her MLS in Library and

Information Science from Simmons in 1998. At Simmons, Megan also teaches graduate and continuing education courses for the Graduate School of Library & Information Science. Her specialties include online resources, searching the Web, business information, and mobile technologies. In addition, Megan is the Special Projects Analyst for Administration and Planning, which entails providing institutional research support for the Simmons Strategic Plan, Diversity Action Plan, Strategic Plan for Technology, and other special projects. Contact Megan at fox@simmons.edu, and see web. simmons.edu/~fox/ for more information and links on mobile technologies in libraries.

Beth Gallaway, a *Library Journal* "Mover & Shaker" (2006), is an independent library trainer/consultant specializing in youth services and technology. She has been playing video games since she was five, and is currently playing Lego Star Wars II, Guitar Hero II, and Rayman Raving Rabbits (not all at the same time). Beth is the founder of the LibGaming e-mail list, co-chair of the YALSA Teen Gaming Interest Group, and a Second Life citizen; her avatar Cerulean Vesperia is a volunteer at the Second Life Library on Info Island. Her chapter is adapted from her forthcoming book on gaming and libraries, tentatively titled *Get Your Game On* (Neal-Schuman).

Joseph Janes is Associate Professor and Associate Dean for Academics at the Information School of the University of Washington. A frequent speaker in the U.S. and abroad, he was the Founding Director of the Internet Public Library and is the co-author of eight books on librarianship, technology, and their relationship, including *Introduction to Reference Work in the Digital Age*. Janes writes the "Internet Librarian" column for *American Libraries* magazine, and is the 2006 recipient of the Isadore Gilbert Mudge award from the American Library Association for distinguished contributions to reference librarianship. He holds the MLS and PhD from Syracuse University, and has taught at the University of Michigan, the University of North Carolina at Chapel Hill, and the State University of New York at Albany, as well as at Syracuse and Washington.

David Lee King is the Digital Branch & Services Manager at the Topeka & Shawnee County Public Library. He has years of experience in Web site creation, planning, and design. He has spoken in the U.S.

and Canada about Web site usability and management, digital experience planning, and managing techie staff, and has been published in many library-related journals. David writes the "Internet Spotlight" column in *Public Libraries* magazine with Michael Porter. David maintains a blog at www.davidleeking.com.

Jenny Levine received her MLS from the University of Illinois, Urbana-Champaign in 1992 and has been a reference librarian, a technology coordinator, and a consultant at a multi-type library system. In 2002, she started "The Shifted Librarian" (theshiftedlibrarian. com), a blog that examines how the coming world of ubiquitous, always-on, broadband Internet will affect libraries and how they can "shift" their services to where their users are. She was named a *Library Journal* "Mover & Shaker" in 2003, received the Illinois Reference & Technical Services Award in 2004, and travels around the world to give presentations about emerging technologies for libraries. In 2006, she became the Internet Development Specialist and Strategy Guide for the American Library Association, where she assists the Publishing and Information Technology Departments with strategic planning for online services and dissemination of digital content.

Tom Peters is the founder of TAP Information Services (www.tap information.com), which provides a wide variety of services supporting libraries, library consortia, government agencies, publishers, and other information-intensive organizations. Tom has worked previously at the Committee on Institutional Cooperation (CIC, the academic consortium of the Big Ten universities and the University of Chicago), Western Illinois University in Macomb, Northern Illinois University in DeKalb, Minnesota State University at Mankato, and the University of Missouri at Kansas City. Tom did his undergraduate work at Grinnell College, where he majored in English and philosophy, and earned his library science degree at the University of Iowa. His second master's degree (in English) was completed at the University of Missouri at Kansas City. His library experience includes reference service, library instruction, collection management, and administration. His current interests include library services in virtual worlds, online programming using Web conferencing software, and digital audio books.

Dorothea Salo recently returned to Wisconsin to become Digital Repository Librarian for MINDS@UW (minds.wisconsin.edu), which serves the entire University of Wisconsin system. She was previously the Digital Repository Services Librarian at George Mason University. She holds a master's degree in Library and Information Studies and another in Spanish from the University of Wisconsin at Madison, and a BA in comparative literature and Spanish from Indiana University at Bloomington. Her previous experience includes typesetting and SGML production for scholarly books and journals, and work on technology standards for electronic books.

John D. Shank has been in the higher education field since 1996, and received his MLS from Drexel's School of Library and Information Science. Since entering the field, he has worked at several academic institutions in various capacities, including Montgomery County Community College, Haverford College, and Bryn Mawr College. Currently, Shank is the Instructional Design Librarian and Director of the Center for Learning Technologies for Pennsylvania State University's Berks campus. He has presented hundreds of faculty development workshops, lectures, and seminars at various universities and colleges, and given presentations at regional and national conferences. John has also authored and co-authored articles and book chapters on the topic of integrating instructional technology into library services, and is co-founder, along with Steven Bell, of the Blended Librarian Online Learning Community.

Michael Stephens is Assistant Professor at Dominican University's Graduate School of Library and Information Science in River Forest, Illinois. Before joining the faculty at Dominican, he spent 15 years working in public libraries. He has presented at library conferences nationally and internationally, consulted with library systems across the U.S., and published with Neal-Schuman, Inc. and the American Library Association. He has written for *Public Libraries, American Libraries, NextSpace, Teacher Librarian, School Library Journal*, and *Library Media Connection*. He co-authors a department in *Computers in Libraries* with Rachel Singer Gordon and is a monthly columnist with Michael Casey in *Library Journal*. He writes for the ALA TechSource Blog (www.techsource.ala.org/blog) as well as his own blog, Tame the Web (tametheweb.com). His Library Technology Report, *Web 2.0 & Libraries 2: Trends, Tools & Technologies*, will be published in September 2007.

Rhonda B. Trueman received an MLIS from the University of North Carolina, Greensboro in 2005 and works as Reference Librarian at Johnson & Wales University, Charlotte. She is currently liaison to the College of Business, providing research and collection development for this area. Rhonda is the treasurer of the Metrolina Library Association, a regional organization encompassing counties in both North and South Carolina; she also serves on the board of and is the book review editor for the North Carolina Genealogical Society. Rhonda joined the volunteer staff of Second Life Library 2.0 soon after its inception and has headed collections, been involved in many Second Life library groups, and currently serves as assistant director.

Jessamyn West is a community technology educator in central Vermont, where she works with public librarians and seniors, helping them use technology to solve problems. Her first technology education position was in 1994, training journalists in Bucharest, Romania to use pine and gopher. She started her Web site, jessamyn.com, in 1995; she is also the editor of the Weblog librarian.net, where she examines the intersection of libraries, technology, and politics. She is a moderator of the online community metafilter.com. She can teach anyone how to use a computer, and still types letters to friends on an Underwood-Olivetti Lettera 22. She will send you a letter if you send her a postcard.

Alane Wilson worked at OCLC (www.oclc.org) from 1997–2007, most recently as a senior library market consultant, working on special projects for the VP of Marketing and Library Services, Cathy De Rosa. After a brief time away from OCLC in 2003, she was recruited by OCLC's president and CEO, Jay Jordan, to return and work on the *OCLC Environmental Scan* (www.oclc.org/reports/escan), which was released in January 2004. In addition to co-authoring and editing the *Scan*, she has written and contributed to other OCLC reports, including the most recent one, *Perceptions of Libraries and Information Resources* (www.oclc. org/reports/2005perceptions.htm). She has spoken to many groups, has facilitated workshops, and was one of five OCLC contributors to the "It's All Good" blog (scanblog.blogspot. com). Her current blog is Missalaney (missalaney.blogspot.com). She holds a BA in English Literature and Classical Civilizations, University of Waterloo, Waterloo, Ontario, and an MLIS, from the University of British Columbia, Vancouver, British Columbia. She is a member of the Association of Professional Futurists.

About the Editor

Rachel Singer Gordon is Consulting Editor for Information Today, Inc., Book Publishing Division, and Webmaster for LISjobs.com. Rachel writes and presents widely on career development issues for librarians and maintains two blogs: the Liminal Librarian (www.lisjobs.com/liminal) and Beyond the Job (with Sarah Johnson; librarycareers.blogspot.com). She is the author of six books on career development and technology topics, including *The Accidental Systems Librarian* (ITI, 2003), *The Librarian's Guide to Writing for Publication* (Scarecrow, 2004), *The Accidental Library Manager* (ITI, 2005), and *The NextGen Librarian's Survival Guide* (ITI, 2006). Her MLIS is from Dominican University, and her MA is from Northwestern University.

Index

245

More Great Books from Information Today, Inc.

The Thriving Library
Successful Strategies for Challenging Times

By Marylaine Block

Here is a highly readable guide to strategies and projects that have helped more than 100 public libraries gain community support and funding during challenging times. Marylaine Block integrates survey responses from innovative library directors with her research, analysis, and extended interviews to showcase hundreds of winning programs and services. The strategies explored include youth services, the library as place, partnerships, marketing, stressing the economic value, Library 2.0, outreach, and more.

352 pp/softbound/ISBN 978-1-57387-277-5 $39.50

Library 2.0
A Guide to Participatory Library Service

By Michael E. Casey and Laura C. Savastinuk

Two of the first and most original thinkers on Library 2.0 introduce the essential concepts and offer ways to improve service to better meet the changing needs of 21st-century library users. Describing a service model of constant and purposeful change, evaluation and updating of library services, and user participation, the book both outlines the theoretical underpinnings of Library 2.0 and provides practical advice on how to get there.

200 pp/softbound/ISBN 978-1-57387-297-3 $29.50

Listen Up!
Podcasting for Schools and Libraries

By Linda W. Braun

Here is a timely—and time-saving—guide for teachers, librarians, and school media specialists who need to get quickly up-to-speed on podcasting. Educational technology specialist Linda Braun explains what podcasting is and why it is such a useful tool for schools and libraries. She covers both content and technical issues, sharing tips for finding and using podcasts and vodcasts, examples of innovative school and library projects, how-to advice for creating great podcasts, and guidance on getting the word out to students, staff, patrons, and other users. Whether you are new to the technology or an experienced podcaster in search of ideas and inspiration, you'll find a unique source of support in *Listen Up! Podcasting for Schools and Libraries*.

120 pp/softbound/ISBN 978-1-57387-304-8 $29.50

Making Search Work
Implementing Web, Intranet and Enterprise Search

By Martin White

This important book is designed to help organizations understand, evaluate, and implement desktop, Web site, intranet, and enterprise search applications. Martin White explains search technology in clear, nontechnical language and describes the benefits and issues for a range of solutions—from high-end to affordable plug-and-play software products. In addition to providing critical guidance, the book features a glossary, suggestions for further reading, and an annotated listing of firms providing Web, intranet, and enterprise search solutions.

200 pp/hardbound/ISBN 978-1-57387-305-5 $69.50

Social Software in Libraries
Building Collaboration, Communication, and Community Online

By Meredith G. Farkas

This guide provides librarians with the information and skills necessary to implement the most popular and effective social software technologies: blogs, RSS, wikis, social networking software, screencasting, photo-sharing, podcasting, instant messaging, gaming, and more. Novice readers will find ample descriptions and advice on using each technology, while veteran users of social software will discover new applications and approaches. Supported by the author's Web page.

344 pp/softbound/ISBN 978-1-57387-275-1 $39.50

The NextGen Librarian's Survival Guide

By Rachel Singer Gordon

This unique resource addresses the specific needs of GenXers and Millenials as they work to define themselves as information professionals. The book focuses on how NextGens can move their careers forward and positively impact the profession. Library career guru Rachel Singer Gordon provides timely advice along with tips and insights from dozens of librarians on issues ranging from image to stereotypes, to surviving library school and entry-level positions, to working with older colleagues.

224 pp/softbound/ISBN 978-1-57387-256-0 $29.50

Information and Emotion

The Emergent Affective Paradigm in Information Behavior Research and Theory

Edited by Diane Nahl and Dania Bilal

Information and Emotion introduces the new research areas of affective issues in information seeking and use, and the affective paradigm applied to information behavior in a variety of populations, cultures, and contexts. The contributions by the editors and authors make this book a unique source of research findings on the user perspective, the user experience, and how emotional aspects can be interpreted, mitigated, or enhanced through design that is informed by use, and by users who directly participate in information design.

392 pp/hardbound/ISBN 978-1-57387-310-9 $59.50

Blogging & RSS

A Librarian's Guide

By Michael P. Sauers

Author, Internet trainer, and blogger Michael P. Sauers shows how blogging and RSS can be easily and effectively used in the context of a library community. Sauers showcases interesting and useful blogs, shares insights from librarian bloggers, and offers step-by-step instructions for creating, publishing, and syndicating a blog using free Web-based services, software, RSS feeds, and aggregators.

288 pp/softbound/ISBN 978-1-57387-268-3 $29.50